THE

AMERICAN SLAVE CODE

IN THEORY AND PRACTICE:

ITS

DISTINCTIVE FEATURES

SHOWN BY

ITS STATUTES, JUDICIAL DECISIONS,

AND

ILLUSTRATIVE FACTS.

"Truth is stranger than Fiction."—(*Modern Maxim.*)
"Statutes against Fundamental Morality are void."—(*Judge M'Lean, U. S. Supreme Court.*)

BY
WILLIAM GOODELL,
Author of the "Democracy of Christianity," and "History of Slavery and Anti-Slavery."

NEW-YORK:
AMERICAN AND FOREIGN ANTI-SLAVERY SOCIETY,
48 BEEKMAN STREET.
1853.

JOHN A. GRAY,

Printer,

95 & 97 Cliff, cor. Frankfort Street.

CONTENTS.

PAGE

PRELIMINARY CHAPTER, ... 15

PART I.

THE RELATION OF MASTER AND SLAVE, ... 21

CHAPTER I.

SLAVE OWNERSHIP.

Fundamental idea of modern Slaveholding, namely, the assumed principle of Human Chattelhood, or Property in Man, constituting the relation of Owner and Property, of Master and Slave, ... 23

CHAPTER II.

SLAVE TRAFFIC.

Sale—Purchase — Barter—Mortgage—Auction—Coffle-gang — Shipments—as absolutely as in the case of any other Property, and by the same tenure, .. 44

CHAPTER III.

SEIZURE OF SLAVE PROPERTY FOR DEBT.

As Property, Slaves may be seized and sold to pay the debts of their Owners, while living, or for the Settlement of their Estates after their Decease, ... 63

CHAPTER IV.

INHERITANCE OF SLAVE PROPERTY.

Slaves, as Property, are transmitted by Inheritance, or by Will, to heirs at law or legatees. In the distribution of Estates they are distributed like other Property, ... 69

CHAPTER V.

USES OF SLAVE PROPERTY.

Slaves, as Property, may be USED, absolutely, by their Owners, for their own profit or pleasure, ... 77

CHAPTER VI.

SLAVES CAN POSSESS NOTHING.

Being Property themselves, they can own no property, nor make any contract, 89

CHAPTER VII.

SLAVES CANNOT MARRY.

Being held as Property, and incapable of making any Contract, they cannot contract Marriage recognized by law, ... 105

CHAPTER VIII.

SLAVES CANNOT CONSTITUTE FAMILIES.

Being Property,—"Goods and Chattels Personal, to all intents, constructions, and purposes whatsoever,"—they have no claim on each other; no security from separation; no Marital Rights; no Parental Rights; no Family Government; no Family Education; no Family Protection, ... 113

CHAPTER IX.

UNLIMITED POWER OF SLAVEHOLDERS.

The Power of the Master or Owner is virtually unlimited; the submission required of the Slave is unbounded; the Slave, being Property, can have no Protection against the Master, and has no redress for injuries inflicted by him, ... 122

CHAPTER X.

LABOR OF SLAVES.

The Slave, being a Chattel, may be worked at the discretion of his Owner, as other working Chattels are, ... 128

CHAPTER XI.

FOOD, CLOTHING, AND DWELLINGS OF SLAVES.

The Slave, as a Chattel, is fed or famished, covered or uncovered, sheltered or unsheltered, at the discretion or convenience of his Owner, like other working animals,.......... 135

CHAPTER XII.

COERCED LABOR WITHOUT WAGES.

The "legal relation of Master and Slave," being the relation of an Owner to a Chattel, is incompatible with the natural and Heaven-sanctioned "relation" of Labor and Wages,.. 150

CHAPTER XIII.

PUNISHMENTS OF SLAVES BY THE OWNER AND HIRER.

Being the absolute Property of the Owner, the Slave is wholly in his power, without any effectual restraint,.. 155

CHAPTER XIV.

OF LAWS CONCERNING THE MURDER AND KILLING OF SLAVES.

The structure of the Laws and the condition of the Slaves render adequate Protection impossible, ... 177

CHAPTER XV.

OF THE DELEGATED POWER OF OVERSEERS.

All the power of the Owner over his Slave is held and exercised also by Overseers and Agents, ... 197

CHAPTER XVI.

OF THE PROTECTION OF SLAVE PROPERTY FROM DAMAGE BY ASSAULTS FROM OTHER PERSONS THAN THEIR OWNERS.

Slaves are better protected as *Property* than they are as *Sentient Beings*,..... 201

CHAPTER XVII.

FACTS ILLUSTRATING THE KIND AND DEGREE OF PROTECTION EXTENDED TO SLAVES.

The Extent, the Atrocity, the Frequency, and the Impunity of barbarous Outrages upon Slaves, show that the laws afford them little or no Protection, 209

CHAPTER XVIII.

FUGITIVES FROM SLAVERY.

The Slave, being Property, may be hampered and confined to prevent his escape; may be pursued and reclaimed; must not be aided or concealed from his Master; and when too wild or refractory to be *used* by his Owner, may be *killed* by him with impunity,.. 225

CHAPTER XIX.

THE SLAVE CANNOT SUE HIS MASTER.

Slave Property cannot litigate with its Owner,.............................. 239

CHAPTER XX.

NO POWER OF SELF-REDEMPTION OR CHANGE OF MASTERS.

The Slave, being a Chattel, has no power of Self-redemption, nor of an exchange of Owners,... 245

CHAPTER XXI.

THE RELATION HEREDITARY AND PERPETUAL.

Slaves, being held as Property, like other Domestic Animals, their Offspring are held as Property in the same manner,................................ 248

CHAPTER XXII.

RIGHT TO EDUCATION — RELIGIOUS LIBERTY — RIGHTS OF CONSCIENCE.

The Slave, being held as a Chattel, is held by a tenure which excludes any legal recognition of his rights as a thinking and religious being,................ 251

CHAPTER XXIII.

ORIGIN OF THE RELATION AND ITS SUBJECTS.

The so-called "legal relation" of Slave Ownership of Negroes originated in that African Slave-Trade which our laws now punish as piracy; but Slavery is, in general, extended over all classes whom the Slaveholders have been able to seize upon and retain—over Indians, free persons of Color, and Whites, ... 258

PART II.

RELATION OF THE SLAVE TO SOCIETY AND TO CIVIL GOVERNMENT, ... 287

CHAPTER I.

OF THE GROUND AND NATURE OF THE SLAVE'S CIVIL CONDITION.

The Civil Condition of the Slave grows out of his relation to his Master, *as Property*, and is determined and defined by it, ... 289

CHAPTER II.

NO ACCESS TO THE JUDICIARY, AND NO HONEST PROVISION FOR TESTING THE CLAIMS OF THE ENSLAVED TO FREEDOM.

"A Slave cannot be a Party to a Civil Suit." (Stroud.) 295

CHAPTER III.

REJECTION OF TESTIMONY OF SLAVES AND FREE COLORED PERSONS.

Slavery is upheld by suppressing the testimony of its victims, ... 300

CHAPTER IV.

SUBJECTION TO ALL WHITE PERSONS.

Submission is required of the Slave, not only to the will of his Master, but to the will of all other *White Persons!*"................................ 305

CHAPTER V.

PENAL LAWS AGAINST SLAVES.

The Laws are unequal; their administration despotic: their execution barbarous. Even this is exceeded by "Lynch Law,"........................... 309

CHAPTER VI.

EDUCATION PROHIBITED.

The Slave, not being regarded as a Member of Society, nor as a Human Being, the Government, instead of providing for his Education, takes care to forbid it, as being inconsistent with the condition of Cattelhood,......... 319

CHAPTER VII.

FREE SOCIAL WORSHIP AND RELIGIOUS INSTRUCTION PROHIBITED.

The Government not only allows the Master to forbid the Free Social Worship and Instruction of his Slaves, but it also steps in with direct prohibitions of its own, which even the Master himself may not relax or abrogate, 326

CHAPTER VIII.

LEGISLATIVE, JUDICIAL, AND CONSTITUTIONAL OBSTRUCTIONS TO EMANCIPATION.

The Statutes of the Slave States not only make no provision for a general Emancipation, but they obstruct and prevent Emancipations by the Master. And the Constitutions of some of the States forbid the Legislatures to abolish Slavery,.. 338

PART III.

RELATION OF THE SLAVE CODE TO THE LIBERTIES OF THE FREE, ... 353

CHAPTER I.

LIBERTIES OF THE FREE PEOPLE OF COLOR.

The free People of Color, though not in a condition of Chattelhood, are constantly exposed to it, and, at best, enjoy only a portion of their rights, ... 355

CHAPTER II.

LIBERTIES OF THE WHITE PEOPLE OF THE SLAVEHOLDING STATES.

The White People of the Slaveholding States, whether Slaveholders or Non-Slaveholders, are deprived, by the Slave Code, of some of their essential Rights, and cannot be regarded as a people in possession of Civil, Religious and Political Freedom, ... 372

CHAPTER III.

LIBERTIES OF THE WHITE PEOPLE OF THE NON-SLAVEHOLDING STATES.

The Rights of the White People of the Non-Slaveholding States are directly and indirectly invaded by the Slave Code of the Slave States; their Liberties, to a great extent, have already fallen a sacrifice, and can never be secure while Slaveholding continues, ... 389

CONCLUDING CHAPTER.

Summary Review of the Slave Code; its Character and Effects—Inquiries concerning the Duty of Christians, Churches, and Ministers—The Responsibilities of Citizens, of Society, of Civil Government, of Legislators, of Magistrates—Scrutiny of the Legality of American Slavery—The Heaven-prescribed Remedy—The Worthlessness of Temporizing Expedients—Closing Appeal, ... 394

LETTER FROM HON. WILLIAM JAY TO THE AUTHOR.

NEW-YORK, 25th January, 1853.

REV. AND DEAR SIR:

On returning the MSS. of your "AMERICAN SLAVE CODE, *in Theory and Practice*," I must ask you to accept my thanks for writing it, as well as for favoring me with its early perusal. Surely, never before has mischief been framed by law with more diabolical ingenuity than in this infernal code. Your analysis of the slave laws is very able, and your exhibition of their practical application by the Southern Courts, evinces great and careful research.

It is more easy to make than to refute a charge of exaggeration against a work of fiction like Mrs. Stowe's; but your book is as impregnable against such a charge as is Euclid's Geometry, since, like that, it consists of propositions and demonstrations. The book is not only true, but it is *unquestionably* true. You show us the rack constructed "according to law;" we examine, at our leisure, the cruel but skilful contrivance of its machinery; we see the ministers of the law bind the victim on the instrument of torture; we see one feature of humanity after another crushed and obliterated, till at last an immortal man, made a little lower than the angels, and for whose redemption the Son of God shed his blood on the cross, is converted into a beast of burden—a vendible animal, scourged at the will of its owner, and offered for sale in the market with horses and oxen.

Your book will take from our Northern dough-faces and slave-catchers the flattering unction they are laying to their souls that

"Uncle Tom's Cabin" is a gross exaggeration; that, of course, slavery is, after all, not so very bad; and that they, in doing its biddings, are not as base as they seem to be. You show them that the most educated and refined among the slaveholders have, for the past century, as legislators, been deliberately enacting the most fiendish of laws, in utter defiance of the moral sense of mankind, and the precepts of the blessed gospel of the Lord Jesus; and that their grave and learned judges have enforced these accursed statutes, in all their execrable rigor, thus giving a solemn sanction to the atrocities portrayed by Mrs. Stowe and others without number, still more aggravated by investing them with legal impunity.

May God make your book a means of awakening the consciences of our cotton divines to the deep sin of upholding, in the name of the blessed and adorable Redeemer, a system so damnable as American Slavery! These reverend pro-slavery champions of Christianity resemble the priests of Juggernaut, recommending the worship of their god by pointing to the wretches writhing, and shrieking, and expiring under his car.

That the blessing of God may rest on your labors for his glory and the good of our suffering and oppressed brethren, is the fervent prayer of

Your friend and servant,

WILLIAM JAY.

REV. WILLIAM GOODELL.

THE AMERICAN SLAVE CODE.

THE AMERICAN SLAVE CODE.

PRELIMINARY CHAPTER.

OCCASIONS AND USES FOR THIS VOLUME.

THE practical importance of an exact knowledge of the Slave Code and of its legitimate workings, will be manifest from the considerations that follow.

It is often maintained that the "legal relation of master and slave" is not a criminal one, and that there is no sin, or moral wrong, in the mere fact of sustaining that relation. On the other hand, it is held that the relation is wrong in itself, and cannot be innocently sustained.

Such a question cannot, intelligently, be settled without a correct understanding of that "legal relation," and of the particulars in which it consists. And it is only by *the Slave Code of the country* that "the legal relation" can be ascertained. By this, and by this only, is it to be defined. "The legal relation of master and slave" is what the Slave Code declares it to be. *And it is nothing else.*

It is worse than mere trifling, it is evasion and sophistry, to ransack the archives of some other age and nation for the laws and usages which *then* constituted slavery, or which we may now choose to *call* slavery; and then, on the assumed (or even the ascertained) innocency or divine sanction or tolerance of *those usages*, to argue the innocency of the existing "relation of master and slave" in this country. Sincere and honest inquirers are bound to ascertain "the legal relation of master and slave" as it now exists in America, in virtue of the code that authorizes and defines it. They are bound to bring "the legal relation," as *thus* defined and ascertained, to the standard of the Divine will, and say to whether or no it corresponds with that standard. The question whether it is right or wrong to sanction *such* a "legal relation" by "sustaining" it, will then be easily settled.

No man, in America, can hold a slave by any other tenure, or in any other "relation," than that which the American Slave Code describes. He cannot hold a slave under the code of Moses, (if it ever could have been done,) nor under the usages of Abraham's day, for no such code or usages now exist. If he relinquishes the hold on his slave that the American Slave Code gives him, he manumits him, at once and entirely. Let him do this, or let that code be blotted out, and he cannot forcibly retain a man in bondage a single day, without becoming a felon in the eye of the law. So that in "sustaining the legal relation," he sustains and sanctions the code, and *its* character becomes *his*. The more unsullied his reputation may be in other respects, the more effectually does his example of slaveholding sanction the system, and rivet the chains of the slave.

It must be futile and absurd to decry the code, and yet attempt to justify him who holds a slave under it. The code would harm no one, if no one ever made use of it. The worst that can properly be said of the code is, that it enables men who are thus disposed to hold the "relation" described by it. For, the very men for whose consideration we make this remark are forward to tell us that the system (in other words, the code) is not to be held responsible for the mere *abuses* committed under it. It must, then, be responsible for the *relation*, and those who sustain the relation must be responsible for *it*.

We propose, then, by an exhibition of the American Slave Code, to test the moral character of American slaveholding. The practice (in the absence of mere abuses) cannot be better than the code, or rule of conduct, that gives it license and sanction.

On the other hand, the usages under any code are seldom or never better than the code itself. Communities are not forward to proclaim themselves worse than they are, by giving public license to evil practices not prevalent among them, and which they do not intend to practise and sustain. "No people," says a learned writer and profound thinker,* "were ever yet found who were better than their laws, though many have been known to be worse."

The only exceptions to this rule are where bad laws

---

* Dr. Priestley.

are forced upon a community without their consent; or where, from their odiousness, or by the progress of civilization since their enactment, they have become obsolete. In our own country, the people (except the victims of the Slave Code) enact their own statutes. And in the present investigation it will be made apparent that the Slave Code has not become obsolete.

The present contest for the abolition of American slavery has encountered a species of opposition which it has been difficult to meet. If existing practices are arraigned, we are told that these are only abuses of the system, which argue nothing against the innocent "legal relation." Thus all efforts for the abolition of that innocent relation are discountenanced and disparaged. At the same time, all adequate, trustworthy, and truthful representations of the cruelties habitually and extensively practised upon slaves, are scouted as incredible or exaggerated. Attempts are made to offset them by the cool remark that parents are sometimes cruel to their children, mechanics to their apprentices, and capitalists to operatives in their employ. To this it is often added that, on the whole, slaves are as well off as other laboring people, and better off than they would be if set free. In this way, the sympathies of the people of the North are withdrawn from the slaves. And whether we arraign "the legal relation," or the so-called "abuses," we find our attacks warded off by the arts of sophistry and evasion. Even ministers of religion and ecclesiastical bodies have been proficients in these arts, and the friends of liberty themselves have thereby been led, in some instances, to make unwise and unfortunate concessions.

In this book we shall endeavor to show what "the legal relation" is; what the usages of slaveholders generally are; and the natural and necessary correspondence and connection between them. In describing the "legal relation," we shall use the testimony of slaveholders themselves, in their own language, set forth in the most solemn and authenticated form, the public testimony of their legislative acts and judicial decisions, made for the very purpose of defining and enforcing that relation. If such testimony cannot be received, there is an end to all rational discussion. Our account of the usages and practices current among slaveholders will be found sufficiently authenticated by their own testimony, and by other unimpeachable witnesses. More than all this: The intelligent and reflecting reader will be compelled, if we mistake not, to perceive that the connection between "the legal relation" and the most frightful "abuses" is that of cause and effect, or more properly, of a WHOLE with its constituent and essential PARTS, insomuch that the presence of the one implies and certifies the presence of the other.

In speaking (as we are compelled by the prevailing use of language to do) of "the legal relation," of the "laws" of slavery and of slave "owners," we must not be understood to concede the "legality" of such a relation, or the validity of such "laws," or the reality of such "ownership," in the proper meaning of those terms. The "law of sin and death" is not obligatory law. "Mischief framed by a law" binds men to nothing but to the repudiation and contempt of it. "If it be found," says Lord Littleton, "that a former decision is manifestly absurd and unjust, it is declared, *not* that such a sentence was *bad* law, but that it was *not* law." "It is generally laid down that acts of Parliament contrary to reason are void." Of the character and validity of the Slave Code the reader of this volume will have an opportunity to judge, when he shall have carefully examined and considered it.

N. B.—It is sometimes alleged that the severe laws against the education and free religious worship of slaves were occasioned by the impertinent interference of abolitionists. But it will be found, on an examination of their dates, that, with few exceptions, they were enacted long before any of the Abolition Societies were formed, and even before the American Revolution.

On the other hand, it is sometimes said that these and other severe enactments are antiquated and obsolete. It is marvellous to see with how much confidence these self-confuting statements are made by the same persons. The careful reader of the following pages will find ample evidence that both these pleas are without a shadow of foundation.

PART I.

THE RELATION OF MASTER AND SLAVE

CHAPTER 1.

SLAVE OWNERSHIP.

Fundamental Idea of modern Slaveholding; namely, the assumed principle of Human Chattelhood, or Property in Man; constituting the relation of Owner and Property—of Master and Slave.

SOUTH CAROLINA.—"Slaves shall be deemed, sold, taken, reputed and adjudged in law to be *chattels personal*, in the hands of their owners and possessors, and their executors, administrators and assigns, *to all intents, constructions, and purposes whatsoever.*" (2 Brevard's Digest, 229; Prince's Digest, 446, &c., &c.)

LOUISIANA.—"A slave is one who is in the power of a master *to whom he belongs.* The master may *sell him, dispose of his person,* his industry and his labor. He can do nothing, *possess nothing, nor acquire* any thing, but what must belong to his master." (Civil Code, Art. 35.)

"*The slave is entirely subject to the will of his master,* who may correct and chastise him, though not with *unusual* rigor, or so as to maim and mutilate him, or expose him to the danger of loss of life, or to cause his death." (Art. 173.)

It will be found, as we proceed, that this attempted

or pretended limitation of power has no real existence, and affords no protection to the slave.

An exception, in Louisiana, to the general tenure of "chattels personal," is expressed as follows:

"Slaves, though movable by their nature, are considered as *immovable* by the operation of law." (Civil Code, Art. 461.)

"Slaves shall always be reputed and considered *real estate*; shall, as such, be subject to be mortgaged, according to the rules prescribed by law, and they shall be seized and sold as *real estate*." (Statute of June 7, 1806; 1 Martin's Digest, 612.)

This provision, if literally carried into effect, would prevent the sale of slaves from off the plantations of their masters. More of this in its proper place.

KENTUCKY.—By the *law of descents*, slaves are con sidered *real* estate, and pass in consequence to *heirs*, and not to executors. (2 Littell & Swigert's Digest, 1155.)

From the following it appears, however, that special care was taken in Kentucky, that the slaves should derive no benefit from the distinction between real estate and chattels personal:

They are, however, liable, *as chattels*, to be sold by the master at his pleasure, and may be taken in execution for the payment of his debts. (Ib; see also 1247.)

VIRGINIA.—In 1705 a law similar to that of Kentucky was enacted, but was soon after repealed. (Note to Revised Code, 432.) Slaves are therefore held as *chattels personal* in Virginia, as in most of the slave States, where, in the absence of *entire written codes*, or such *general* enunciations as those of South Carolina and Louisiana, the chattel principle has, nevertheless, been affirmed and maintained by the courts, and involved in legislative acts. A specimen of the latter description we have in the following:

MARYLAND.—"In case the personal property of a ward shall consist of specific ARTICLES, *such as* SLAVES, WORKING BEASTS, ANIMALS of any kind, STOCK, FURNITURE, plate, books, AND SO FORTH, the Court, if it shall deem it advantageous to the ward, may, at any time, pass an order *for the sale thereof*," &c., &c. (Act of 1798, chap. CI. No. 12.)

Without further citation (as might be made) of particular enactments in this place, it may be sufficient to state that the "Roman civil law," as existing at an early period, before its modification under professedly Christian Emperors, is generally referred to in our slave States, as containing the principles of their "peculiar institution." Where other usages or statutes, in any of the States, fail of furnishing the requisite definition of the "legal relation," recourse is generally had to the "Roman civil law." Those also who defend the "legal relation" as an innocent one, and who claim that Christ and his apostles did not disapprove it, but gave it their sanction, are forward to remind us that it existed in the Roman Empire at that period. It seems desirable, therefore, in more aspects than one, to ascertain precisely what that relation was. We find that information in Dr. Taylor's Elements of the Civil Law.

"Slaves were held *pro nullis: pro mortuis, pro quadrupedibus;* they had no head in the State; no name, title or register; *they were not capable of being injured,* nor could they take by purchase or descent; they had no heirs, and could therefore make no will; exclusive of what was called their *peculium*, whatever they acquired was their master's; they could not plead or be pleaded for, but were excluded from all civil concerns whatever. They could not claim the indulgence of absence *reipublicæ causa: they were not entitled to the rights and considerations of matrimony*, and therefore had no relief in case of adultery; nor were they proper objects of cognation and affinity, but of *quasi-cognation* only: they could be sold, transferred, or pawned as goods or personal estate, for goods they were, and as such they were esteemed; they might be tortured for evidence, *punished at the discretion of their lord, or even put to death by his authority.*" (Taylor's Elements, p. 429.)

Such was the "legal relation" said to have been sanctioned by Christ and his apostles as innocent, or (as others express it) not condemned, disapproved or censured by them. Such was the heathen "institution" now held to have been adopted as Christian. It must be added that the ancient heathen "relation" of owner and property has been more rigidly enforced in Christian America than it ever was in Pagan Rome. *Our* slavery allows no *peculium* or exempted property to be held by the slave. It denies education and literature to its human brutes. It ignores their religious nature, and bars the door of redemption and release. But we anticipate topics of future examination.

The testimony already presented is corroborated by jurists who have examined the subject. Judge Stroud, in his "Sketch of the Laws relating to Slavery," has fully expressed his views on this point. Having explained the maxim of the civil law, "partus sequitur ventrem," by which the condition of the slave *mother* is for ever entailed on all her remotest posterity, he remarks as follows:

"This maxim of the civil law, the genuine and degrading principle of slavery, inasmuch as it places the slave upon a level with *brute* animals, prevails universally in the slaveholding States." (Stroud's Sketch, p. 11.)

The same writer also says:

"It is plain that the dominion of the master is as unlimited as that which is tolerated by the laws of any civilized country in relation to brute animals—*to quadrupeds*, to use the words of the civil law." (Stroud's Sketch, p. 24.)

"The cardinal principle of slavery—that the slave is not to be ranked among *sentient beings,* but among *things*, as an article of property, a chattel personal—obtains as undoubted law, in all these (the slaveholding) States." (Ib. pp. 22, 23.)

This, then, is the definition of the terms, Slavery, Slave, and Slaveholding, as furnished by slaveholding communities, and as understood by jurists who have studied their legislation and jurisprudence. This is the theory of American Slavery. This is its fundamental Law, if it has any. This is the "legal relation of master and slave," if there be any such relation.

The next point of inquiry is, Whether these definitions correspond with existing realities, or facts? Whether this theory is an empty abstraction; or whether it is carried out into actual practice? Whether this law is merely a nominal one, (as is sometimes alleged,) antiquated and obsolete; or whether it furnishes the rule of *action* to the slaveholder, the rule of *condition* to the slave?

From statutory enactments and recognized codes, we now turn to the courts. Their reported decisions, in the hands of the lawyers, and in daily use in the decision of new causes, will tell us whether or no the Code of Slavery is obsolete, and the statute book of the slave states a dead letter.

Chief Justice Kinsey, of the Supreme Court of New-Jersey, in 1797, said:

"They" (Indians) "have so long been recognized as *slaves* in our law, that it would be as great a *violation of the rights of property* to establish a contrary doctrine at the present day, as it would in the case of Africans, and as useless to investigate the manner in which they originally lost their freedom." (The State *vs.* Wagoner, 1 Halstead's Reports, 374 to 378.)

To be a *slave* then, even in New-Jersey, is to be *property*, upon the same tenure upon which *other* property is held. This is "the legal relation of master and slave" *there*, if the courts understand it correctly.

We will now travel further south, and look into the courts for information. As our guide we will take "Wheeler's Law of Slavery," a regular law-book, made for the use of slaveholders.* Slave property, like other property, is the subject of frequent litigation between the different owners or claimants of it, or with their neighbors. From these suits chiefly, and for use in future suits, the volume of Mr. Wheeler is compiled. The incidental testimony of such a work to the nature and incidents of slavery is the strongest and the most unobjectionable that can be conceived. We shall refer to it frequently in this volume. On the property tenure and chattelhood by which slaves are held, its testimony is clear and explicit. The idea is involved and implied throughout the entire volume. A few direct statements of the doctrine will be sufficient. Let it; be understood that our quotations are the decisions of Courts, stated in the language of the Judges.

"Slaves, *from their nature*, are CHATTELS, and were put in the hands of executors, before the act of 1792

---

* "A Practical Treatise of the Law of Slavery, being a Compilation of *all the Decisions* made on that subject, in the *several Courts* of the United States, and State Courts; with copious notes and references to the Statutes and other authorities, systematically arranged. By Jacob D. Wheeler, Esq., Counsellor at Law. New-York: Allan Pollock, Jr. New Orleans: Benjamin Levy. 1837." 476 pages, octavo. This work is recommended by Hon. Judge H. Hichcock, of Alabama, and by the New-York *Mercantile Advertiser*, and New-York *Star*.

declaring them to be personal estate." (Wheeler's Law of Slavery, p. 2.)

"The phrase '*personal estate*,' in wills and contracts, should be understood as embracing slaves." (Ib.)

"Slaves were declared by law to be *real estate*, and descend to the heir at law. They are considered real estate in case of descents." (Ib.)

"Although for some purposes slaves are declared by statute to be real estate, they are nevertheless, intrinsically personal, and are therefore to be considered as included in every statute or contract in relation to *chattels* which does not, in terms, exclude them. They are liable, as chattels, to the payment of debts," &c. (Ib. p. 37.)

In the case of Harris *vs.* Clarissa and others, March Term, 1834, (6 Yerger's Tenn. Rep., 227; Wheeler's Law of Slavery, pp. 319–26,) the Chief Justice, in delivering the opinion of the Court, found occasion (p. 325) to say:

"In Maryland, *the issue*" (*i. e.*, of female slaves) "is considered not an accessory, but as a part of the *use*, like that of *other* female animals. (1 Har. & McHen. Rep., 160, 352; 1 Har. & John's Rep., 526; 1 Hayw. Rep., 335.) Suppose a *brood mare* be hired for five years, *the foals* belong to him who has a part of the *use* of the dam. (2 Black. Com., 290; 1 Hayw. Rep., 335.) *The slave, in Maryland, in this respect, is placed on no higher or different ground.*"

Mr. Gholson, of the Virginia Legislature, by the use of similar language, (as will hereafter be quoted,) offended the delicacy of some, who supposed him to be *peculiarly* brutish and gross; but we here find it to be in accordance with the ordinary language of the courts of law!

About forty-five pages of "Wheeler's Law of Slavery" are occupied with judicial decisions concerning the "warranty of slaves" sold, in respect to their soundness, health, "freedom from all redhibitory vices, diseases," &c. It is impossible to look over the revolting details, and to notice the cold-hearted insensibility with which the rules and decisions of the Courts are laid down and recorded, without being deeply impressed with the unhumanizing effects of the process, particularly in the systematic forgetfulness that the slave is any thing more than a brute animal. The section concerning "*the warranty of moral qualities*" may be claimed as an exception, and is certainly one of the most remarkable pieces of law literature extant:

"The 2500th article of the Code of Louisiana divides the defects of slaves into two classes: vices of *body*, and vices of *character*." "But with regard to those of *character*, the next article expressly declares that they are *confined* to cases where the slave has committed a capital crime, where he is convicted of *theft*, and where he is in the habit of *running away*." (p. 133.)

"Drunkenness is a mental, not a physical defect, and is not ground of redhibition." (Ib.) "But a fraudulent concealment of it will be a ground for rescinding the contract." (Ib., p. 134.)

"In South Carolina there is no *implied* warranty

of the moral qualities of the slave;" "as where a slave was sold who had committed burglary, the fact being unknown to both the seller and purchaser." (Ib., p. 136.)

These quotations are made to prove the bona fide, matter-of-fact *chattelhood* of the slave, or his being degraded to the condition of mere *property*, either real or personal. And they show that the condition adheres not merely to the *body*, but to the *soul;* to the moral qualities that distinguish a man from a brute! It is an *honest* servant that the vender sells. If the article is proved to have been *dishonest*, the sale is vitiated. The *honesty* of the man, then, is a commodity in the market!

"Craziness or idiocy is an absolute vice; and, where not apparent, will annul the sale." (Ib., p. 139.)

The God-like intellect of the human chattel is, therefore, the commodity sold and warranted! On the same page, a case is cited—"Icar vs. Suars, Jan. Term, 1835. 7 Louisiana Reports, 517"—in which Judge Bullard, after stating the law and the facts, gave judgment for the plaintiff, saying, "We are satisfied that the slave in question was wholly, and perhaps worse than useless."

In the case of the State *vs.* Mann, the defendant was indicted for an assault and battery on a hired slave, named Lydia. Judgment was rendered for the State; but, on an appeal, the judgment was reversed. In giving his decision, Judge Ruffin thus disposes of the plea that the relation of master and slave resembles other domestic relations:

"This has indeed been assimilated, at the bar, to the other domestic relations; and arguments drawn from the well-established principles which confer and restrain the authority of the parent over the child, the tutor over the pupil, the master over the apprentice, have been pressed upon us. *The Court does not recognize their application. There is no likeness between the cases. They are in opposition to each other, and there is an impassable gulf between them.* The difference is that which exists between freedom and slavery, and a greater cannot be imagined. In the one, the end in view is the happiness of the youth, born to equal rights with that governor on whom the duty devolves of training the youth to usefulness, in a station which he is afterwards to assume among freemen. To such an end, and with such a subject, moral and intellectual instruction seem the natural means; and, for the most part, they are found to suffice. Moderate force is superadded, to make the others effectual. If that fail, it is better to leave the party to his own headstrong passions, and the ultimate correction of the law, than to allow it to be immoderately inflicted by a private person. *With slavery it is far otherwise. The end is the profit of the master*, his security, and the public safety. The subject is doomed, in his own person and his posterity, to live without knowledge, and without capacity to make any thing his own, and *to toil that others may reap the fruits*," &c.

From such premises the Judge infers the necessity of absolute power in the master over the slave, and the impossibility of any legal protection to the slave from that power, while the slave system continues. We shall cite his words, to this effect, in another connection.

It would be easy to multiply appropriate quotations from the courts, but we reserve them for a still more appropriate use, in treating of the various features of slavery, all of which spring out of the principle of *property in man*, and attest its existence and activity.

Let us next see how this matter is understood among slaveholders themselves. Hear the testimony of their statesmen.

THOMAS JEFFERSON, in his letter to Governor Coles, of Illinois, dated August 25th, 1814, asserts that slaveholders regard their slaves as property and as brutes, in the paragraph that follows:

"Nursed and educated in the daily habit of seeing the degraded condition, both bodily and mental, of these unfortunate beings, FEW MINDS HAVE YET DOUBTED THAT THEY WERE AS LEGITIMATE SUBJECTS OF PROPERTY AS THEIR HORSES OR CATTLE." (Am. Slavery as it is, pp. 110–11.)

HENRY CLAY, in his celebrated speech in the U. S. Senate, in 1839, based his argument against the abolition of slavery on the value of the slaves, AS PROPERTY. This was his language:

"The third impediment to immediate abolition is to be found in the immense amount of *capital* which is invested in *slave property*." "The total value of slave property then, by estimate, is twelve hundred millions of dollars. And now it is rashly proposed, by a single fiat of legislation, to annihilate this immense amount of property! To annihilate it without indemnity, *and without compensation to* THE OWNERS." "I know that there is a visionary dogma which holds that negro slaves cannot be the subject of property. I shall not dwell on the speculative abstraction. *That* IS *property which the law declares* TO BE *property.* Two hundred years of legislation have sanctified and sanctioned negro slaves as property."

This argument identifies slaveholding with human chattelhood, and the relinquishment of this claim of property with abolition. It bases the practice upon the theory, and rests the justification of its perpetuity upon the practical efficacy of the law, as being neither a dead letter nor obsolete. In this argument the slaveholders confide, the nation consents, and therefore slavery exists, with all the evils it brings in its train.

By claiming their slaves as "property," the "owners" of this property are naturally led to forget and even to deny that they are human beings. For proof of this we cite the speech of Mr. SUMMERS of Virginia, in the Legislature of that State, January 26, 1832, as published in the *Richmond Whig:*

"When in the sublime lessons of Christianity, he (the slaveholder) is taught to 'do unto others as he would have others do unto him,' *he never dreams* that the degraded *negro* is within the pale of that holy canon."

We learn from this that the Southern pulpit has failed to teach the community a contrary lesson. The innocent "legal relation" has been suffered to circumscribe the jurisdiction of the golden rule.

Col. DAYTON, formerly member of Congress from South-Carolina, in a work entitled, "The South vindicated from the Treason and Fanaticism of Northern Abolitionists," holds the following language:

"The Northerner looks upon a band of negroes as so many *men*, but the planter or Southerner *views them in very different light.*"

Mr. GHOLSON, of Virginia, in his speech in the Legislature of that State, Jan. 18, 1831, as published in the *Richmond Whig*, (in reply to some members who had proposed abolition,) said:

"Why, I really have been under the impression that I *owned* my slaves. I lately purchased *four women* and ten children, in whom I thought I obtained a great bargain, for I really supposed they were *my property*, as were my *brood mares.*"

Mr. WISE, in the United States House of Representatives, said:

"The right of petition belongs to the people of the United Staves. *Slaves are not people* in the eye of the law. They have *no legal personality.*"

Another gentleman (as quoted by Mr. Vanderpool, of New-York) said: "SLAVES had no more right to be heard than HORSES AND DOGS,"

Mr. VANDERPOOL, of New-York, himself said: "He should be ashamed of himself, if he ever could have supposed that slaves had a right to petition this or any other body where slavery exists."—"Had *any one*, before to-day, ever dreamed that the appellation of THE PEOPLE embraced SLAVES? Sir! (said he,) I hesitate not to say, that were I a Southern man, I would not submit to the doctrine that slaves have a right to petition, if Congress were ever mad enough to sanction it. Nay, I go farther, and say, that *as a Northern man* I would not submit to it."

Mr. PICKENS, of South Carolina, said:

"The offense of Mr. Adams consisted in his announcing, that he had a petition from the slaves, THUS DESTROYING THE RELATION BETWEEN MASTER AND SLAVE, and denying the doctrine that the slave can BE HEARD ONLY THROUGH HIS MASTER."

The doctrine, thus explained and advocated, was deliberately and solemnly sanctioned by the House of Representatives of the United States, in a resolution adopted Feb. 11, 1837—yeas 162, nays 18, as follows:

"*Resolved*, that SLAVES do not possess the right of petition secured to THE PEOPLE of the United States, by the Constitution."

Thus was the national sanction given to the definition of "the legal relation between master and slave," which denies that "the relation" can consist with the recognition of personality and humanity in the slave.

Ecclesiastical bodies have been equally explicit in their definition of the relation.

The Charleston Baptist Association addressed a memorial to the Legislature of South Carolina, maintaining that "the Divine Author of our holy religion" adopted this institution "as one of the allowed relations of society," and they further say:

"Neither society nor individuals have *any more* authority to demand a relinquishment, without an equivalent, in the *one* case than in the OTHER," (that is, their right to) "the *money and lands* inherited from ancestors, or derived from industry." "We would resist to the utmost every invasion of *this right*, come from what quarter and under what pretence it may."

In the settlement of the estate of Rev. Dr. Furman, of the same sect, in the same State, his legal representatives exercised this "right," in an advertisement of a public sale of his property at auction, as follows:

"A plantation or tract of land on and in Wateree swamp, a tract of the first quality of fine land on the waters of Black River; a lot of land in the town of Camden; a library of a miscellaneous character, chiefly theological; twenty-seven negroes, some of them very prime; two mules; one horse; and an old wagon."

"Slaves are neither considered nor treated as human beings."* This is the testimony of Mr. L. Turner, a regular and respectable member of the Second

* Nothing else than the prevalence of this feeling can account for the preposterous effort to discredit the unity of the negro race with the rest of mankind! It is very remarkable that Mr. Jefferson, who wrote so eloquently against slavery, and whose kindness to his own mulatto slave children was so commendable, should have published to the world such crude speculations of this character—

Presbyterian church in Springfield, Illinois; who was brought up in Caroline County, Virginia. And the testimony is approvingly communicated by Rev. William T. Allan, of Chatham, Illinois, pastor of a Presbyterian church in that place. Mr. Allan is son of Rev. Dr. Allan, pastor of the Presbyterian church in Huntsville, Alabama. (Weld's "Slavery as it is," p. 46.)

"Slaveholders regard their slaves *as property*, the mere instruments of their convenience and pleasure. One who is a slaveholder at heart, *never recognizes a human being in a slave*." This is the testimony of Angelina Grimke Weld, daughter of the late Judge Grimke of the Supreme Court of South Carolina, and sister of the late Hon. Thomas S. Grimke of Charleston. (Ib., 57.)

When a slave is accidentally killed, the Southern newspapers speak of it merely as a *loss of property* to the *owner*. Nothing is said of the bereaved widow, children, or parents of the deceased. It would be easy to present numerous instances in proof.

The Natchez (Miss.) *Free Trader* of February 12, 1838, contained the following advertisement:

"FOUND.—A NEGRO'S HEAD was picked up on the railroad, yesterday, which THE OWNER can have by calling at this office and paying for this advertisement." (Ib., 169.)

---

not less unphilosophical than unscriptural. It is still more remarkable that professed believers in the Bible should express doubts on the subject!

The idea of the advertiser probably was, that the head would be of use to the owner in establishing his claim on the Railroad Company, or some one, for damages in the destruction of his property.

The Vicksburg (Miss.) *Register*, December 27, 1838, contains the following item of news for the amusement of its readers:

"ARDOR IN BETTING.—Two gentlemen at a tavern having summoned the waiter, the poor fellow had scarcely entered when he fell down in a fit of apoplexy. 'He's dead!' exclaimed one. 'He'll come to,' replied the other. 'Dead for five hundred!' 'Done!' retorted the second. The noise of the fall, and the confusion which followed, brought up the landlord, who called out to fetch a doctor. 'No, no! we must have no interference—there's a bet depending!' 'But, sir, I shall lose a valuable servant!' 'Never mind, you can put him down in the bill!'"

This is shocking: but, aside from the moral wrong of betting, the *principle* involved differs nothing from that avowed by the Charleston Baptist Association already quoted, so far as the matter of human chattelhood is concerned. Admit the doctrine, as held by the Association, and as defended by Mr. Clay, and the life of the negro was no more sacred than the life of a horse. "The innocent legal relation" "sanctifies and sanctions" the whole.

The same principle finds daily expression in the ordinary vocabulary of slaveholders. Their slaves, like their other domestic animals, are called "stock." The children of slaves are spoken of, prospectively, even before they are born, as anticipated "increase." Female slaves that are mothers are called "breeders," till past child-bearing. Those who compel the labor of slaves are called "drivers." Like horses they are warranted, when sold, to be "sound," and are returned by the purchaser when "unsound."

The same principle is recognized by the free citizens and professed Christians of the North, whenever they speak of the slaveholder's "rights of property," or entertain the idea of "compensation" to them, in case of a general abolition of slavery, or of the redemption of particular slaves, in any such sense as implies that such appropriation or purchase money would be equitably due.

It remains to be observed that this claim of property in slaves, both in theory and practice, as defined by legislation and jurisprudence, as defended by theologians and as sanctioned by ecclesiastical bodies, as carried out into every-day practice by the pious and by the profane, is manifestly and notoriously a claim, not only to the bodies and the physical energies of the slave, but also to his immortal soul, his human intelligence, his moral powers, and even (in the case of a pious slave) to his Christian graces and virtues.

This is proved by the fact, that the body of the slave without his soul would be a dead carcass of no value. Or, if it be objected that the same distinction obtains between a dead horse and a living one, our proposition is proved by the fact, that if the slave had only the intellectual powers of a horse, his inferiority to a horse in physical strength would sink him below the pecuniary value of a horse, instead of his commanding, as he now does, the price of a number of horses.

In advertisements of slaves to be sold or to be hired out, their intelligence, their skill, their honesty, their sobriety, their benevolent dispositions are specified and insisted on, as items of primary importance in estimating their value. Their *piety* is not unfrequently mentioned in the inventory, and they are recommended as being worthy members of Methodist, Baptist, or Presbyterian churches. And church members of the same sects both buy and sell them on the basis of these recommendations.

This, in the United States of America, in this nineteenth century, is "the legal relation of master and slave"—a relation that challenges as "goods" and "chattels personal, to all intents, constructions, and purposes whatsoever," the immortal soul of man, the image of the invisible Creator, the temple of the Holy Spirit, the purchase of a Redeemer's blood. The statement is no rhetorical flourish. It is no mere logical inference. It is no metaphysical subtlety. It is no empty abstraction. It is no obsolete or inoperative fiction of the law. It is veritable matter-of-fact reality, acted out every day wherever and whenever a negro or any one else is claimed as an American slave. If any slaveholder denies it, let him be challenged to put the denial in writing, duly attested, and in such a shape that the courts of law can take cognizance of it. Whenever he does this, and puts the paper in the hands of his slave or trusty friend, his slave is set free. Every intelligent slaveholder knows this.

The evidence already presented is sufficient, but there is much more in reserve. In the chapters that follow, the various features of the slave system will be presented, as defined by the Slave Code and as exhibited in daily practice. And each one of these features will be seen to grow out of the foundation principle of American Slavery—to wit, human chattelhood, as exhibited in this chapter, thus proving the presence and the vitality of that principle by its practical operations and bearings. The whole system may be educed from this parent stock, as any science, in detail, is educed from its fundamental axioms. Let any reflecting person assume that human chattelhood, or property in man, is the foundation of the system; then let him follow out, in his own mind, the natural and necessary workings of such a principle *reduced to practice*, and he will be able to anticipate beforehand almost the entire code of slavery, and the practices existing under it.

CHAPTER II.

SLAVE TRAFFIC.

Sale—Purchase—Barter—Mortgage—Auction—Coffle-gang—Shipments—As absolutely as in the case of any other Property, and by the same Tenure.

THIS feature must result, of necessity, from "the legal relation" of ownership exhibited in the first chapter. The quotations there made cover explicitly this ground.

"The master may sell him." "Slaves shall be sold." "Sold, transferred, or pawned as goods, or personal estate, *for* goods they were, and as such they were esteemed."

Any modification of this feature must evidently relax the application of the principle of ownership, and limit its operation. In the Spanish, Portuguese, and French colonies, such modifications, nevertheless, obtained. The *Code Noir*, art. 47, prohibits the selling of the husband without the wife, the parents without the children, or *vice versa.* In cases of *voluntary* sales, made contrary to this regulation, the wife or husband, the children or parents, though expressly retained by the seller, pass, by the same conveyance, to the purchaser, and may be claimed by him without any additional price. (See Stephen's Slavery, 69 ;* Stroud's Sketch, 51.)

What bearing this humane regulation would have upon our internal slave-trade, if it were established in this country, the reader will see by the following account of its operation.

Says the compiler of the Annals of the Sovereign Council of Martinique:

"This law has always been rigidly executed, whenever a claim has been set up on the part of *the purchaser*. I have known slaves who have been sent to Guadaloupe or St. Domingo to be expatriated and sold, to reclaim *their children* remaining in our colony, with success, through the action of the purchasers in the colonies to which they were sent." (See Stephen's Slavery, 69 and 70, citing Annals de la Martinique, tome i., p. 285. Vide Stroud, p. 51.)

It would not, probably, be quite as easy for slave children to recover their *aged parents*, or for husbands to reclaim their feeble and *sickly wives*, by this "action of the purchasers." Humanity, nevertheless, would gain much. The principle of human chattelhood would be weakened. Perhaps it was partly through the influence of this and similar relaxations of the principle that the entire system was swept away in Mexico and the South American Republics. By this feature of the *Code Noir*, the bondage under its ju-

* This remarkable provision arises, doubtless, from the fact that the laws respecting slavery in those colonies are framed in the mother country, and not (as in the British colonies) by colonial legislatures, composed of slaveholders.

risdiction was made to resemble, in this aspect, the feudalism or serfdom of northern Europe, where the villein is attached to the soil, rather than the chattel slavery of the American slave States.

In Pennsylvania, in New-York, perhaps in other American States, when measures were taken for the prospective abolition of slavery, the sale of slaves to be sent out of the State was prohibited by express statute. Except in these instances, we know of no departure, in the matter of sale and transfer, in our American slave States, from the principle of unrestricted and absolute human chattelhood, unless the anomaly be found in the State of Louisiana, as hinted in our first chapter, where it was stated that slaves are held in Louisiana as *real* estate. "In the slaveholding States," (says Judge Stroud,) "*except in Louisiana*, no law exists to prevent the violent separation of parents from their children, or even from each other." (Stroud's Sketch, p. 50.) Again, after dwelling upon these cruelties of the domestic slave-trade, as being peculiar to "the republican States of North America," the same writer adds in a note, (p. 52,) "From the generality of this remark, the State of Louisiana must be excepted." "The slaves are declared to be *real* estate, to be ranked among *immovable* property. *When*, therefore, the owner of slaves is, as I presume is most commonly the case, possessed of *land*, the slave cannot be separated from it by process of law. Besides this humane regulation, there are several others which deserve to be signalized, viz.: 'If, at a public sale of slaves, there happen to be some who are disabled through old age or otherwise, and who have children, such slaves shall not be sold but with his or her children, whom he or she may think proper to go with.'" (1 Martin's Digest, 612; Act of July 7, 1806; Stroud's Sketch, p. 52–3.)

How far these provisions are, at this late day, available for the benefit of the slaves of Louisiana, we have no means of knowing. Louisiana has been a purchasing, rather than a slave-exporting State. The striking contrast between these enactments and the known usages and scenes of other States, mark their anomalous character, as exceptions which prove and illustrate the general rule of unrestricted chattelhood in our slaveholding States.

It is to be noticed that these refreshing anomalies are witnessed in only *one* of the slave States: a State coming within our jurisdiction from under that of France, and receiving its earlier features of polity under the laws of Spain. Louisianian slavery took its type from the *Code Noir*, and from the usages growing up under what our citizens are pleased to denominate Spanish despotism and superstition. Anglo-Saxon civilization and religion, with all their "republican" and "Protestant" boastings, have not yet reached the same point of progress; nor do we learn that in Florida, acquired from Spain, the mild features of Spanish slavery have survived the transfer. The reason may be, that too many Northern citizens (the most merciless of all slaveholders) have planted themselves there. Be this as it may, it is certain that the "legal relation of master and slave," as commonly understood, practised, vindicated, and protected, in these United States, differs widely, in the feature now under consideration, from that defined by the *Code Noir*. We may venture to affirm that the commonly received exposition, as it exists in theory and practice, in the Church and the State, has been truthfully set forth by one of our most prominent and popular statesmen, the late Henry Clay, in his speech in the U. S. Senate, Feb. 7, 1839, in which he said:

"The moment that the incontestable *fact* is admitted, that the slaves are *property*, the law of movable property *irresistibly* attaches itself to them, and *secures the right* of carrying them from one State to another."*

* It may be said that there is an exception to this statement of Mr. Clay, in the laws of some of the slave States, prohibiting the importation of slaves from other States; also, in the restrictions recently imposed, on motion of Mr. Clay himself, upon the prosecution of the slave-trade from the Federal District.

Those State regulations were, for reasons of policy or supposed interest, to encourage slave-breeding at home, instead of receiving supplies from abroad. Whether consistent or inconsistent with the rights of property, they have their precedent in the prohibitions of importations of other kinds of property, by different nations and States. But, under our Federal Constitution, the power of regulating commerce between the several States is committed to Congress, not to the States; and hence, in Mississippi, notwithstanding the prohibitory enactment, the slave-dealers in 1836–7 brought into that State and sold slaves to the value of ninety millions of dollars! It is true that when they undertook the collection of their debts, the purchasers pleaded the illegality of the sales; the

This definition, which is acted upon every day, identifies "the legal relation" and the slave system with the domestic slave-trade, and its constant and violent disruption of the most sacred and tender ties of consanguinity and affection. If the "legal relation" does not produce this effect in respect to each slave, it *does*, in each instance, uphold and sanction the principle of chattelhood upon which alone the traffic in slaves rests. It recognizes the rightfulness of the traffic by recognizing the rightfulness of slave ownership, which includes the right of purchase and sale. This is what Mr. Clay affirmed, and, thus far, he spoke truthfully. The moment the right of property in man is admitted, (and here lies the core of the "relation,") that moment the right of purchase and sale is virtually conceded likewise. It was a triumph of human sympathy over legal congruity and logical consistency, that enacted the *Code Noir*.

The exposition of Mr. Clay reduces slaves to a level with poultry and swine; it denies to them personality and the attributes of human beings. It does this not merely in theory, but on a point of the most pressing practical importance. It certifies us that the chattel principle is neither a dead letter nor an unmeaning abstraction. It exhibits the practical statesmanship, not of Henry Clay only, but of all

---

State courts sustained them, and thus they obtained the greater part of the importation without payment!

The restriction in the Federal District prevents *dealers* from bringing in supplies from the States, for sale and shipment abroad, but does not prevent purchases and sales among the citizens.

who admit the validity of the so-called "legal relation."

A similar exposition we have from Rev. James Smylie, of the Amite Presbytery, Mississippi, in a pamphlet written in defense of slaveholding. Alluding to the charges of abolitionists, he admits the facts adduced by them, but denies their criminality. And he says:

"If slavery be a sin, and advertising and apprehending slaves with a view to restore them to their masters, is a direct violation of the divine law, and if the BUYING, SELLING, and holding a slave, FOR THE SAKE OF GAIN, is a heinous sin and scandal, then verily, THREE FOURTHS of all the Episcopalians, Methodists, Baptists, and Presbyterians, in eleven States of this Union, are of the devil. They hold, if they do not buy and sell slaves, and (with few exceptions) they hesitate not to apprehend and restore runaway slaves, when in their power."

It will be noticed that the *holding*, the *buying*, and the *selling* of a slave are here put together, as being essentially of the same character. And common sense as well as "the *law*" of the peculiar "relation," as expounded by Henry Clay, attests the same thing.

A large portion of "Wheeler's Law of Slavery" is occupied with legal decisions connected, directly or indirectly, with cases growing out of the transfer of slaves. One division, or chapter of the work, treats "Of the Increase of Slaves—to whom the increase belongs—of the grant or devise of the increase." Another topic is, "Of the Title to Slaves;" another, "Of Warranty;" another, "Of Hiring of Slaves;" another, "Of Mortgage of Slaves;" another, "Of Dower of Slaves;" another, "Of the Division of Slaves;" another, "Of the Remainder in Slaves." Upwards of one hundred and fifty pages of the book (nearly one third of the entire work) are occupied with these topics. From the extent and variety of litigation coming before the courts and demanding these complicated legal rules and decisions, it would seem that a very large part of the business transactions of the people must consist in the reception or transfer, in some form, of this species of property. And, at every step, it appears that transfers of slave property are made upon the same principles that govern the transfer of other property, that it is held and conveyed under the same tenure, and with as little sense of the impropriety of the transaction; thus placing, *in practice,* a human being upon a level with a *mere thing.* Thus, when the judge, the lawyer, or the law compiler or author would lay down the legal rule by which the decision should be made in a litigated case, in a matter of sale, delivery, possession, warranty, &c., he looks up the precedents and rules originally occurring or laid down in respect to "*a mare*" or "a colt," and then, with the utmost coolness and gravity, applies it, as valid law, to the sale, delivery, or warranty of "*a girl!*" An instance of this occurs in "Wheeler's Law of Slavery," pp. 119, 120, in a note on the case of Smith *vs.* Rowzee, Spring Term 1821; a case in which "the girl" purchased was unable to travel home with her new master, eight miles distant, and

soon died. A lawsuit followed, and the law concerning *other* live stock determined the case!

In one instance (p. 68) we find "a negro woman slave named Peg," sold for $300, with leave to return her in three weeks, if the purchaser did not like her. With her new master she became *frost-bitten*, which rendered her "*of little value.*" Hence a suit between the parties, judgment given, an appeal taken, judgment reversed—just as in the case of a horse or an ox.

On page 79 we learn that "five years' peaceable possession gives a title to a slave, and which, if lost, may be regained." We infer that if possession, as between contending claimants of slave property, be thus potent, it would be at least equally powerful, as between the possessor and the slave's legal right to freedom.

Of the extent of the slave traffic between the slave-growing and planting States (of which we shall speak presently) some tolerably reliable approximation towards the true statistics may be gathered. But of the extent of local and neighborhood transfers, with which Wheeler's reported cases seem mostly occupied, very little can be accurately known. We can only say that a perusal of "Wheeler's Law of Slavery" has very greatly swelled our own estimate or apprehension of that extent. It can hardly be supposed that more than a tithe of such transfers would occasion lawsuits. But we seem to see the courts crowded with them, and a compilation of the reported cases swelling a law volume. It must be folly to pretend that the slave traffic occupies only the vulgar portion of Southern society, when it figures so largely in the courts.

"Slaves may be sold and transferred from one to another, *without any statutory restriction or limitation, as to the separation of parents and children, &c.*, except in Louisiana." (Wheeler's Law of Slavery, p. 41.)

It can hardly be necessary to cite witnesses to prove that this feature of the Slave Code, which licenses the slave-trade and the separation of families, is not a dead letter. But it might be useful to impress upon the reader some idea of the magnitude and the atrocity of this traffic. This would open a wide field. We might refer the inquirer to Weld's "Slavery as it is," to Jay's "Inquiry," and to Goodell's "History of Slavery and Anti-Slavery," for collections of facts and testimonies on this subject, upon which we cannot enlarge here.

The extent of the slave-trade in America may be conceived, from the testimony of the Presbyterian Synod of Kentucky, that "these scenes" (i. e. coffle-gangs) are "*daily* occurring in the midst of us;" that "there is *not a neighborhood* where these heart-rending scenes are not displayed;" that "there is not a *village or road* that does not behold the sad procession of manacled outcasts, whose chains and mournful countenances tell that they are exiled by force from all that their hearts hold dear."

Its general prosecution may be seen by the numerous advertisements of both purchasers and venders, in the most respectable newspapers in the slave States, as, for example, the following:

"NEGROES FOR SALE.—A negro woman, 24 years of age, and her two children, one eight and the other three years old. Said negroes will be sold SEPARATELY or together, *as desired.* The woman is a good seamstress. She will be sold low for cash, or EXCHANGED FOR GROCERIES. For terms, apply to

"MATTHEW BLISS & Co., 1 Front Levee."

[*New-Orleans Bee.*

"I will give the highest cash price for likely Negroes, from 10 to 25 years of age.

"GEORGE KEPHART."

[*Alexandria* (*D. C.*) *Gazette.*

"FIFTY NEGROES WANTED IMMEDIATELY.—The subscriber will give a good market price for fifty likely negroes, from 10 to 30 years of age.

"HENRY DAVIS."

[*Petersburg* (*Va.*) *Constellation.*

Having obtained their supplies and driven or shipped them South, the dealers offer them for sale, in advertisements like the following, which appeared in the papers of Charleston, S. C.:

"ONE HUNDRED AND TWENTY NEGROES FOR SALE.—The subscriber has *just arrived from Petersburg, Virginia,* with one hundred and twenty *likely young negroes* of both sexes and every description, which he offers for sale on the most reasonable terms. The lot now on hand consists of plough-boys, several likely and well-qualified house servants of both sexes, *several women with children, small girls* suitable for nurses, and SEVERAL SMALL BOYS WITHOUT THEIR

MOTHERS. Planters and *traders* are earnestly requested to give the subscriber a call previously to making purchases *elsewhere*, as he is enabled to sell as cheap or cheaper than can be sold by *any other person in the trade.* BENJAMIN DAVIS.

"*Hamburg, S. C., September* 28, 1838."

The respectability and profitableness of the traffic may be inferred from the fact, that some of the largest shipping merchants are slave merchants, that they own, and charter, and freight numerous vessels to transport their slaves coastwise, and invest princely fortunes as capital in the business.

The importance of this branch of commerce will be apparent from the speeches of leading statesmen, and the paragraphs of prominent editors.

HENRY CLAY, in his speech before the Colonization Society, in 1829, said:

"It is believed that *no where*, in the farming portion of the United States, would slave labor be generally employed, if the proprietor were not tempted to RAISE slaves, by the HIGH PRICE of the SOUTHERN MARKET which keeps it up in his own."

Mr. GHOLSON, of Virginia, in the same speech in the State Legislature before quoted, after claiming his negro women as his property, like his "brood mares," expatiated upon the profitableness and the rightfulness of the investment. "The owner of land had a reasonable right to its annual products, the owner of brood mares to their product, and the owner of female slaves to their increase." "The value of the property justifies the expense; and I do not hesitate to say that in it *consists much of our wealth.*"

The Editor of the *Virginia Times*, in 1836, made a calculation that 120,000 slaves went out of that State during the year, that 80,000 of them went with their owners who removed, leaving 40,000 who were SOLD, at an average price of $600; amounting to twenty-four millions of dollars.

Similar estimates and testimonies might be added.

The annexation of Texas and the conquest of Mexico were openly advocated, and notoriously prosecuted, for the object of extending the area of slavery, and thereby opening a new slave marke, for the breeders of slaves. And the coastwise slave trade has been protected by the National Govern ment, and its diplomacy prostituted to this purpose The particulars may be found in Jay's "View of the Action of the Federal Government in behalf of Slavery," and Jay's "Review of the Mexican War;" also (briefly) in Goodell's "History of Slavery and Anti-Slavery."

Of the *character* of this traffic little more need be said. By our own National Government the African slave-trade is branded "piracy." But Thomas Jefferson Randolph, in the Virginia Legislature, in 1832, declared the domestic slave-trade to be "*much worse.*"

About 1100 citizens of the Federal District, including Judge Cranch and the principal clergy of the District, petitioned Congress against it, (as there existing;) and, comparing it with the African slave-trade, they said that it is "scarcely less disgraceful in its character, and even more demoralizing in its influence." This was in 1828. The Grand Jury of the District had, many years before, (1802,) presented it as a nuisance.* Its character there, at that time, differs nothing from its character in the different States, at present.

The New-Orleans *Courier*, February 15th, 1839, says: "The United States law" (prohibiting the African slave-trade) "may, and probably does put MILLIONS into the pockets of the people living between the Roanoke and Mason and Dixon's line; still we think it would require some casuistry to show that the *present slave-trade from that quarter is a whit better than the one from Africa.*"

It may be asked, *who are they*, at the South, that prosecute this domestic slave-trade? The Presbyterian Synod of Kentucky, describing its extent, its common occurrence and its barbarities, inform us, in the same paragraph, that "professors of the religion of mercy," "who hold to our communion," have "torn the mother from the children, and sent them into returnless exile. Yet acts of discipline have rarely" [never†] "followed such conduct." In the Presbyterian General Assembly of 1835, it was stated

* By the Act of Congress of 1850, the slave dealers are prohibited from making the Federal District a deposit for slaves. But this does not prevent any citizen of the District from selling his slave, or purchasing a slave from abroad.

† James G. Birney, long resident in Kentucky, and a Presbyterian, says "*never.*"

by an elder, Mr. Stewart, of Illinois, and without contradiction, that "even ministers of the gospel and Doctors of Divinity may engage in this unholy traffic, and yet sustain their high and holy calling." "Elders," said he, "ministers and Doctors of Divinity, are, with both hands, engaged in the practice." Yet nothing was done or said by the Assembly in condemnation of it. The testimony of Rev. James Smylie, already cited for another purpose, implicates "three fourths" of four leading religious sects in the practice.

If a distinction be set up between the Virginian breeders and Mississippi purchasers, gentlemen planters, on the one hand, and the human drovers, commonly called "soul-drivers," on the other, who ply between the two, disposing at the far South of their "stock" purchased at the North, we maintain that there is no legal or moral distinction between them. "The legal relation" is as innocent and as criminal in the one as in the other. The "growers," the "consumers" and "dealers" so necessary to them, stand on the same level.

Besides, the "dealers" are sometimes *esteemed* as respectable and as pious as the "growers" and "consumers." A number of authentic narratives assure us that itinerant preachers, in more sects than one, carry on the double avocation of *converting* souls, and *buying up* the souls and bodies of men, women and children, for sale. An instance, in "the fine old Methodist preacher who dealt in slaves," may be found in Weld's "Slavery as it is," p. 180. In the higher circles of society at the South, this would be thought low and vulgar—equally so with buying up horses and swine. But slave-trading on a sufficiently large scale is considered a reputable employment, just as the large importers and distillers of rum are respected among us, while the dealer of drams is despised. The items that follow are from the work of Mr. Weld, just mentioned, and which, for thirteen years past, has had an extensive circulation and eager perusal in our widely extended country, without having had one of its vast collection of facts disproved or even questioned, to our knowledge.

"That they" (the smaller dealers) "are not despised because it is their business to trade in *human beings* and bring them to market, is plain from the fact that when some 'gentleman of property and standing,' and of a 'good family,' embarks in a negro speculation, and employs a dozen 'soul-drivers' to traverse the upper country and drive to the South coffles of slaves, expending hundreds of thousands in his wholesale purchases, *he does not lose caste.*

"It is known in Alabama that Mr. ERWIN, *son-in-law of* HENRY CLAY, and brother of J. P. Erwin, formerly postmaster and late Mayor of the city of Nashville, laid the foundation of a princely fortune in the slave-trade carried on from the Northern slave States to the planting South; that Hon. H. HITCHCOCK, brother-in-law of Mr. E., and *since* one of the Judges of the Supreme Court of Alabama, was interested with him in the traffic; and that a late member of the Kentucky Senate, (Col. WALL,) not only carried on the same business a few years ago, but accompanied his droves in person down the Mississippi. Not as the *driver*, for that would be vulgar drudgery, beneath a gentleman, but as a nabob in state, ordering his understrappers.

"It is also well known that President JACKSON was a 'soul-driver,' and that even so late as the year before the last war, he bought up a coffle of slaves and drove them down to Louisiana for sale.

"THOMAS N. GADSDEN, Esq., the principal slave auctioneer in Charleston, S. C., is of one of the first families, and moves in the very highest class of society there. He is a descendant of the distinguished General Gadsden, of revolutionary memory," and "member of the Continental Congress," "afterwards Governor of the State." "The Rev. Dr. Gadsden, rector of St. Philip's Church, Charleston, and Rev. Philip Gadsden," and "Col. James Gadsden, of the U. States' Army, are his brothers." "Under his hammer, men, women and children go off by thousands; its stroke probably sunders, *daily*, husbands and wives, parents and children, brothers and sisters, perhaps to see each other's faces no more. Now, who supply the auction table of this Thomas Gadsden, Esq., with its loads of human merchandise? These same 'detested soul-drivers,' forsooth, (as they are sometimes called, even at the South.) They prowl through the country, buy, catch, and fetter them, and drive their chained coffles to his stand, where Thomas Gadsden, Esq., knocks them off to the highest bidder, to Ex-Gov. Butler, perhaps, or to Ex-Gov. Hayne, or to Hon. Robert Barnwell Rhett," (M. C.,) "or (it may be) to his own Reverend brother, Dr. Gadsden." (Weld's "Slavery as it is," p. 174.)

One illustration more must suffice. During the great negro speculation of 1836, when all the negro-consuming States were insanely eager to purchase at high prices, and all the negro-breeding States were enriching themselves with the sales, the 'soul-drivers,' now multiplied beyond all former precedent, were separating wives and husbands, parents and children, with unwonted celerity, and driving them in chained coffles, or droves, as speedily as possible to the market. The whole South was feverish and in motion. Money for the operation was in brisk demand. The banks extended their loans, and were drained. Capitalists demanded high rates of interest. Through the banks they made loans to the speculators. Then it was that the Trustees of the General Assembly of the Presbyterian Church, lured by these high rates of interest, though well knowing, as every body did, the purposes for which their capital was wanted, withdrew their funds, to the amount of $94,692.88, from a Northern institution where they were drawing the usual interest, and invested them in the Southwestern banks, where they would be loaned to the speculators in the bodies and souls of men, women, and children. In the re-action and general bankruptcy that followed, the Presbyterian Church lost $68,893.88 of their funds. Had the General Assembly and its Trustees understood and felt, as they should have done, the sinfulness of "the legal relation of master and slave," they would have understood and felt the sinfulness of this abominable slave-trade which the relation involves, and the consequent sinfulness of loaning money to carry it on. But they deemed it "ultra" and "fanatical" to recognize these self-evident truths. And therefore they lost the greater part of their funds.

We dismiss this feature of the Slave Code, presuming that its paternity, its character, its vitality, and its practical workings have now been made sufficiently clear. In this feature of the system, *its Slave Traffic*, the people have been found no better than their laws, and the Church no better than the people.

CHAPTER III.

SEIZURE OF SLAVE PROPERTY FOR DEBT.

As Property, Slaves may be seized and sold to pay the Debts of their Owners, while living, or for the settlement of their Estates, after their decease.

THIS is evident from the very nature of property, especially of chattels personal, as well as from the fact that slaves may be bought and sold, and pawned or mortgaged for the security of debts. A pawn or mortgage is of the nature of barter. If not redeemed, it becomes a barter in the end. And barter is only one form of purchase and sale. Whatever may be bought and sold may be bartered, consequently mortgaged; and, if unredeemed, seized, taken possession of.

The very definition of slave property, as cited in Chapter I., specifies this incident. They "may be sold, transferred, and *pawned*." They are "chattels personal, to *all intents*, constructions and purposes whatsoever."

"The slave, being a *personal chattel*, is *at all times* liable to be sold absolutely, or *mortgaged*, or leased, at the will of his master. He may also be *sold by process of law* for the satisfaction of the debts of a living, or the debts and bequests of a deceased master, at the suit of creditors or legatees." (Stroud's Sketch, pp. 25, 51.)

"If a slave *sold*, remains with the vender, he is liable to be seized for his *debts*." (Wheeler's Law of Slavery, p. 54.)

"Slaves are considered as *property*, and in most of the States they are considered as *chattels personal*. They are *therefore* subject to those rules and regulations which society has established for the purchase and sale, and transmission from one to another, of that species of property. *They therefore may be mortgaged as personal property*, or are the subjects of a qualified or conditional sale, to suit the wants of the owner or purchaser of them. They are declared to be personal estate by the Revised Code of Mississippi, 379; Revised Code of Virginia, vol. I., pp. 431–47. Indeed, *they are considered the subjects of mortgage in all the States by custom*, and which exists in many of the States by express statutory provisions." By the Black Code of Louisiana, vol. I., Dig., p. 102, sect. 10, it is declared that slaves shall be reputed and considered real estate; shall be, as such, *subject to be mortgaged*, according to the rules prescribed by law, and they shall be *seized and sold* as real estate. (Ib., Note, pp. 164–5.)

"Slaves may be sold by creditors for debts of their owners, in all the States but Louisiana, where they cannot be separated from the land." (1 Martin's Dig., 612, Act of July, 1806; cited in Wheeler's Law of Slavery, p. 41.)

"The *children* of a female slave mortgaged, born after the execution of the mortgage, are as much liable to the demand of the mcrtgagee as the slave herself." (Ib., p. 167.)

In contrast with the preceding, we present the following:

"Plantation slaves, not only in the Spanish and Portuguese, but in the French colonies also, are *real* estate, and attached to the soil they cultivate, partaking therewith all the restraints upon voluntary alienation to which the possessor of the *land* is there liable, and they cannot be seized or sold by creditors for the satisfaction of the debts of the owner. It has already been stated that by the *Code Noir*, art. 47, the husband cannot be sold without the wife, nor the parents without the children. Sales made contrary to this regulation, by process of law, *under seizure for debts*, are declared void. (See Stephens' Slavery, 68–9; Stroud's Sketch, p. 53.)

It is evident that this feature of liability to seizure for the master's debt is, in many cases, more terrific to the slave than that which subjects him to the master's voluntary sale. The slave may be satisfied that his master is not willing to sell him—that it is not for his interest or convenience to do so. He may be conscious that he is, in a manner, necessary to his master or mistress, or that, being a favorite and tried servant, they would not sell him at any price. He may even confide in their Christian benevolence and moral principle, or promise that they would not sell him, especially that they would not thus separate him from his wife and children. But all this affords him no security or ground of assurance that his master's creditor will not seize him, or his wife or his children, against even his master's entreaties. Such occurrences are too common to be unnoticed, or out of mind.

Advertisement in the *Georgia Journal* of January 2d, 1838.

"WILL be sold, the following PROPERTY, to wit: one CHILD, by the name of James, *levied on* as the property of Gabriel Gunn."

From the *Southern Whig*, March 2, 1838.

"WILL be sold, in La Grange, Troup County, one negro girl, by the name of Charity, aged about ten or twelve years, as the *property* of Littleton L. Burk, to satisfy a *mortgage* fi. fa. from Troup Inferior Court, in favor of Daniel S. Robertson *vs.* said Burk."

Neither the Court, the sheriff, the plaintiff, the defendant, nor the negro girl, appear to have been instructed in the literature which assures willing dupes that the Slave Code is obsolete—a dead letter.

From the *Milledgeville Journal*, Dec. 26, 1837.

"EXECUTORS' SALE.—Agreeable to an order of the Court of Wilkinson County, will be sold on the first Tuesday of April next, before the Court-House door in the town of Irwington, ONE NEGRO GIRL, about *two years old*, named Rachel, belonging to the estate of William Chambers, deceased. Sold for the benefit of the *heirs* and CREDITORS of said estate.

"SAMUEL BELL,
"JESSE PEACOCK, } *Executors.*"

Here, again, the "chattel principle" appears not to have been regarded as "a mere metaphysical, speculative abstraction," as some would persuade us to believe it is.

From the *Natchez Courier*, April 2, 1838.

"NOTICE is hereby given that the undersigned, pursuant to a certain Deed of Trust, will, on Thursday, the 12th day of April next, expose to sale at the Court-House, to the highest bidder, for cash, the following negro slaves, to wit: Fanny, aged about twenty-eight years; Mary, aged about seven years; Amanda, aged *about three months;* Wilson, aged about nine months. Said slaves to be sold *for the satisfaction of the debt secured in said Deed of Trust.*

"W. J. MINOR."

The "legal relation" was here defined and exemplified, as likewise in the following:

Extract of a letter to a member of Congress from a friend in Mississippi, published in the *Washington Globe*, June, 1837.

"The times are truly alarming here. Many plantations *are entirely stripped of their negroes and horses*, by the marshal or sheriff. Suits are multiplying," &c.

Truly alarming times, indeed, for slave mothers and their babes—for slave wives and their husbands. But of *their* alarms the writer, the publisher, and the readers generally, it may be presumed, thought no more than they did of the alarms of the "horses" associated and seized with them.

In all this we have only the natural workings of

the "legal relation;" the legality of which was understood and enforced by the sheriff. It were idle to talk of his act or of the act of the creditors as an *abuse* of the relation. The relation is that of owner and chattels, and nothing else. It would be absurd (not to say dishonest) for the law to sanction such a relation, and then leave the rights unprotected which the relation implies. Were it true that *such* a relation existed, and that it was truly legal and valid, there would be manifest injustice to the attaching creditor, as well as to the voluntary slave vender, in the *Code Noir*. The truth is, no such "legal relation" can be valid; and to this fact, the *Code Noir* gives its attestation, by its *veto* upon the exercise of its involved rights.

We dismiss also this feature of the Slave Code, with the remark that, in respect to it, we find the people to be no better than their laws, and their usages no worse than "the legal relation" that gives sanction to them.

CHAPTER IV.

INHERITANCE OF SLAVE PROPERTY.

Slaves, as Property, are transmitted by Inheritance or by Will to Heirs at law or to Legatees.—In the distribution of Estates, they are distributed like other Property.

THIS feature of the slave system, like all its other features, is derived from its cardinal principle of PROPERTY in the bodies and souls of men. Without this principle, the whole edifice falls to the ground. With it, the entire system, in all its parts, and entire, is sustained.

We have already stated the law on this subject. The slave "may be sold" "at the suit of creditors OR LEGATEES." (Stroud, p. 51.)

A more specific recognition of this feature is found in a law of North Carolina, substantially copied by other States, in which, after prohibiting, in a great measure, the further introduction of slaves into their limits,* a proviso is added that "nothing in this act

---

* It has already been seen that these prohibitions have not prevented an immense slave traffic between the States. In some of the States, these prohibitions have been repealed.

shall prohibit any citizen of this State who may obtain slaves, &c., by *marriage, gift, legacy, devise, or descent*," "from bringing the slaves, &c., into this State by land or water." (Hayward's Manual, 533–4. Act of 1794, chap. 2, &c., &c., &c. Vide Stroud, p. 55.)

This indicates what is the known fact, that slaves had previously been inherited in the several States.

The inheritance of slave property appears to have occasioned much litigation in the courts, and accordingly the topic occupies no little space in the reported decisions collected together in "Wheeler's Law of Slavery."

In the case of Beatley *vs.* Judy, &c., in Kentucky, it was determined that the phrase "personal estate" in *wills* and contracts should be construed as embracing slaves. (2 Wash. Rep., 1–8.) The same in the case of Plumpton *vs.* Cook. (2 Marshall's Ky. Rep., 450; copied by Wheeler, p. 2.*)

In the case of Banks, Admr., *vs.* Marksbury, it was decided that "the owner of a female slave may give *her to one* of his children, and the *future increase*, (that is, unborn children!) *to another*." (Wheeler, p. 28.) [The case is reported at length. We give here, as in many other instances, the brief marginal statement of the compiler.]

* In our quotations from Wheeler, we often (to save room) omit his statements of the names of the litigants, the judges, and the "Reports" from which he has copied. We preserve these, in some instances, that the reader may be impressed with the *matter-of-fact* nature of the record, and not fancy himself reading "*legal fiction*." Whatever may be said of statutes, the daily decisions of courts are not "obsolete," nor are they "theoretical abstractions."

In the case of Carroll et al. *vs.* Connet, (in Kentucky,) ROBINSON Ch. J., it was held that "The administrator is liable for failure to distribute slaves. Although *for some purposes* slaves are declared by statute to be real estate, they are nevertheless intrinsically personal, and therefore are to be considered as included in every statute or contract in relation to chattels which does not, in terms, exclude them. They are liable, as chattels, to the payment of debts. They may be attached as chattels, and they have *invariably been treated* as chattels, in both Virginia and Kentucky, *so far as the rights and duties of administrators are concerned.*" (Wheeler's Law of Slavery, pp. 37–8.)

And yet Kentucky is one of the only two States in which the statutes have declared slaves to be real estate, a tenure which, *if adhered to*, would attach the slave to the soil, and prevent the separation of families. The *practice*, as sanctioned by custom and the courts, is in this case found to be less favorable to the slaves than the words of the statute, in their plain import. The people have been worse than their statutes, and the judges have conformed to the people.

"Enlaws *vs.* Enlaws, Spring Term, 1821; 3 Marshall's Ky. Rep., 228. The Court held that the slaves of a female, immediately on the marriage, vest in the husband, and although she may survive him, her right to the slaves is not revived." (Wheeler, p. 39.)

"A wife's estate in dower of slaves, by a former

husband, on her marriage vests in her husband; *and her right to manumit them is gone.*" (Ib., p. 182.)

"Slaves are subject to dower, in all the States. Not only are they subject to dower, but the widow's interest in them is protected by statutory provisions. If the husband manumits his slaves, whereby creditors and the dower are affected, the manumission is so far ineffectual, that the manumitted slaves may be sold for a period, and the proceeds applied to the creditors of the former owner and his widow." (Wheeler, p. 181.)

"Slaves are devisable, like any other chattel. A distinction, however, exists, where slaves are considered as real property. In these cases they pass immediately to the legatee, and not to the executor as personal estate." (Wheeler, p. 57.)

"If a father, at the time of his daughter's marriage, puts a negro or *other* chattel into the possession of his son-in-law, it is, in law, a gift, unless the contrary can be proven." (Ib., p. 62.)

"The *increase*" (*i. e.* the *children*) "of slaves born during the life of a legatee for life, belong to the *ulterior* legatee, who is the absolute owner." (Ib., p. 23.)

"By the Revised Code of Mississippi, p. 50, slaves descending from an intestate *may be sold* by order of the Orphan's Court, where equal division cannot be made; and persons holding life estate in slaves, or guardians for infants, are required to deliver a list of slaves to the register of the Orphan's Court, and also the *increase*, p. 51. And *similar provisions* exist in the *other States* for the division of slaves." (Ib., p. 183.)

On the same page appears, however, the following, which seems less inflexible. It appears, from the "Table of Cases," that the court was held in Virginia:

"Held, by the Court, that an equal division of slaves in number and value is not always possible, and sometimes improper, when it cannot be exactly done without separating infant children from their mothers, which humanity forbids, and will not be countenanced in a court of equity; so that a compensation for excess must, in such cases, be made and received in money." (Ib.)

Here, the humanity of the judge appears to have modified the statute.

Every one is familiar with the phrases "inherited" or "entailed slave property." Such an one is said to have been "born to a slave inheritance," or "born a slaveholder." These phrases occur in almost every plea for the blamelessness of the slaveholder, and for the "innocency of the legal relation." "The man was born into it, and how can he be blamed for it?" This plea is never more confidently urged than by a class of clergymen who are forward to teach that *all* men are born sinners and shapen in iniquity; but who would, nevertheless, be shocked at the impiety of the reprobate who should urge his "birth" in sin, his "inherited" or "entailed" depravity, in excuse of his obstinate and voluntary transgression. Perhaps it never occurs to them that "inherited" and "entailed" slaveholding, like other "inherited" and "entailed" transgressions, incur guilt when they are voluntarily adopted and cherished. In the case of any other "inherited" sin, they would readily make the requisite explanation.

This feature of the "legal relation," deemed so "innocent," so capable of white-washing with the supererogation of its meritorious innocency the crimes of successive generations and whole nations of slave-breeders and slave-venders, with their approving Senates and Synods, will be found, on a close scrutiny, to embody one of the most foul and damning features of the whole system—the feature of self-perpetuity—of self-transmission to the future; the quality of seducing and cursing posterity—securing the sin and the shame, the wretchedness and the hopelessness of the unborn. It is an "innocent relation," forsooth! because it embodies, and because (as is claimed) it even *necessitates* these results.

No feature of the slave system is more terrific to the poor slave than this. The hazards of a voluntary sale, by his master, he and his loved ones may escape. The dreaded mortgage, and creditor, and sheriff, may pass them by untouched. But there is a mortgage hanging over them, that all the gold of California cannot lift. There is a creditor whose debt against the master must be cancelled, but seldom without touching some of them. There is a sheriff, whose warrant is already out, who may seize at any day, and *will* soon seize, but probably not without touching *them*, if alive! The death of the master is the close of their respite. They are liable to be "distributed," like other "property," among the "heirs," whoever and wherever they may be, "for goods they are, and as goods they are esteemed,"—"chattels personal, in the hands of their owners and possessors, THEIR EXECUTORS, ADMINISTRATORS AND ASSIGNS, to all intents, constructions, and purposes whatsoever." This is the very definition of an American slave, and there is no escape from the condition it describes, but by the "fanaticism of abolition." This is the "legal relation" too innocent to be questioned, claiming relationship with Abraham and Moses, the sanction of Jesus and Paul!

From the *Georgia Journal.*

"TO BE SOLD.—One negro girl, *about eighteen months old*, belonging to the estate of William Chambers, deceased. Sold for the purpose of *distribution.*

"JETHRO DEAN,
"SAMUEL BEALL, } *Ex'rs.*"

Here, again, the practice corresponds with the theory, and the people are in harmony with their laws.

How the distribution of slave property among heirs and legatees is effected under the *Code Noir*, or where slaves are held as *real estate*, as in Louisiana, we are not minutely informed. If the soil and the slaves must remain together, a distribution would seem to require the whole to be sold, and to one purchaser. We doubt whether such a restriction obtains, at present, in that State. Under the old feudal system, the estate, consisting of soil and serfs, was kept together by the law of primogeniture, entailing it to the eldest son, in perpetuity. The repeal of that law has been justly regarded as a step in the march of human progress; but if the "peculiar institution" of slavery is to remain, humanity might, perhaps, invoke its re-enactment, as it might prevent the separation of slave families, or rather, permit their existence.

CHAPTER V.

USES OF SLAVE PROPERTY.

Slaves, as Property, may be *used*, absolutely by their owners at will, for their own profit or pleasure.

PROPERTY is that which may be *used* by the owner. "The slave is one who is in the power of a master, *to whom he belongs*." "Goods they are, and as goods they are esteemed." This is the law of the relation. "As goods," therefore, they may be *used*, while, like other goods, they "perish with the using." 'Have I not a right to do what I will with mine own?' is a question affirming a prerogative universally claimed. Admit the validity of the ownership, and the *right of use* follows of course. If the "legal relation" be an innocent one, the right of use and the exercise of that right are innocent likewise, provided the use be a legitimate one. We shall see what uses are *deemed* legitimate by those who have shaped, defined, and administered "the relation."

It is true that the use of property by the owner is limited by the rights of other persons. But slaves are *not* persons in the view of the law, for any purposes of benefit to them; as will hereafter be more fully shown. The rights of a slave are not recognized, and no limitation of the master's use of him can come from that quarter. "The slave" (says the law) "is entirely subject to the will of his master." Nothing, therefore, can *prevent* the master from putting him to any use he pleases.

It is also true, that the use of property by the owner is limited by the nature of that property. Thus, a living horse, or other domestic animal, may not lawfully be hacked and hewed to pieces, as a block of wood may be. The barbarity may be punished. The most that can be claimed for the Slave Code, on this point, is, that by placing slaves upon a level with other live cattle, it entitles them to the same kind and degree of protection. Beyond this, the Slave Code, so far as we know, never attempts or pretends to protect them. It knows them only as mere animals. Their rational and moral natures, not being recognized by the laws, can claim no legal protection. Sufficient evidence of this has already been adduced, but it will accumulate as we proceed. And it will be seen that as a mere animal, the slave has not equal protection, in some respects, with other animals.

We will specify some of the uses of slave property.

1. A prominent use of slave *property* is unrequited *slave labor*. The hired laborer is employed. The slave laborer is used as a horse or an ox is used. His labor is held to be the property of his owner. At this point he is degraded to the level of a brute,

whether moderately or excessively worked. The *use* of a slave as a brute laborer is an injury and an insult. It is a denial of his nature as a man, and of his rights as a free moral agent.

"The *end* of slavery," said Judge Ruffin, "is the *profit of the master.*" The slave "is doomed to *toil*, that *others may reap the fruits.*" STATE *vs.* MANN. (N. Carolina Reports, p. 263. Wheeler's Law of Slavery, p. 246.)

This honest judicial decision should shame the pretense that slaves are held for their own benefit.

In a separate chapter, we shall look more directly into the particulars of slave *labor*, and in another, shall consider the withholding of *wages*. Additional light will then be thrown upon *this* use of slave property. In the mean time, it will be easy to show that in this use of slave property, in some of the slave States, it is systematically and deliberately *so* used as to be *used up*, and destroyed in a manner that would be shameful and wicked, even if brute beasts were the victims.

Dr. Deming, a gentleman of high respectability, residing in Ashland, Richland county, Ohio, stated to Prof. Wright, at New-York city:

"That during a recent tour at the South, while ascending the Ohio river on the steamboat Fame, he had an opportunity of conversing with a Mr. Dickinson, a resident of Pittsburg, in company with a number of cotton-planters and slave-dealers from Louisiana, Alabama, and Mississippi. Mr. Dickinson stated as a fact, that the sugar-planters upon the sugar coast in Louisiana had ascertained that, as it was usually necessary to employ about *twice* the amount of labor during the boiling season that was required during the season of raising, they could by *excessive driving*, day and night, during the boiling season, accomplish the whole labor *with one set of hands*. By pursuing this plan they *could afford to sacrifice one set of hands once in seven years!* He further stated, that this horrible system was now practised to a considerable extent. The correctness of this statement was substantially admitted by the slaveholders then on board." (Weld's "Slavery as it is," p. 39.)

"The late Mr. Samuel Blackwell, a highly respected citizen of Jersey City, opposite the city of New-York, and a member of the Presbyterian Church, visited many of the sugar plantations in Louisiana, and says: "That the planters *generally* declared to him that they were *obliged* so to overwork their slaves, during the sugar-making season, (from eight to ten weeks,) as to USE THEM UP *in seven or eight years*. For, said they, after the process is commenced, it must be pushed without cessation, night and day, and we cannot *afford* to keep a sufficient number of slaves to do the *extra* work at the time of sugar-making, as we could not *profitably* employ them the rest of the year." (Ib.)

Rev. Dr. Reed, of London, who went through Kentucky, Virginia, and Maryland, in the summer of 1834, gives the following testimony:

"I was told, confidently, from *excellent authority*,

that recently, at a meeting of planters in South Carolina, the question was seriously discussed whether the slave is more profitable to the owner, if well fed, well clothed, and worked lightly; or, if made the most of *at once*, and exhausted in some eight years. The decision was in favor of the last alternative. That decision will, perhaps, make many shudder. But to my mind, this is not the chief evil. The greater and principal evil is considering the slave *as property*. If he is only property, and *my* property, then I seem to have some right to ask how I may make that property *most available*." ("Visit to the American Churches," by Drs. Reed and Mattheson, vol. II., p. 173.)

Other testimony might be added. Southern newspapers have published the proceedings of Agricultural Societies, in which, after discussion, it had been agreed that the more profitable method was to "*use up*" a gang of negroes once in seven or eight years, and then purchase a fresh supply of the dealers.

A terrible sacrifice of life arises from a change of climate. A writer in the New-Orleans *Argus*, of 1830, says: "The loss by death, in bringing slaves from a northern climate, which our planters are under the necessity of doing, is not less than *twenty-five per cent*." Advertisements like the following are not uncommon:

"I offer my plantation for sale. Also twenty fine *acclimated negroes*. O. B. COBB." (*Vicksburg Reg.*, Dec. 27th, 1838.)

"I will sell my Old River Plantation, near Columbia, in Arkansas; also one hundred and thirty *acclimated negroes.* BEN. HUGHES.—Port Gibson, 14th Jan."

"PROBATE SALE.—Will be offered for sale, at public auction, to the highest bidder, one hundred and thirty *acclimated slaves.* G. W. KEETON, Judge of the Parish of Concordia, La., March 22d, 1837."

General Felix Houston advertises in the Natchez *Courier*, April 6th, 1838, "Thirty very fine *acclimated negroes.*" (See Jay's View, pp. 98, 99.)

Dr. Reed was correct in charging the murderous *use* of slave property to the principle or law of *slave ownership*, which constitutes what is called "the legal relation." Such treatment may be called an "abuse," but is a result which will be almost certain to follow, where laborers can be owned and *used*, instead of being bargained with and *hired.* Even on the low ground of "consequences," such a "relation" is to be condemned.

2. Another prominent use of slave property, in the case of females capable of being mothers, is that of *breeders* of slaves. And if the tenure of slave property be legitimate, and the ownership valid, by what rule of law or of logic shall this use of slave property be condemned? The argument of Mr. Gholson, of Virginia, on that assumption, holds good. (See Chapter II.) If the owners of lands, of orchards, and of brood mares had a right to their products, why had he not a right to the products of the slave women he had purchased? Had not the Slave Code, the legislatures and the courts secured to him his

claim upon them as "chattels personal, *to all intents*, constructions and *purposes* whatsoever?" Might he not, with other great statesmen,* affirm that "that *is* property which the law declares *to be* property," and that "two hundred years of legislation have sanctified and sanctioned negro slaves as property"? Did he not sustain to those women the relation of owner? And had not Doctors of Divinity, Northern and Southern, attested the lawfulness and the innocency of sustaining the relation? And how could there be a relation without its implied rights? Thus fortified, was not his inference warranted by his premises, when he spoke as follows? (we quote again from his speech :)

"The legal maxim of '*Partus sequitur ventrem*' is coeval with the existence of the rights of property, and is founded in wisdom and justice. It is on the justice and inviolability of this maxim that the master foregoes the service of his female slave; has her nursed and tended during the period of her gestation, and raises the helpless and infant offspring. The value of the property justifies the expense, and I do not hesitate to say that in its increase consists much of our wealth." (Speech in Leg. of Va.)

The closing sentence indicates the extent and importance of *this use* of slave property. According to the estimate of Henry Clay as before cited, (Chap. II.,) this use (to "raise slaves" for the "Southern market") is of more pecuniary value to "the farming portion

---

* Henry Clay. Speech in U. S. Senate, 1839.

of the slave States" than all their agricultural operations!

The value, indeed, cannot fall short of the receipts for exports of surplus slaves to the South. Professor Dew, afterwards President of William and Mary University, (Va.,) speaking of the slave-trade from Virginia, said: "It furnishes every inducement to the master to attend to his negroes, to ENCOURAGE BREEDING, and to cause the greatest number of slaves to be raised," &c. "Virginia is, indeed, a negro-raising State for other States." To which may be added the far-famed announcement—"The noblest blood of Virginia runs in the veins of slaves."

In the *Charleston Mercury*, the leading political paper of South Carolina, appeared the following advertisement:

"NEGROES FOR SALE.—A girl, about 20 years of age, (raised in Virginia,) and her two female children, one four, and the other two years old—is remarkably strong and healthy—never having had a day's sickness, with the exception of the small-pox, in her life. The children are fine and healthy. She is very prolific in her generating qualities, and affords a rare opportunity to any person who wishes to raise a family of healthy servants for their own use. Any person wishing to purchase will please leave their address at the *Mercury* office."

The coarseness of this language disgusts us, and so does the language of Mr. Gholson. But *the facts* involved differ nothing from the statements of Henry Clay, as quoted in our chapter on the Traffic in Slaves.

And whoever will take up AND STUDY the judicial decisions cited in "Wheeler's Law of Slavery" concerning "the increase of slaves," will find that the newspaper advertisements of which we have furnished a specimen, are merely descriptive of a business recognized and protected as respectable, in courts of justice. And this remark will be found to apply not merely to the supply raised for the inter-State slave-trade. The litigation reported in Mr. Wheeler's book under the head of "Increase of Slaves," is mainly that which grew out of neighborhood transactions and the inheritance of slave property.

And we have already, in discussing the nature of slave ownership, (Chap. I.,) taken occasion to quote from Wheeler's Law of Slavery (p. 325) the *express language* of the judges, placing the issue of female slaves, when *hired out* for five years, upon the same footing, and to be awarded upon the same rules, as in the case of the increase of "*brood mares*" or other "*female animals*."

3. Another use of slave property (sometimes, probably, connected with the preceding) is indicated by advertisements of beautiful young mulatto girls for sale; and by the fact that these commonly command higher prices than the ablest male laborers, or any other description of slaves. A reputed daughter of Thomas Jefferson was said to have been sold at auction in New-Orleans for one thousand dollars. Many have been sold for $2,000. One young woman was sold at public auction to a rich young

planter for $7,500. It must be an able field hand that commands $800.

Forced marriages of slaves with slaves, including second and third marriages after separations from former companions by sale, constitute a class of well attested facts. The Savannah River Baptist Association decided that in case of such separation of Baptist slave husbands and wives, it was lawful for them, without church censure, to form such new connections, "*in obedience to their masters*," whose right to enforce such arrangements was thus tacitly acknowledged.

Forced concubinage of slave women with their masters and overseers, often coerced by the lash, constitutes another class of facts, equally undeniable. Vide Weld's "Slavery as it is," p. 15. "Rape committed on a female slave is an offense not recognized by law." (MSS. by Judge Jay.)

Such facts, in their almost interminable varieties, corroborate the preceding, and illustrate the almost innumerable USES *of slave property!*

4. Another use of slave property, and a very remarkable one, assures us that the Southern "owners" of this "peculiar" kind of property have ways of turning it to account that even Northern ingenuity could scarcely have devised, unless, indeed, it *be* a Yankee's invention. Assortments of diseased, *damaged*, and disabled negroes, deemed incurable and otherwise worthless, are *bought up*, it seems, (cheap, no doubt, like old iron,) by medical institutions, to be experimented and operated upon, for purposes

of "medical education" and the interests of "medical science!" The *Charleston* (S. C.) *Mercury*, Oct. 12, 1838, contained an advertisement, by Dr. T. Stillman, on behalf of the "Medical Infirmary," setting forth its objects, and closing as follows:

"TO PLANTERS AND OTHERS.—Wanted, *fifty negroes.* Any person, having sick negroes, considered incurable by their respective physicians, and wishing to dispose of them, Dr. S. will *pay cash* for negroes affected with scrofula, or king's evil, confirmed hypochondriasm, apoplexy, diseases of the liver, kidneys, spleen, stomach and intestines, bladder and its appendages, diarrhœa, dysentery, &c. *The highest cash price* will be paid, on application as above," (viz., "Medical Infirmary, No. 110 Church street, Charleston.")

5. It seems indeed difficult to foresee or imagine all the *uses* to which slave property may be put by the owner. "The slave is entirely subject to the will of his master." He is supposed to have no conscience and no rights. What his "owner" commands him to do he must do. What he requires him to be he must be. What he chooses to inflict upon him he must suffer. He must never lift a hand in self-defense. He must utter no word of remonstrance. He has no protection and no redress. This will more fully be shown as we proceed.

The slave, however pious, and whatever his scruples, must do the work allotted to him—it may be the drudgery of a tippling shop, a gambling house, a brothel, or a den of counterfeiters or shop-lifters.

And he must witness in silence whatever he sees there, if it be murder. He cannot testify against a white man. *He is merely property* TO BE USED!

6. A class of murders of slaves by slave masters may as well be put down in this category.

The monster, Lillburn Lewis, nephew of Thomas Jefferson, who chopped in pieces a living article of slave property, in presence of his other slaves, only USED UP that article to awe the others into subjection, as he told them.

But this was "an abuse" of the relation, a violation of the law! Perhaps it was. In *words*, the law prohibits the murder of slaves. How much it *intends* or *effects*, will be seen in another chapter.

A slaveholder flogged a little slave girl, and put her feet in the stocks. She was found dead. A prominent lawyer, of a respectable family, was asked "whether the murderer of this little helpless child could not be indicted." He coolly replied that "the slave was Mr. P.'s *property*, and if he chose to suffer *the loss*, no one else had any thing to do with it." (Vide Weld's "Slavery as it is," p. 54.)

The slave child was "property," and had only been *used!* "It is believed that no record exists of a *white* man having been executed in the United States, simply for the murderof a *slave*." (MSS. by Judge Jay.)

In another chapter this point will be examined.

Again we find the people to be no better than their laws. If these practices are to be considered unauthorized "abuses," the people are *worse* than their laws, for they are practised with impunity.

CHAPTER VI.

SLAVES CAN POSSESS NOTHING.

Being Property themselves, they can own no Property, nor make any Contract.

MAN was created proprietor of the earth, with dominion over the beasts of the field. The humanity of the slave is denied, by denying to him any share in this original right of human nature or capability of its exercise. He is "not ranked among sentient beings, but among things." A chattel cannot be the owner of a chattel. The slave "can possess nothing nor acquire any thing but what must belong to his master." (Civil Code, Art. 35.) They "cannot take by purchase or descent."

"Slaves have no legal rights in things, real or personal; but whatever they may acquire, belongs, *in point of law*, to their masters." (Stroud, pp. 25, 45.)

"Slaves can make no contract." (Ib., 25, 61.)

"Slaves are incapable of inheriting or transmitting property." (Civil Code, Art. 945.)

By the Roman law, the slave might possess what was called his *peculium*, or what his master might, by stipulation, accord to him, and which, having thus stipulated, he could not afterwards take from him. By this law, slaves acquired property, sometimes embarked in commerce, redeemed themselves and amassed fortunes; or, in other cases, without an absolute purchase of themselves, paid their masters an annuity, as the price of their services, and attended to their own affairs. Not so in republican and Christian America! The "legal relation" here is another thing. The only exception, approximating the Roman code in this particular, so far as we know, is found in the Civil Code of LOUISIANA, as follows:

"All that a slave possesses belongs to his master, he possesses nothing of his own except his *peculium*, that is to say, the sum of money or movable estate, *which his master chooses he should possess*." (Art. 175; see 1 Martin's Digest, 616.)

Yet, in the same Code stands the following:

"Slaves cannot dispose of or receive by donation, *inter vivos or mortis causa*, unless they have been previously and expressly enfranchised conformably to law, or unless they are expressly enfranchised by the act by which the donation is made to them." (Art. 1462.)

"The earnings of slaves and the price of their service belong to their owners, who have their action to recover the amount of those who have employed them." (Louisiana Code of Practice, Art. 103.)

Except in the permission of a *peculium*, the laws of the other States on this subject are similar to those of Louisiana.

SOUTH CAROLINA.—"Slaves cannot take by descent or purchase." (4 Desaussure's Chancery Reports, 266, Bynum *vs.* Bostwick.)

NORTH CAROLINA.—"Slaves cannot take by sale, or devise, or descent." "A devise of land to be rented out, for the maintenance of a slave, was adjudged to be void." (1 Cameron and Norwood's Reports, 353; same decision, 1 Taylor's Reports, 209.)

MARYLAND.—A gift, bequest, or devise, made to a slave, by any one *not* his owner, would be void, (see Dulany's opinion, 1 Maryland Reports, 561,) though such a devise of real or personal estate, made by the *owner* of a slave, has been held to entitle him to *freedom*, as the *implied* intention of the owner. (Hall *vs.* Mullin, 5 Harris and Johnson's Reports, 190.)

In "Wheeler's Law of Slavery" may be found ample evidence that this feature of the Slave Code (the incapacity of the slave to possess property) is not a dead letter, but recognized by the courts, and enforced whenever there is occasion, not only to the *letter* of the statute, but by an application of the principle and *spirit* of the enactment, in a contingency which legislative sagacity did not, probably, foresee.

A slave, for instance, accidentally found a sum of money, in bank bills, which some one took from him and carried to the bank. The *owner* of the slave boy brought an action of trover against the bank for the sum, and recovered it by judgment of court.

Judge Safford said:

"Our slaves can do nothing in their own right,

can hold no property, can neither buy, sell, barter, nor dispose of any thing, without express permission from the master or overseer; so that every thing they can possess or do is, in legal contemplation, on authority of the master."

Judge Crenshaw said:

"A slave is in absolute bondage; he has no civil right, and can hold no property, except at the will and pleasure of his master. A slave is a rational being, and endowed with understanding and volition, like the rest of mankind; and *whatever* he lawfully acquires, and gains possession of, *by finding* or otherwise, is the acquirement and possession of the master. A slave cannot take property by descent or purchase." (Brandon et al. *vs.* Merchants' and Planters' Bank of Huntsville, 1 Stewart's Ala. Report, 320; S. P. Bynum *vs.* Bostwick, 4 Desaussure, 266; Wheeler's Law of Slavery, pp. 6, 7.)

In the preceding decision, the manhood, the reason, the understanding, the volition of the slave are distinctly recognized, and for the express purpose of claiming all the acquirements of *such* a being as the property of his master—equivalent to the claim of absolute proprietorship in the human soul itself! The theory and the practice of slavery are here found to be in harmony, and the courts enforce the enactments of the legislatures.

In a note to the preceding decision, Mr. Wheeler says, (p. 7:) "These principles prevail in *all* the States, and are taken from the civil law, and were adopted in all, except Connecticut, and perhaps Massachusetts."

"Hall *vs.* Mullin, 5 Har. and John's Md. Report, 190. The Court held that no legal contract, whatever, could be made with a slave, without the consent of his master." (Ib., p. 7.)

"In Jackson *ex. dem.* the People *vs.* Lervey, 5 Cowen's Rep., 397, the Court held that a slave at common law could not contract matrimony, nor could the child of a slave take by descent or inheritance." (Ib., p. 7.)

"Free Lucy and Frank, Fall Term, 1826, 4 Monroe's Rep., 167; Emmerson *vs.* Howland, 1 Mason's Rep., 45. The Court held that contracts made by negroes while in slavery, do not bind them when liberated; and consequently a plea by a free negro, that a writing sued on was delivered when he was a slave, is good." (Ib., p. 190.)

In a note on this topic, Mr. Wheeler says: "One general principle prevails in all the States, and in the British, Spanish, and Portuguese West Indies, and that is, that *a slave cannot make a contract, not even the contract of matrimony.*" And he cites numerous authorities for the statement. (Ib., p. 190.)

The slave is thus taught that his promises and agreements are of no binding force! Even the free negro, as has been seen, is taught the same lesson in respect to his former condition! Yet those by whom these lessons are taught affect to marvel at the moral obtuseness of the negroes, and consider themselves as occupying a high moral eminence above them.

A warrant for one thousand acres of land, issued to a slave in Tennessee, for military services as a musician during the revolutionary war, was adjudged to be the property of his owner, in 1834. This decision was made against the claims of an heir of his *former* owner, Col. Patton, a revolutionary officer, who caused his slave to be enlisted. No claim appears to have been set up on behalf of the slave. (See Wheeler's Law of Slavery, p. 229.)

Though "a slave can make no contract" on his own account, yet his master may constitute a slave his agent for the most important pecuniary transactions. We once knew of a prominent public man, whose personal credit in his market town was so low that his written order on his merchant for fifty dollars' worth of goods was rejected; but when his managing slave stepped forward and promised that the next loads of produce should be delivered in payment, the answer was: "Very well, Cuffee, if you say so, I'll deliver ten times the amount of goods."

"Chastain *vs.* Bowman et al., May Term, 1833, 1 Hill's S. C. Reports, 276. The Court charged the jury that a slave might be the agent of his master, and if his agency was established, the master was bound. Verdict for the plaintiff, and motion for a new trial.

"*Per Cur.*, Johnson J.—It is not questioned that a master may constitute his slave his agent, and I cannot conceive of any distinction between the circumstances which constitute a slave and a freeman an agent. They are both the creatures of the principal, and act upon his authority. There is no condition, however degraded, which deprives one of the right to act as a private agent. Motion dismissed." (Wheeler's Law of Slavery, p. 228.)

It is certainly remarkable that a man should "have a right" to act as an agent for another who can have no right to act for himself. Equally remarkable is the plea that slaves cannot take care of themselves and must be benevolently superintended for *their* benefit, while they conduct the business of their masters. The slave is adjudged to be a mere thing, except where his master's interests or convenience require that he should be regarded a man.

Another curiosity of slave jurisprudence deserves notice here. Although it is adjudged an offense against the State for a free white citizen to hold honest commerce with a slave, for the beneficial and useful purposes of life, to employ a slave to labor and to pay him just wages—an offense, likewise, for the master of a slave to permit and authorize such transactions, (as will be shown presently,) yet, according to Wheeler, "It is *not* an offense, either at common law or by statute, *to gamble* with slaves." This statement is his marginal title to the law case of "The State *vs.* Pemberton and Smith, Dec. Term, 1829, 2 Devereaux's N. Carolina Rep., 281," in which, "after verdict for the State, his Honor Judge Strange arrested the judgment, being of opinion" as before stated. "From this judgment the solicitor for the State appealed," but the judgment of the Court below was affirmed. (Wheeler's Law of Slavery, p. 441.)

With exception of Louisiana, as already mentioned, our American slave States have signalized themselves by special enactments to *prohibit* the possession of the smallest amount of property by the slave, *even with the consent of the master!* The Greeks, the Romans, the ancient Germans, the Poles, with the Portuguese, the Spanish and the French of our own times, had provided, both by law and by custom, for the possession of property by the slave, which could not be seized by his master. In the *British* West Indies, though no written law had sanctioned the custom, a public sentiment had indulged the slave in the enjoyment of some petty possessions, and had forbidden the master to interfere with them.

But this lenity was manifestly inconsistent with the absolute and unlimited chattelhood of the slave. A *principle* was seen to be involved, which, if tolerated *in an age of inquiry*, would undermine the whole system. If the slave could possess property, he could dispose of it; he could make contracts; he might contract marriage; he might become a man, and, becoming such, cease to be a slave. The safety of the entire fabric required that not one stone in the edifice should be missing. And besides, the idea that a slave can *possess property*, however trifling the amount, is the idea that the slave has *rights*, an idea that must by no means be permitted to enter the mind of the slave, or be entertained by the community around him. Especially must this not be done in a land wherein human rights have been discussed and proclaimed. The jealousy, the vigilance, the sagacity, the appliances of a grim despotism are never so severely tasked as in the presence of the spirit and the doctrines of freedom. This single thought solves the enigma, and repels the opprobrium, of an unprecedented tyranny in a land wherein are taught the principles of liberty. A despotism, in such a country, must be doubly despotic or die instantly. The reader has, in these suggestions, our philosophy of the remarkable enactments that follow.

South Carolina.—"It shall not be lawful for any slave to buy, sell, trade, &c., for any goods, &c., without a license from the owner, &c. Nor shall any slave be permitted to keep any boat, periauger, or canoe, or raise and breed for the benefit of such slave any horses, mares, cattle, sheep, or hogs, under pain of forfeiting all the goods, &c., and all the boats, periaugers or canoes, horses, mares, cattle, sheep, or hogs. And it shall be lawful for *any person whatsoever* to seize and take away from any slave, all such goods, &c., boats, &c., &c., and to deliver the same into the hands of any justice of the peace, nearest to the place where the seizure shall be made, and such justice shall take the oath of the person making such seizure, concerning the manner thereof; and if the said justice shall be satisfied that such seizure has been made according to law, he shall pronounce and declare the goods so seized to be forfeited, and order the same to be sold at public outcry; one half of the moneys arising from such sale *to go to the State, and the other half to him or them that sue for the same.*" (James's Digest, 385–6; Act of 1740.)

GEORGIA.—The statute is nearly the same as in South Carolina, with this additional prohibition: Lest the master should sometimes permit the slave to hire himself to another for his own benefit, the State imposes a penalty of thirty dollars "for every weekly *offense* on the part of the master, unless the labor be done on his own premises." (Prince's Digest, 453, 457.)

KENTUCKY.—The same, with a slight modification. (2 Litt. & Sui. Digest, 1159–60.)

TENNESSEE.—Similar. (Act of October 23, 1813, chap. 135.)

VIRGINIA.—If the master shall permit his slave to hire himself out, it is made *lawful for any person*, and the *duty* of the Sheriff, &c., to apprehend such slave, &c., and the master shall be fined not less than ten dollars, nor more than twenty, &c. (1 *Revised* Code, A. D. 1819, 374–5.)

MISSISSIPPI.—Same as in Georgia and Kentucky, before stated. (*Revised* Code, 375.)

A slave, in Mississippi, is forbidden to raise cotton for his own use; and should the master permit him to do so, he incurs a fine of fifty dollars. (*Revised* Code, 379.)

Further: "If any master, &c., of a slave, license such slave to go at large and trade as a freeman, he shall forfeit the sum of fifty dollars for each and every offense." (*Revised* Code, 374. See also North Carolina.)

An equal fine is imposed upon any master *convicted* of permitting his slave to keep "*stock of any description.*" (Act of Jan. 29, 1825; Pamph. Laws of Mississippi, of 1825.)

MISSOURI.—Same as Virginia, before stated. (2 Missouri Laws, 743; Hayward's Manual, 534.) Also, same as Mississippi, third specification, just stated. (2 Missouri Laws, 743.)

NORTH CAROLINA.—Act of 1779: "All horses, cattle, hogs, or sheep, that, one month after the passage of this act, shall belong to any slave, or be of any slave's mark, in this State, shall be seized and sold by the County Wardens, and applied, one half to the support of *the poor of the county*, and the other half to the *informer!*" (Hayward's Manual, 526.) Same or similar law also in Mississippi. (*Revised* Code, 378.) Same also in Maryland. (Act of 1723, chap. 15, sect. 6; Kilty's Laws of Maryland.)

And so the *white* poor are to be fed by plundering the *colored* poor!

MARYLAND.—See last preceding item. Also Mississippi, third item there stated. See Kilty's Laws of Maryland, Act of April, 1787, chap. 33.

By act of April sessions, 1787, any person who shall permit and authorize any slave belonging to him or herself, &c., to go at large himself or herself within this State, shall incur the penalty of five pounds ($13.33) current money *per month*, except ten days *at harvest.* The penalty was increased to twenty dollars, excepting, however, an additional ten days in harvest. (Act of December Sessions, 1817.

chap. 104, sect. 1.) By both acts, a slave being *a pilot* is not included in the prohibition.

"No person shall trade, barter, commerce, or in any way deal with any servant or slave, &c., &c., without leave or license first had from such servant or slave's master, dame, or overseer, for his or her so doing, under penalty of two thousand pounds of tobacco," &c. (Laws of Maryland, 1715, chap. 44, sect. 11, 12, 13.)

DISTRICT OF COLUMBIA.—"Under exclusive jurisdiction of Congress." Same as in Maryland.

It may easily be conceived that this law would be inconvenient and disadvantageous to many owners of slaves in or near maritime towns, where job labor, or labor by the day or the hour, might be picked up by the laborers themselves, better than by their owners. In such localities the strict letter of the law could not always be rigidly enforced. The public convenience, the wants of every body who must needs employ transient laborers, would interpose obstacles. It is known that in Wilmington, N. C., a port from which much lumber used to be shipped, which needed much cooper's labor in the preparing, the work was often or commonly carried on by slaves, who paid a large monthly stipend to their owners. Stevedores, (who stow away cargoes,) caulkers, riggers, and perhaps ship-blacksmiths, and even sail-makers, being slaves, were allowed the same privilege. The custom had an elevating effect on the slaves, and was therefore looked upon with jealousy by masters not interested in such arrange-

ments. This was thirty years ago. The present usages are unknown to the writer, who gladly presents this one brighter spot in the picture. But it must not be forgotten that all the *surplus* earnings of these slaves, *if any*, over and above their support, (after having paid ten or fifteen dollars monthly to their masters for their time,) is nevertheless, *in the eye of the law*, the property of their masters, and they can take away, if they please, whatever they find in their possession.

The convenience and interest of the planter might permit or even direct the slaves to cultivate small patches of vegetables near their cabins, for food, by Sunday labor, for the most part. In Spanish Florida this was a custom. It may obtain to a small extent in other States, without serious violation of the letter or spirit of the statutes quoted. Such small and transient supplies would hardly be accounted *possessions or property*.

That the statutes quoted are not commonly regarded a dead letter, may be seen by reports of judicial decisions, as compiled by Mr. Wheeler, who expressly refers to the statutes as the ground of the decisions. And in a note he adverts to some of their provisions which we have not yet mentioned:

"By the Revised Code of Virginia, (A. D. 1819,) vol. I., p. 442, sect. 81, it is declared that a slave going at large, or hiring himself out, may be committed by a magistrate, who may fine the owner, and *may order the slave to be sold*." "Also, by the Revised Code of Mississippi, 374, sect. 25"—"in certain cases, the *slave may be sold*. And by sect. 20, any citizen may seize a slave offering articles for sale, and take him before a justice of the peace, and the justice *shall order the slave to be whipped, and forfeit the article* TO THE PERSON APPREHENDING THE SLAVE"! (Wheeler's Law of Slavery, p. 153.)

It is preposterous to suppose that such modern enactments, holding out such inducements to informers and prosecutors, should remain a dead letter. Mr. Wheeler adds:

"Similar provisions are to be found in the statute books of *those States* where this species of property is recognized." (Ib.)

In the same note he had before said:

"The statutes of *the States* contain a prohibition with a penalty against the slave going at large, *or* hiring himself out." (p. 152.)

He cites the law of Alabama, in particular; and Judge Hitchcock, of Alabama, says of his book: "I have no doubt it will be a valuable work for the use of the members particularly of the *Southern bar* of the United States." He understands, of course, that these laws are to be enforced, as in the following instance recorded in the same "valuable" auxiliary of "the Southern bar":

"Jarrett *vs.* Higbee, 5 Monroe's Ky. Report, 546. Jarrett brought trespass against Higbee for taking and imprisoning his slave." "Defendant admitted that when he took the slave up he produced *a pass* from his master" which gave him permission "to bargain and trade for himself until the first day of May next; and also for to pass and repass from Livingston county, Kentucky, to Monongahela county, State of Virginia," &c., dated 26th Sept., 1822. The following is from the judicial decision:

"*Per Cur.*, Bibb Ch. J. That the master shall not let loose his slave, with a permit for him to *violate the established order and economy prescribed by law in relation to slaves, is due to society.*" "Without abridging the lawful powers of the master to use his property in the slave, it may safely be declared that this paper, given by the master in (to) the slave, violated that duty which he, as owner, owed to the laws of society." "These permissions, and such acts of the slave, are violations by master and slave of the policy, spirit, and letter of the statute of 16th Dec., 1802, against permitting the slaves to go at large and hire themselves." "Such licenses would tend to beget idle and dissolute habits in the particular slaves so indulged, as well as in others, and to lead to depredations upon the property of others, and to crimes and insubordination. To such licenses and indulgences society are not bound to submit; the master has no right to give such." "*It was not a lawful pass or permit. It was a species of temporary and unlawful manumission,*" &c. (Wheeler's Law of Slavery, pp. 269–70.)

In other language, the statute and its enforcement are deemed necessary to the security and the perpetuity of slavery.

It deserves especial notice that this decision was made in Kentucky, where slavery is said to be exhibited in its mildest form, and where the privileges of slaves are greater than in most of the other States.

It is not known that in any other nation, ancient or modern, the robbery of the poor has been carried, by system, to such a pitch as to prohibit the mass of the laboring people from holding the smallest article of property as their own, or from making any bargain or contract.

And it ought to be noticed and remembered that this condition of things has resulted from an extreme solicitude to protect from danger the so-called "legal relation" of owner and owned, of master and slave.

CHAPTER VII.

SLAVES CANNOT MARRY.

Being held as Property, and incapable of making any Contract, they cannot contract Marriage recognized by Law.

MEN may forget or disregard the rules of logic in their reasonings about slavery, but the genius that presides over American slavery never forgets or disregards them. From its well-defined principle of human chattelhood it never departs, for a single moment. If any thing founded on falsehood might be called a science, we might add the system of American slavery to the list of the strict sciences. From a single fundamental axiom, all the parts of the system are logically and scientifically educed. And no man fully understands the system, who does not study it in the light of that axiom.

The slave has no rights. Of course he, or she, cannot have the rights of a husband, a wife. The slave is a chattel, and chattels do not marry. "The slave is not ranked among sentient beings, but among things," and things are not married.

"Slaves are not people, in the eye of the law.

They have no legal personality." So said Mr. Wise. So, by their votes, said the Federal Congress. But none except "people" and "persons" ever marry.

"The slave is one who is in the power of a master *to whom he belongs*." How, then, can the slave marry?

"The legal relation of master and slave," with all the vestal robes of its spotless innocency, and saintly Biblical paternity, has *never, in this country*, been held to be compatible with marriage. So early as in colonial times, when parish ministers, all over New-England, owned slaves, it was held by learned civilians, in good old Connecticut, that when a slave master, though inadvertently, gave verbal license to a female slave *to marry*, the license made her free. Being married, she was not a slave, and the husband bore off his prize in triumph, before her master!

The same doctrine has always been held (though differently enunciated) at the South. Slave mothers are there licensed by their masters to be "breeders," not wives, and thus they are retained as slaves.

"A slave cannot even contract matrimony, the association which takes place among slaves, and is *called* marriage, being properly designated by the word *contubernium*, a relation which has no sanctity, and to which no civil rights are attached." (Stroud's "Sketch of the Slave Laws," p. 61.)

"A slave has never maintained an action against the violator of his bed. A slave is not admonished for incontinence, or punished for fornication or adultery; never prosecuted for bigamy, or petty treason for killing a husband being a slave, any more than admitted to an appeal for murder." (Opinion of Daniel Dulaney, Esq., Attorney General of Maryland. 1 Maryland Reports, pp. 561, 563.)

"Slaves were not entitled to the conditions of matrimony, and therefore they had no relief in cases of adultery; nor were they the proper objects of cognation or affinity, but of *quasi-cognation* only." (Dr. Taylor's "Elements of the Civil Law," p. 429.)

"It is clear that slaves have no legal capacity to assent to any contract. With the consent of their master they may marry, and their *moral* power to agree to such a contract or connection cannot be doubted; *but while in a state of slavery* it cannot produce any *civil effect*, because slaves are deprived of all civil rights. Emancipation gives to the slave his civil rights, and a contract of marriage, legal and valid by the consent of the master, and moral assent of the slave, *from the moment of freedom*, ALTHOUGH DORMANT DURING SLAVERY, produces all the effects which result from such contract among free persons." (Opinion of Judge Matthews, case of Girod *vs.* Lewis, May Term, 1819; 6 Martin's "Louisiana Reports," p. 559. Wheeler's "Law of Slavery," p. 199.)

The most favorable inference from this ingenious decision is, that the joint action of master and slave can legalize a slave's marriage *when he ceases to be a slave!*

The obligations of marriage are evidently inconsistent with the conditions of slavery, and cannot be performed by a slave. The husband promises to protect his wife and provide for her. The wife promises to be the help-meet of her husband. They mutually promise to live with and cherish each other, till parted by death. But what can such promises by slaves *mean?* The "legal relation of master and slave" renders them void! It forbids the slave to protect even himself. It clothes his master with authority to bid him inflict deadly blows on the woman he has sworn to protect. It prohibits his possession of any property wherewith to sustain her. His labor and his hands it takes from him. It bids the woman assist, not her husband, but her owner! Nay! it gives him unlimited control and full possession of her own person, and forbids her, on pain of death, (as will be shown,) to resist him, if he drags her to his bed! It severs the plighted pair, at the will of their masters, occasionally, or for ever! The innocent "legal relation" of slave-ownership does or permits all this, and without forfeiting clerical favor, or a high seat in the Church, or in the Senate, or Presidential chair. What, then, can the marriage vows of slaves *mean?*

The laws annulling slave marriage are explicit, as has been seen. The corresponding position of the judiciary, as attested by the Maryland Reports, has been adduced. Will any one inquire whether or no, in this particular, the Code be a "dead letter"? or whether the institution of marriage among slaves may not have survived the annulling action of the legislatures and the courts? As a recognized "legal relation," most assuredly the marriage relation among slaves does not and cannot exist. The petted "legal relation" of owner and slaves crowds it off from the platform of human society. The *two* "legal relations" cannot coëxist. A choice must be made between the two. And those who will still persist in affirming the innocency and the validity of the "relation" of slave owner, are bound, if sincere and truthful men, to repudiate the "relation" of slave marriage. The Savannah River Baptist Association had the nerve and the consistency to do this.

"In 1835, the following query relating to slaves was propounded to the Savannah River Baptist Association of ministers: Whether, in case of involuntary separation of such a character as to preclude all future intercourse, the parties may be allowed to marry again?"

"ANSWER.—That such separation, among persons situated as our slaves are, is, civilly, a separation by death, and they believe that, in the sight of God, it would be so viewed. To forbid second marriages in such cases, would be to expose the parties not only to greater hardships and stronger temptations, but to *church censure* for acting in *obedience to their masters*, who cannot be expected to acquiesce in a regulation at variance with justice to the slaves, and to the spirit of that command which regulates marriage between Christians. *The slaves are not free agents*, and a dissolution by death is not more entirely without their consent and beyond their control than by such separation."

The Church is here seen submitting, with complacency, to that feature of the Slave Code that annuls marriage! What the Southern Baptists have avowed, the other religious sects there practise.

Some of the facts stated concerning the "*uses of slave property*" illustrate the absence of slave marriage. And so do the statistics of the domestic *slave-trade.* The restored institution and sanctity of marriage would cut off the supplies that gorge the slave markets.

The Presbyterian Synod of Kentucky, in their address, have given us their testimony to the general fact and its effects. They say:

The system "produces general licentiousness among the slaves. Marriage, as a civil ordinance, they cannot enjoy. Our laws do not recognize this relation as existing among them, and, of course, do not enforce, by any sanction, the observance of its duties. Indeed, until slavery waxeth old, and tendeth to decay, there CANNOT BE any legal recognition of the marriage rite, or the enforcement of its consequent duties. *For*, all the regulations on this subject *would limit the master's absolute* RIGHT OF PROPERTY in the slaves. In his disposal of them he could no longer be at liberty to consult merely his own interest. He could no longer separate the wife and the husband to suit the convenience or interest of the purchaser, no matter how advantageous might be the terms offered." "Hence, all the marriages that could ever be allowed them, would be a mere contract, violable at the master's pleasure. Their present *quasi* marriages are continually thus voided. They are, in this way, brought to consider their matrimonial alliances as a thing not binding, and they act accordingly. We are then assured by the most unquestionable testimony that licentiousness is the necessary result of our system." (Address, pp. 15, 16.)

"Chastity is no virtue among them; its violation neither injures female character in their own estimation, nor in that of their master or mistress. No instruction is ever given—no censure pronounced. I speak not of the world. *I speak of Christian families generally.*" (Lexington, Ky., *Luminary.*)

Even in Puritan New-England, seventy years ago, female slaves, in ministers' and magistrates' families, bore children, black or yellow, without marriage. No one inquired who their fathers were, and nothing more was thought of it than of the breeding of sheep or swine. We had the facts from those who well remembered them.

The universal testimony concerning "slave quarters" connected with plantations is, that "the sexes are herded together, promiscuously, like beasts."

Said a sister of President Madison to the late Rev. George Bourne, then a Presbyterian minister in Virginia: "We Southern ladies are complimented with the name of wives; but we are only the mistresses of seraglios."

The report of the Presbyterian Synod of Georgia, December, 1833, sustains, on this general subject, the testimony of the Synod of Kentucky.

We have seen a well-authenticated account of a respectable Christian lady at the South, who kept a handsome mulatto female for the use of her genteel son, as a method of deterring him, as she said, from more indiscriminate and vulgar indulgences. Undoubtedly he passed current in the first circles of respectable young ladies. In our chapter *on the uses* of slave property, this item would have been in place.

The rapid and constant bleaching of colors, at the South, assures us that there is no exaggeration in these pictures. And if the Synod of Kentucky were not mistaken, the innocent "legal relation" of slave ownership is to be held responsible for it all. Where the laws annul marriage, we may be certain that "the people are not better than their laws."

CHAPTER VIII.

SLAVES CANNOT CONSTITUTE FAMILIES.

Being Property, "Goods" and "Chattels Personal," to all intents, constructions and purposes whatsoever, they have no claim on each other—no security from Separation—no Marital Rights—no Parental Rights—no Family Government—no Family Education—no Family Protection.

THE family relation originates in the institution of marriage, and exists not without it. We have already proved that slaves cannot have families or be members of families, by proving that they cannot be married. To this latter point, in its connection with the former, we cite the words of Judge Jay:

"A *necessary consequence* of slavery is the absence of the marriage relation. No slave can commit bigamy, because the law knows no more of the marriage of slaves than of the marriage of brutes. A slave may, indeed, be formally married, but so far as legal rights and obligations are concerned, it is an idle ceremony." "*Of course*, these laws do not recognize the *parental* relation, as belonging to slaves. A slave has no more legal authority over his child than a cow has over her calf." (Jay's Inquiry, p. 132.)

The fact that the slave, as a chattel personal, may be bought, sold, transported from one place to another, mortgaged, attached, leased, inherited, and "distributed" in the settlement of estates, shows plainly that slaves cannot constitute families.

"In the slaveholding States, except in Louisiana, no law exists to prevent the violent separation of parents from their children, or even from each other." (Stroud's Sketch, p. 50.)

"Slaves may be sold and transferred from one to another without any statutory restriction or limitation, as to the separation of parents and children, &c., except in the State of Louisiana." (Wheeler's Law of Slavery, p. 41.)

This has been the condition of American slaves in every period of our history, since their first introduction among us. *John Woolman*, the philanthropist, a minister of the Society of Friends, residing in New-Jersey, bears the following testimony concerning the slaveholders of his times, (A. D. 1757:)

"They often part men from their wives by selling them far asunder, which is common when estates are sold by executors at vendue." (Journal of the Life of John Woolman, London edition, p. 74.)

At a later period than this, according to a well-authenticated tradition in the neighborhood, a Congregational minister at Hampton, Conn., (Rev. Mr. Moseley,) separated by sale a husband and wife who were both of them members of his own church, and who had been, by his own officiating act as a minister, united in marriage. Yet no legal or ecclesiastical proceedings grew out of the transaction. Some thought it a hard case, but the sufferers were only negroes and slaves.

It is the common understanding at the South, that slaves do not constitute families. It is the common understanding of the country at large. The American Bible Society, many years ago, proposed to supply *each family* in the United States with a Bible. After a long effort, it was announced by the Society that the great work was completed. It was afterwards ascertained that no part of the supply went to the then two and a half millions of slaves. The Society made no apology for its mistake, nor acknowledged that it had committed any. Public sentiment in general (with exception of abolitionists) attributed to them no error. The nation knew nothing about *families of slaves!*

The practice corresponds with the theory. The statement that follows is from Sarah M. Grimke, daughter of the late Judge Grimke, of Charleston, S. C.:

"A slave who had been separated from his wife, because it best suited the convenience of his owner, ran away. He was taken up on the plantation where his wife, to whom he was tenderly attached, then lived. His only object in running away was to return to her; no other fault was attributed to him. For this offense he was confined in the stocks *six weeks*, in a miserable hovel, not weather-tight. He received *fifty lashes weekly* during that time, was allowed food barely sufficient to sustain him, and when released from confinement, was not permitted to return to his wife. His master, although himself a husband and a father, was unmoved by the touching appeals of the slave, who entreated that he might only remain with his wife, promised to discharge his duties faithfully; his master continued inexorable, and he was torn from his wife and family. The owner of this slave was a professing Christian, in full membership with the church, and this circumstance occurred while he was in his chamber, during his last illness." (Weld's "Slavery as it is," p. 23.)

The following is from Mrs. Angelina Grimke Weld, sister of the preceding witness:

"Chambermaids and seamstresses often sleep in their mistresses' apartments, but with no bedding at all. I know of an instance of a woman who has been *married eleven years, and yet has never been allowed to sleep out of her mistress's chamber.* This is a *great* hardship to slaves. When we consider that *house* slaves are rarely allowed social intercourse during *the day*, as their work generally *separates* them, the barbarity of such an arrangement is obvious. It is peculiarly a hardship in the above case, as the husband of the woman does not 'belong' to her 'owner,' and because he is subject to dreadful attacks of illness, and he can have but little attention from his wife *in the day.* And yet her mistress, who is an old lady, gives her the highest character as a faithful servant, and told a friend of mine that she was entirely dependent on her for all her comforts;

she dressed and undressed her, gave her all her food, and was so *necessary* to her that she could not do without her. I may add that this couple are tenderly attached to each other."

"I know an instance in which the husband was a slave, and the wife was free. During the illness of the former, the latter was *allowed* to come and nurse him; she was obliged to leave the work by which she made a living, and come to stay with her husband, and thus lose weeks of her time, or he would have suffered for want of proper attention; and yet this 'owner' made her no compensation for her services. He had long been a faithful and a favorite slave, and his owner was a woman very benevolent to the poor whites." "She, no doubt, only thought how kind she was to *allow* her to come and stay so long in her yard." (Ib., p. 56.)

"Persons who own plantations and yet live in the cities often take their children from them as soon as they are weaned, and send them into the country; because they do not want the time of the mother taken up with attendance upon *her own children*, it being too valuable to the mistress. As a *favor* she is sometimes permitted to go to see them once a year. So, on the other hand, if the field slaves happen to have children of an age suitable to the convenience of the master, they are taken from their parents and brought to the city. *Parents are almost never consulted as to the disposition to be made of their children, and they have as little control over them as have domestic animals over the disposal of their young. Every natural and social feeling and affection are violated with indifference.* Slaves are treated as though they did not possess them." (Ib., pp. 56–7.)

If such be the condition of domestic or house servants, in the best and most refined families of the South, what must be the condition of field slaves, under the direction of overseers, on the plantations?

"Among the gangs there are often young women, who bring their children to the fields, and lay them in a fence corner while they are at work, only being permitted to nurse them at the option of the overseer. When a child is three weeks old, a woman is considered in working order. I have seen a woman, with her young child strapped to her back, laboring the whole day beside a man, *perhaps the father of the child*, and he not permitted to give her any assistance, himself being under the whip." (Testimony of L. Sapington, a native of Maryland. Ib., p. 49.)

On page 157 of the same book may be found the particulars of the public execution of a negro in a barbarous manner, by burning and beheading, after which his head was stuck up on a pole. His crime was the killing of a white man. The provocation was, that the white man "*owned* his wife, and was in the habit of sleeping with her. The negro said he killed him, and he believed he should be rewarded in heaven for it."

The bearing of "the legal relation" of slave *ownership* upon the "*family*" relation may be seen by such advertisements as the following, which abound in the Southern papers. They are selected from about *thirty* similar ones in Weld's "Slavery as it is," pp. 164–166:

From the *Richmond Enquirer*, Feb. 20, 1838.

"$50 REWARD.—Ran away from the subscriber, his negro man Pauladore, commonly called Paul. I understand Gen. R. Y. HAYNE* *has purchased his wife and children* from H. L. PINCKNEY, Esq.,† and has them now on his plantation at Goose-creek, where, no doubt, the fellow is frequently *lurking*.

"T. DAVIS."

"$25 REWARD.—Ran away from the subscriber, a negro woman named Matilda. It is thought she may be somewhere up James River, as she was claimed as *a wife* by some boatman in Goochland.

"J. ALVIS."

"$10 REWARD for a negro woman named Sally, 40 years old. We have reason to believe said negro to be lurking on the James River Canal, or the Green Spring neighborhood, where, we are informed, *her husband* resides. POLLY C. SHIELDS.

"*Mount Elba, Feb.* 19, 1838."

From the *Savannah Georgian*, July 8, 1837.

"Ran away from the subscriber, his man Joe. He visits the city occasionally, where he has been *harbored by his mother and sister*. I will give one hundred dollars for proof sufficient to *convict his harborers*.

"R. P. T. MONGIN."

---

* Ex-Governor of South Carolina, and U. S. Senator.

† Member of Congress from South Carolina.

We add another, on page 156:

From the *Wilmington* (N. C.) *Advertiser* of July 13, 1838.

"Ran away, my negro man RICHARD. A reward of $25 will be paid for his apprehension, DEAD or ALIVE. Satisfactory proof only will be required of his being KILLED. He has with him, in all probability, HIS WIFE ELIZA, *who ran away from Col. Thompson*, now a resident of Alabama, about the time he commenced his journey to that State.

"DURANT H. RHODES."

We have some reason to believe that this Rhodes was originally from New-England. When he visits the North he will probably tell his friends that he has never known any cruel treatment of slaves. Should he dine with the parish pastor, the result would perhaps be a sermon on "the innocent legal relation!"

The hair-splitters in logic will nevertheless persist in admonishing us to distinguish between the "relation" and its "abuse." But what, we demand, must be the nature of a "relation" that is constantly producing such fruits?

Undoubtedly there are slaveholders who would not thus advertise slaves. But if, in refraining, they are governed by any *moral principle*, it must be a principle at variance with the "legal relation" of slave-ownership which authorizes such acts and interposes no check or disapprobation of them. The very idea of slave-*ownership* naturally suggests *the right* of doing such things. And when slave-ownership is held to be legalized, and is dignified with the name of a "legal relation"—and when these results (which some call "abuses") are neither forbidden nor discountenanced by the authorities that establish the said "legal relation," it is sheer sophistry to attempt discriminating between them so as to approve the one and condemn the other.

CHAPTER IX.

UNLIMITED POWER OF SLAVEHOLDERS.

The Power of the Master or "Owner" is virtually unlimited—The submission required of the Slave is unbounded—The Slave being "Property" can have no protection against the Master, and has no remedy or redress for injuries inflicted by him.

THIS proposition is substantially involved in the legal definition of slavery, as presented in our first chapter. The proof and illustration of it has been gradually evolving as we have proceeded thus far. It will continue to accumulate as we shall in future chapters examine the topics of slave labor, slave sustenance and clothing, slave punishments, and the intellectual and religious condition of slaves. At every step, the slave will have been found wholly subject to his master, dependent upon him, and defenseless. In this chapter we shall aim only to present, in a condensed form, the precise doctrine of the Slave Code on this subject.

If the slave be the absolute property of his master —"entirely subject to his will"—"incapable of being injured"—"chattels personal, to all intents, constructions, and purposes whatsoever"—"not ranked among sentient beings, but among things"—the subjects of absolute purchase and sale—of seizure for debt—of inheritance and distribution—incapable of possessing property—"not entitled to the conditions of matrimony"—"not capable of constituting families"—(and all this has been shown)—then the master is indeed absolute, and the slave defenseless, of course. And any attempt by the Legislature or by the Courts to afford him protection, would be, in effect, an attempt to subvert "the legal relation of master and slave," and overturn the tenure of slave-ownership entirely.

The question before us is, whether any such attempts have been made, and if so, how much, in a way of limitation and protection, has been accomplished.

We repeat, here, a quotation before made from Judge Stroud: "It is plain that the dominion of the master is as *unlimited* as that which is tolerated by the laws of any civilized country in relation to brute animals—to *quadrupeds*, to use the words of the civil law." (Stroud's Sketch, p. 24.)

We quote further and still more specific statements of the law, from the same writer:

"The master may determine the kind, and degree, and time of labor to which the slave shall be subjected.

"The master may supply the slave with such food and clothing only, both as to quantity and quality, as he may think proper or find convenient.

"The master may, at his discretion, inflict any punishment upon the person of his slave.

"All the power of the master over his slave may be exercised not by himself only in person, but by any one whom he may depute as his agent.

"A slave cannot be a party before a judicial tribunal, in any species of action, against his master, no matter how atrocious may have been the injury received from him.

"Slaves cannot redeem themselves, nor obtain a change of masters, though cruel treatment may have rendered such change necessary for their personal safety."

"Slaves being objects of *property*, if injured by others, their *owners* may bring suit, and recover *damage* for the injury." (Stroud's Sketch, p. 25.)

To this we will add:

The *master* may wholly forbid and prevent the education, the moral and religious instruction of his slaves—their attendance on religious meetings and religious worship, either among themselves or at meetings conducted by white persons.

There is not a slave in the United States that can claim these benefits as legal rights, or that can enjoy these privileges, in any degree, except with the leave of their "*owners*" or their agents.

There is not a slave-owner in the United States, however ignorant, vulgar, degraded, immoral, and irreligious, that does not hold this authority over each and all of his slaves, however pious or intelligent they may be. And this authority, involved in slave-ownership, is part and parcel of "the legal relation of master and slave."

There is not a slave State, or slave Territory or District under the Federal jurisdiction, that does not, by its Slave Code, extend its sanction and its guaranty to this power of the slave-owner.

We speak here only of the power of the individual who holds slaves. The *laws forbidding* education and the free exercise of religion will be considered in another connection.

"A *statu liber*" (a slave minor, entitled to freedom at the age of twenty-one) has (in the mean time) "no action at law for *ill treatment*." Dorothee *vs.* Coquillon et al., Jan. Term, 1829. (19 Martin's Louisiana Rep., 350. Wheeler's Law of Slavery, pp. 108–9.)

No resistance must be made by a slave to his master.

"*While the institution of slavery exists,* every thing like resistance to the master's lawful authority should be decisively checked. Strict subordination must be exacted from the slave, or bloodshed and murders will unavoidably ensue. The laws of the slave-holding States demand, however, a much larger concession of power to the master than is here granted: *they demand that* THE LIFE *of the slave shall be in the* MASTER'S KEEPING—that the slave, having the physical ability to avoid the infliction of a *barbarous* and vindictive punishment by his master, shall not be permitted to do so." (Stroud's Sketch, p. 97.)

We reserve a quotation from Prince's Digest and from several statutes, until, in treating of the *civil* relations of the slave, we shall use them to prove *more* than our present argument requires, viz.: that the same absolute submission of the slave is required by the laws, not merely towards the "owner" and his agent, but towards "*all white persons!*"

Judge Ruffin, of North Carolina, in the case of State *vs.* Mann, decided as follows: "The power of the master must be *absolute*, to render the *submission* of the slave *perfect*. It would not do to allow the rights of the master to be brought into discussion in the courts of justice. The slave, to REMAIN a slave, must be sensible that there is NO APPEAL from his master." (2 Devereaux's N. Carolina Rep., 263.)

This justifies our statement that "the legal relation of master and slave" is responsible for all this despotic power.

In Wheeler's Law of Slavery, pp. 244–8, there is a full report of the opinion of Judge Ruffin, from which we have taken the preceding extract. We shall revert to it again, and make further extracts, when, in another chapter, we come to treat of "Punishments of Slaves by the owners and hirers." An examination of that topic will more fully illustrate the general proposition at the head of this chapter, for the correctness of which we here cite a few personal testimonies.

"The whole commerce between master and slave is a perpetual exercise of the most boisterous passions, the most unremitting DESPOTISM on the one part, and degrading SUBMISSION on the other."

"Thus nursed, educated, and *daily exercised in tyranny*," &c. (Jefferson.)

"I knew a gentleman of great benevolence and generosity of character," "speak of breaking down the spirit of a slave, under the lash, as perfectly right." (Angelina Grimke Weld, "Slavery as it is," p. 54.)

"There was *no law* for the negro, but that of the overseer's whip." (L. Sapington, Ib., p. 49.)

The Savannah River Baptist Association approvingly recognized the unlimited authority of the master, when they maintained his authority to annul slave marriages, and to compel new sexual connections between Baptist husbands and wives whom he had forcibly severed! The people are here found to be no better than their laws, and the Church no better than the people. Hence they consider the "legal relation an innocent one." It stands precisely on their own moral level.

This chapter may serve as a key to a number of the chapters that follow, as it contains the *principle* upon which their specifications are based, *the absolute authority of the master*. Those chapters, in their turn, will furnish illustrations and evidences of the truth of this.

CHAPTER X.

LABOR OF SLAVES.

The Slave, being a Chattel, may be worked at the discretion of his Owner, as other working Chattels are.

If the Legislature of one of our Northern States should enact a law restricting farmers to a specified number of hours per day, in which their oxen and horses should be worked; and if the Act should be prefaced with a preamble, stating that many farmers were in the habit of over-working their cattle, it would be thought a severe reflection upon the farmers. A stranger would conclude that they were an inhuman as well as a short-sighted class of people, to treat their working beasts in that manner. They would eagerly read the Act, to see how many hours were allowed as a relief to the poor beasts. And they would necessarily infer that the practice had been to work the cattle a longer time than that prescribed by the law.

Let us now look at some of the laws of the slave States.

South Carolina, (Act of 1740.)—"Whereas, many owners of slaves, and others who have the care, management, and overseeing of slaves, *do confine them so closely to hard labor that they have not sufficient time for natural rest*, Be it therefore enacted, That if any owner of slaves, or other persons, who shall have the care, management, or overseeing of slaves, shall work or put any such slave or slaves to labor *more than fifteen hours* in twenty-four hours, from the 25th day of March to the 25th day of September; or *more than fourteen hours* in twenty-four hours, from the 25th day of September to the 25th day of March, every such person shall forfeit any sum not exceeding twenty pounds nor under five pounds current money, for every time he, she, or they shall offend herein, at the discretion of the justice before whom the complaint shall be made." (2 Brevard's Digest, 243.)

How much longer than fourteen or fifteen hours per day, in winter and summer, the South Carolina planters had been in the habit of working their slaves, we are left to conjecture! But we know that "the laws of Maryland, Virginia, and Georgia forbid that the *criminals* in their penitentiaries shall be compelled to labor more than *ten* hours a day," (Jay's Inquiry, p. 130;) and not exceeding *nine* hours in some portions of the year, and *eight* during the three other months, (Stroud's Sketch, p. 29.) In Jamaica, (before emancipation,) "besides many holidays which are by law accorded to the slave, *ten* hours a day is the extent of the time which the slave is compelled, *ordinarily*, to work." (2 Edwards' W. Indies, book iv., chap. 5, &c.)

6*

GEORGIA, (Act of 1817.)—"Any *owner* of a slave or slaves, who shall cruelly treat such slave or slaves by unnecessary or excessive whipping, by withholding proper food and nourishment, *by requiring greater labor* from such slave or slaves than he or she or they may be able to perform, by not affording proper clothing, *whereby the health* of such slave or slaves may be *injured or impaired*, every such owner or owners of slaves shall, *upon sufficient information* being laid before the grand jury, be by said grand jury presented, whereupon it shall be the duty of the attorney or solicitor general to prosecute said owner or owners, who, on conviction, shall be sentenced to pay a fine, or be imprisoned, at the discretion of the Court." (Prince's Digest, 376.)

In this act, the "*owner*" only is specified, and not the overseer, or agent.

LOUISIANA, (Act of July, 1806.)—"As for the hours of work and rest which are to be assigned to slaves in summer, the old usages of the territory shall be adhered to, to wit: The slaves shall be allowed half an hour for breakfast during the whole year; from the first day of May to the first day of November they shall be allowed two hours for dinner; and from the first day of November to the first day of May, one hour and a half for dinner: *Provided*, however, that the owners who will themselves take the trouble of causing to be prepared the meals of their slaves, be, and they are hereby authorized to abridge, by half an hour per day, the time fixed for their rest." (1 Martin's Digest, 610–12.)

This relic of "the old usages" under the Spanish and French laws may be considered, like the Louisiana laws before quoted, an exception to the general code of American Slavery. Yet even here the hours of beginning and ending the day's labor are not specified, and consequently, the hours of labor, per day, are not limited nor ascertained. The known custom of night-work in boiling sugar is not touched by this statute.

In Georgia and in Mississippi, there are laws forbidding the unnecessary labor of slaves on the Sabbath.—This is all the information before us. In most of the slave States, there are no laws limiting slave labor. (See Stroud, p. 26.)

One single consideration is sufficient to show that the limitations just quoted are of no practical value. NO SLAVE AND NO FREE COLORED PERSON, IN THE SLAVE STATES, CAN BE A WITNESS AGAINST A WHITE PERSON. (Ib., 27.) Slaveholders would not be forward to prosecute each other for ill treatment of slaves. And many of the non-slaveholding whites, at the South, are a servile and degraded class, not daring to offend the slaveholders.

The celebrated George Whitefield, in a "Letter to the Inhabitants of Maryland, Virginia, North and South Carolina," in 1739, (after having travelled among them,) says: "Your slaves, I believe, work as hard, if not harder, than the horses whereon you ride. *These*, after their work is done, are fed, and taken proper care of, but many negroes, when wearied with labor in your plantations, have been obliged to grind their own corn, after their return home."

John Woolman, in his Journal, under date of 1757, speaks of the labor of slaves as "heavy, being followed at their business in the field by a man with a whip, hired for that purpose." (Life of Woolman, p. 74.)

The following are specimens of a great amount of similar testimony recorded in Weld's "Slavery as it is," p. 35 and onward:

"*So laborious* is the task of raising, beating, and cleaning rice, that had it been possible to obtain European servants in sufficient numbers, thousands and tens of thousands of them must have perished." (History of Carolina, vol. I. p. 30.)

Hon. Alexander Smythe, of Va., in a speech in Congress on the Missouri question, January 28, 1820, argued, on the ground of humanity, in favor of extending slavery into Missouri, that the slaves would be *more comfortable* there than in the older States, where they are "forced to incessant toil," "hard-worked," &c. If you "hem them in where they are," you "doom them to hard labor." It would be "*extreme cruelty* to the blacks."

Henry Clay, in 1834, in a conversation with James G. Birney, expressed a belief (contrary to his former impressions) that at the far South, the births among the slaves were not equal to the deaths. He related what he had heard and believed, that an overseer in Louisiana "worked his hands so closely, that one of the women brought forth a child while engaged in the labors of the field." He was also told of a plantation containing from "twenty to thirty young women in the prime of life," and the proprietor told him there had not been a child born among them for the last two or three years, although they all had husbands.

We have before us much more testimony to the same point; also, to the fact, that the slaves are commonly "obliged to work from daylight till dark, or as long as they can see."

"Every body here (Natchez, Miss.) knows *over-driving* to be one of the most common occurrences. The planters do not deny it, except, perhaps, to Northerners." (A. A. Stone, Theological Student.)

In our Chapter V. on the "*Uses* of Slave Property," it was shown how coolly and deliberately gangs of slaves are *used up* on the sugar plantations of Louisiana, once in seven or eight years. In Mr. Weld's book, before us, we have many testimonies that corroborate the general fact. We spare room for only one, which comes on the authority of Rev. John O. Choules, Baptist minister, once of New-Bedford, Mass., afterwards of Buffalo, New-York. "While attending the Baptist Triennial Convention at Richmond, Va., in 1835," says Mr. C., "I had a conversation with an officer of the Baptist church in that city, at whose house I was a guest. I asked him if he did not apprehend that the slaves would eventually rise and exterminate their masters? 'Why,' said the gentleman, 'I did use to apprehend such a catastrophe, but God has made a providential opening, *a merciful safety valve*, and now I do not feel alarmed, in the prospect of what is coming.' 'What do you mean,' said Mr. Choules, 'by Providence opening a merciful safety valve?' 'Why,' said the gentleman, 'I will tell you. The slave-traders come from the cotton and sugar plantations of the South, and are willing to *buy up* more slaves than we can part with. We must keep a stock for the purpose of *rearing* slaves, but we part with the most valuable, and at the same time the most *dangerous;* and the demand is very constant, and is likely to be so, for when they go to those Southern States, the average existence is ONLY FIVE YEARS!"

The people, including church members, are not better than their laws.

CHAPTER XI.

FOOD, CLOTHING, AND DWELLINGS OF SLAVES.

The Slave, as a Chattel, is fed or famished, covered or uncovered, sheltered or unsheltered, at the discretion or convenience of his Owner, like other working Animals.

LOUISIANA.—"Every owner shall be held to give his slaves the quantity of provisions hereinafter specified, to wit, one barrel of Indian corn,* *or*, the equivalent thereof in rice, beans, or *other grain*, and a pint of salt, and to deliver the same to the slaves, in kind, every month, and never in money, under penalty of a fine of ten dollars for every offense." (1 Martin's Digest, p. 610. Act of July 7, 1806.)

"The slave who shall not have, on the property of his owner, a lot of ground to cultivate on his own account, shall be entitled to receive from said owner *one* linen shirt and pantaloons for the summer, and a linen shirt and woollen greatcoat and pantaloons for the winter." (1 Martin's Digest, 610.) Neither the quantity nor the quality of the "lot of

---

* Meaning a flour barrel full of Indian corn in the ear, equal to about 1½ bushels of shelled corn.

ground" is specified, nor the amount of time to be allowed for tilling it.

NORTH CAROLINA.—"In case any slave or slaves, who shall not appear to have been fed and clothed according to the intent and meaning of this Act, that is to say, to have been *sufficiently* clothed, and to have constantly received for the preceding year an allowance of not less than *a quart of corn** per day, shall be convicted of stealing any corn, cattle, &c., &c., from any person not the owner of said slave or slaves, such injured person shall and may maintain an action of trespass against the master, owner, or possessor of such slave, &c., and shall recover his or her damages." (Hayward's Manual, 524–5.)

GEORGIA.—The Act of 1817 (as quoted in the last previous Chapter on *Labor*) provides for the punishment of "owners" of slaves who "by excessive whipping, *by withholding proper food and sustenance*, by requiring greater labor," &c., shall "cruelly treat" such slaves, "whereby the *health* of such slave, &c., may be *injured or impaired*."

Another Act, of Dec. 12, 1815, is as follows:

"Sect. 1. From and after the passing of this Act, it shall be the duty of the *inferior* courts of the several counties in this State, on receiving information, *on oath*, of any *infirm* slave or slaves in a suffering condition, from the neglect of the owner or owners of said slave or slaves, to make particular inquiries into

---

* It will be observed that in neither of these *legal rations* of food is any mention made of *meat*.

CHAPTER XI.

FOOD, CLOTHING, AND DWELLINGS OF SLAVES.

The Slave, as a Chattel, is fed or famished, covered or uncovered, sheltered or unsheltered, at the discretion or convenience of his Owner, like other working Animals.

LOUISIANA.—"Every owner shall be held to give his slaves the quantity of provisions hereinafter specified, to wit, one barrel of Indian corn,* *or*, the equivalent thereof in rice, beans, or *other grain*, and a pint of salt, and to deliver the same to the slaves, in kind, every month, and never in money, under penalty of a fine of ten dollars for every offense." (1 Martin's Digest, p. 610. Act of July 7, 1806.)

"The slave who shall not have, on the property of his owner, a lot of ground to cultivate on his own account, shall be entitled to receive from said owner *one* linen shirt and pantaloons for the summer, and a linen shirt and woollen greatcoat and pantaloons for the winter." (1 Martin's Digest, 610.) Neither the quantity nor the quality of the "lot of

* Meaning a flour barrel full of Indian corn in the ear, equal to about 1½ bushels of shelled corn.

the situation of such slave or slaves, and render such relief as they in their discretion shall think proper.

"Sect. 2. The said courts *may* and are hereby authorized to *sue* for and recover from the owner or owners of such slave or slaves, the amount that may be appropriated for the relief of such slave or slaves, in *any court* having jurisdiction of the same; any law, usage, or custom, to the contrary notwithstanding." (Prince's Digest, 460.)

SOUTH CAROLINA.—"In case any person, &c., who shall be owner, or who shall have the care, government, or charge of any slave or slaves, shall deny, neglect, or refuse to allow such slave or slaves, under his or her charge, sufficient clothing, covering, or food, it shall and may be lawful for any person or persons, on behalf of said slave or slaves, to make complaint to the next neighboring justice in the parish where such slave or slaves live, or are usually employed, and the said justice shall summon the party against whom such complaint shall be made, and shall inquire of, hear, and determine the same; and if the said justice shall find the said complaint to be true, *or* that such person will not exculpate or clear himself from the charge *by his or her own oath*, which such person shall be at liberty to do, in all cases where positive proof is not given of the offense, such justice shall and may make such orders upon the same, for the relief of such slave or slaves, as he in his discretion shall think fit; and shall and may set and impose a fine or penalty on any person who may offend in the premises, in any sum not exceeding hungry slave's exemption from punishment by his master or by the magistrate, for his "stealing" to appease hunger. There is no humanity in this law. It is a monument of the barbarity of its framers and of the slaveholders.

4. The Georgia Act of 1817, strictly construed, imposes no punishment on a master who shall "cruelly treat" his slave by "excessive whipping," *or* by withholding proper food, *or* by "requiring greater labor," &c. *All* these acts of "cruelty" must be combined in each instance, or the statute fails to apply to the case. Even then, it is not reached, unless "the health" of the slave be "injured or impaired." There may be "cruelty" by "excessive whipping," by hunger, *and* by excessive labor, but if the subject of all this "cruelty" retains his "health," the "cruelty" is not to be punished.

5. The Georgia Act of 1815 applies only to the case of "*infirm* slaves." Other slaves "in a suffering condition from the neglect of the owner" are not provided for. It requires "information *on oath*," (which no *colored* person can give,) before a legal inquiry can be commenced! The facts must be first proved before the process can begin, and proved, too, without the testimony of the sufferer! It shall be "*the duty*" of the courts to render such relief as they think proper. From whence the supply is to be obtained, unless from the pockets of the judges, does not appear. (We have copied the entire act.) They are not authorized to order an execution against the delinquent "owner" on their judgment.

Instead of this, the judges are authorized (not directed) to become SUITORS themselves, as a "court," in ANOTHER court, to collect of the owner the amount of the appropriation, if they can; and if not, put up with the loss as they can, costs and all! Where shall we find a parallel to this farce?

6. The South Carolina Act must also be useless for the want of "positive proof," (as the slave cannot testify,) in the absence of which the defendant is cleared by his *own oath.*

7. We conclude, therefore, that these laws, on the whole, are no better than none. We should not anticipate, from their operation, any better provision for the clothing and sustenance of slaves, in these four States, than in the other slave States, where no laws exist. We are not aware that there is any perceptible difference in fact. And we may extend the remark to the laws of the four States mentioned in the previous chapter, on the subject of slave labor. *The principle of slave-ownership, viz., human chattelhood, is not impaired or infringed by them. The master has the power in his own hands. He may do what he wills with his own.* Such, at every point, is "THE LEGAL RELATION OF MASTER AND SLAVE."

From the law, we now turn to the prevailing practice. From the former we may anticipate the latter. In the work to which we have so often referred (Weld's "Slavery as it is") may be found a great amount of authentic testimony of highly respectable witnesses, of former and later times, for which we cannot spare room, but the substance is as follows:

HUNGER.—Slaves in Virginia (1820) are "ill fed." They are "doomed to scarcity and hunger." (Alex. Smythe, M. C.) In 1739, they "had not sufficient food to eat; they were scarcely permitted to pick up the crumbs that fell from their masters' tables." (Rev. Geo. Whitefield.)—They are "deprived of needful subsistence." (Rev. Geo. Bourne.)—In 1791 "they were supplied with barely enough to keep them from starving." (Dr. Jonathan Edwards, of *Connecticut.*)—In Georgia "their allowance is *often* not adequate to the support of a laboring man." (Thomas Clay, Esq., a slaveholder.)—In Tennessee "thousands are pressed with the gnawings of hunger." (Rev. John Rankin.)—In North Carolina, 1826, "the greater part of them go half starved, much of the time." (Moses and Wm. Swain.)—In Louisiana, 1835, "there is a good deal of suffering from hunger"—"utter famishment, during a great portion of the year." (A. A. Stone.)—In Mississippi, "half starved." (Tobias Boudinot.)

KINDS OF FOOD.—The general testimony is, that slaves are allowed meat only as an occasional "indulgence or favor"—"at Christmas," &c. &c. Experiments have been made with cotton seed, as a substitute in part for corn. Gen. Wade Hampton is said to have tried the experiment, till, as he himself declared with an oath, his slaves "died like rotten sheep." This statement was furnished by "a lady of high respectability and great moral worth," to "a clergyman in the West, extensively known both as a preacher and a writer. His name is with the Executive Committee of the American Anti-Slavery Society." (Weld's "American Slavery as it is," p. 29.)

QUANTITY.—"The quantity allowed by custom is a peck of corn a week." (Thos. Clay, Esq., Georgia, 1833.) Same testimony by W. C. Gildersleeve, now of Wilkesbarre, Pa.; and Rev. Horace Moulton, of Marlboro, Mass.—both once resident in Georgia.

Maryland: Same quantity, 1788. (Baltimore *Advertiser.*)—Florida: A quart of corn a day, to a full task hand, with a modicum of salt. *Kind* masters allowed a peck of corn a week. Some masters allowed no salt." (Wm. Ladd, once a Florida slaveholder, since of Minot, Me.)—North Carolina: Seven quarts of *meal*, or eight quarts of small rice, for one week.' (Nehemiah Caulkins, Waterford, Ct.; resident in North Carolina eleven winters.)—Virginia: A pint of corn meal and a salt herring is the allowance, (for one meal,) or, in lieu of the herring, a 'dab' of fat meat of about the same value. I *have known* the sour milk and clauber to be served out to the hands, when there was an abundance of milk on the plantation. This is a luxury, not often afforded." (Rev. C. S. Renshaw, a native Virginian.)

John Woolman, in his Journal, (1757,) makes the general statement, that "they have in common little else allowed but *one peck of Indian corn* and some salt, for one week, with a *few potatoes;* the potatoes they commonly raise by their labor on the *first day of the week.*" (Life of Woolman, p. 74.)

QUALITY OF FOOD.—"There is often a defect here."

(Thos. Clay, Esq., Georgia.)—"The feed of slaves is generally of the poorest kind." (Rev. Horace Moulton.)—In Kentucky, "They live on a coarse, crude, unwholesome diet." (*Western Medical Reformer.*)—"Large numbers of *badly fed* negroes were swept off by a prevailing epidemic."—"The best remedy for that horrid malady, '*Cachexia Africana,*' is to feed the negroes with *nutritious* food." (Prof. A. G. Smith, of New-York Medical College, once physician in Louisville, Ky.)

NUMBER AND TIMES OF MEALS, EACH DAY.—"The slaves eat *twice* during the day." (Dr. Jonathan Edwards, Connecticut, 1791.)

Florida: "The slaves go to the field in the morning; they carry with them meal, wet with water, and at *noon* build a fire on the ground, and bake it in the ashes. After the labors of the day are over, they take their *second* meal of ashcake. (Philemon Bliss, Esq., Elyria, Ohio; resident in Florida, 1834–5.)

Mississippi, 1837: "The slaves received two meals during the day. Breakfast about 11 o'clock; the *other* meal after night." (Eleazer Powell, now of Chippewa, Pa.)

North Carolina: "The breakfast of the slaves was generally about 10 or 11 o'clock A. M." (Nehemiah Caulkins.)

Virginia: "Two meals a day. Breakfast from 10 to 11 o'clock A. M. Supper from 6 to 9 or 10 at night, as the season and crops may be." (Rev. C. S. Renshaw.)—"Meals generally taken without knife, dish, or spoon." (Wm. Leftwitch, a Virginian.)

Georgia: "The corn is ground in a hand mill, by the slave, *after his task is done.* Generally there is but one mill on a plantation, and as but one can grind at a time, the mill is going sometimes very late at night." (W. C. Gildersleeve, Esq., a native Georgian.) Similar testimony from other States.

South Carolina: "Only two meals a day are allowed *to the house slaves;* the *first* at 12 o'clock. If they eat before this time it is by stealth, and I am sure there must be a good deal of suffering among them from *hunger*, particularly by children. Besides this, they are often kept from their meals by way of punishment. No table is provided for them to eat from. They know nothing of the comfort and pleasure of gathering round the social board; each takes his plate or tin pan, and holds it in the hand or on the lap. I *never* saw slaves seated round a *table*, to partake of any meal." (Angelina Grimke Weld.)

"Stealing food is a crime, punished by flogging. A woman was punished for stealing four potatoes." (P. Bliss, Esq.)

"Cooks, waiters, chambermaids, &c., generally get some meat every day—the remaining bits and bones of their masters' tables." (Weld, p. 31.)

The law of Louisiana of 1806, (Chap. X.,) prescribing the time allotted to meals, by its mention of breakfast and dinner, seems to indicate a *third* meal, though it is not directly mentioned.

The fare of slaves is doubtless better in the slave-*growing* than in the slave-*consuming* States. And there are *exceptions* to the *general* picture we have presented.

CLOTHING.—Mr. Weld has shown by abundant and unimpeachable testimony, that "the clothing of slaves by day, and their covering by night, is not adequate either for comfort or decency." (p. 40, &c.)

Virginia: Hon. T. T. Bouldin, a slaveholder, in a speech in Congress, Feb. 16, 1835, said: "He *knew* that many negroes had *died* from exposure to weather," and added, "They are clad in a *flimsy fabric* that will turn neither wind nor water."

Maryland: "The slaves, *naked* and starved, often fall victims to the inclemencies of the weather." (Geo. Buchanan, M.D., of Baltimore, 1791.)

Georgia, &c.: "We rode through many rice swamps, where the blacks were very numerous"—"working up to the middle in water, *men and women nearly naked.*" (Wm. Savery, of Philadelphia, Minister Friends' Soc., 1791.)

Tennessee, &c.: "In *every* slaveholding State many slaves suffer extremely, both while they labor and when they sleep, *for want of clothing* to keep them warm." (Rev. John Rankin.)

The South generally: "Men and women have many times scarce clothes enough to hide their nakedness, and boys and girls, ten and twelve years old, are often *quite* naked among their masters' children." (John Woolman, 1757. Journal, &c., p. 150.)

"Both male and female go *without clothing* at the age of 8 or 10 years." (John Parrish, Minister Soc.

Friends, 1804.) Same testimony from many others more recently.

Alabama, 1819: "Hardly a rag of clothing on them."—"Generally the only bedding was a blanket." (S. E. Maltby.)

Virginia: "Two old blankets." (Wm. Leftwich.) Advertisements of fugitives *every year* often describe them as "ragged" or "nearly naked."

Florida: "They were allowed two suits of clothes a year; viz: one pair of trowsers with a shirt or frock of osnaburgh, for summer; and for winter, one pair of trowsers and a jacket of negro-cloth, with a baize shirt and a pair of shoes. Some allowed hats, and some did not; and they were generally, I believe, allowed one blanket in two years. Garments of similar materials were allowed the women." (Wm. Ladd, late of Minot, Me.)

"The slaves are generally without beds or bedsteads."—"I have seen men and women at work in the fields, more than half naked." (Testimony furnished by Rev. C. S. Renshaw, from his friend.)

"In Lower Tennessee, Mississippi and Louisiana, clothing made of cotton bagging"—"no shoes." (G. W. Westgate.)

"WILL" of the celebrated JOHN RANDOLPH of Roanoke, Va., distinguished as a "kind master": "To my old and faithful servants Essex and his wife Hetty, I give and bequeath a pair of strong shoes, a suit of clothes, and a blanket each, to be paid them annually; also an annual hat to Essex." No socks, stockings, bonnets, cloaks, handkerchiefs, or towels—no *change* either of outside or inner garments! And a solemn "Last Will and Testament" was deemed necessary to secure to them even the articles specified!

Family servants, waiters, &c., and hotel attendants, must needs appear decently clad. And kept mistresses of gentlemen are often arrayed extravagantly. Superficial observers and shallow thinkers, seeing this, report the happy condition of slaves in general, having never seen the "negro quarters" on the plantations.

DWELLINGS.—These "generally contain but *one* apartment, and that without a floor;"—"no partition to separate the sexes;"—nothing that a Northern laborer "would call a bed";—sometimes "built by themselves of stakes and poles, and thatched with palmetto leaf; sometimes of clay;"—"no window glass or sashes;"—"not sufficient to keep off the inclemency of the weather;—sometimes built of logs; on old plantations sometimes of frame and clapboards, size, 8 feet by 10, or 10 by 12, and but 8 feet high;"—"without any chimney—a hole at top to let the smoke out;"—"*generally* put up (in Georgia) without a *nail;*"—"ill ventilated;"—"surrounded with filth;"—"with neither chairs, table, nor bedstead;"—"on the cold ground they must lie without covering, and shiver while they slumber." Such is the picture attested by competent witnesses. (Weld's "Slavery as it is," p. 43, &c.)

TREATMENT OF THE SICK, THE INFIRM, AND THE AGED.—On this topic we have not room here to enter.

In Mr. Weld's work, pp. 44, 45, may be found statements from the late Rev. Dr. Channing, of Boston, once resident in Virginia, (extracted from his work on Slavery;) from Miss Sarah M. Grimke, formerly of Charleston, S. C.; from Geo. A. Avery, merchant, Rochester, N. Y., once living in Virginia; from Rev. Wm. T. Allan, once of Alabama; the late Rev. Elias Cornelius, (p. 161;)* and several others, all showing that great barbarity characterizes the slaveholders, generally, in their ill treatment or neglect of these unfortunate beings, held dependent upon them, and defenceless, as slaves.

Into *all* the particulars which go to make up the dreadful *condition* of the slave, the plan and limits of the present treatise do not permit us to go. We select mainly such facts as illustrate the *slave laws*, and the consequent "legal relation" of master and slave. At every step we find it a relation identified with wretchedness and wrong.

From Wheeler's "Law of Slavery" it would seem that slaveholders are in the habit of refusing to pay physicians for medical attendance on their slaves, and that suits at law are the consequence, which are variously decided, the decisions of a lower court being sometimes reversed by a higher. The following points are put down by Mr. Wheeler in his marginal titles:

Dunbar *vs.* Williams. 10 John's New-York Rep. 249: "No action lies by a physician against the

* See Edwards' Life of Rev. Elias Cornelius, pp. 101–3.

master for attendance upon his slave without his knowledge, unless it be a case of extreme necessity." (Wheeler, p. 225.)

Wells *vs.* Kennerly, 4 McCord's S. C. Rep. 123: "The *owner* is not liable for medical attendance upon a *hired* slave, given at the request of the *hirer.*" (Ib., p. 226.)

It is hardly to be expected that the temporary *hirer* of a slave would be forward to incur the expense of much medical attendance.

In the case of Johnson et al. *vs.* Barrett, Judge Johnson, South Carolina, said: "If a slave be *in peril* in the absence of his master, the *interest of the owner* is most effectually subserved by rendering assistance to the slave, and in good conscience *the owner* is bound to make satisfaction." (Ib.)

The *legal* rule then is, to give medical aid when the *interest of the owner* demands it!

CHAPTER XII.

COERCED LABOR, WITHOUT WAGES.

The "legal relation of Master and Slave"—being the relation of an Owner to a Chattel, is a relation incompatible with the natural and heaven-sanctioned "relation" of Labor and Wages.

CHRISTIANITY is "a swift witness against those that oppress" even "the *hireling* IN his wages." It also proclaims: "Woe unto him that useth his neighbor's service WITHOUT wages, and giveth him not for his work."

To "oppress the *hireling* IN his wages," is to pay him *inadequate* wages, or to withhold a *part* of his earnings. To use a neighbor's service WITHOUT wages, is to pay him no wages at all. This latter is the definition of *slave* labor, and that labor is extorted by brute force. The slave is *not* a "hireling." He is not hired at all, any more than a working horse or ox is hired. In saying this, we only state the legal and the inevitable fact of the case. More particularly:

1. Wages is "that which is *stipulated* to be paid for services." There is, in this, of necessity, the concurrent action of two parties who stipulate, namely: the employer and the employed; the payer and him

that receives pay. The wages are determined by a mutual stipulation, agreement, or contract between the parties.

2. Wages, to be legitimate, must be equitable, or equal. There must be, by both the parties, an equivalent given and received. The labor must be equal in value to the wages, and the wages must be equal in value to the labor.

3. Wages is that which, when received by the laborer, becomes *his own, his property.* The very ideas of *property* and of the *rights* of property have their origin here. He who receives wages, possesses, appropriates, and disposes of his wages; and no one, without an equivalent, or without his leave, can take them from him.

4. Wages for the faithful services of an able-bodied man, during the proper working hours of the day, in order to be adequate and equitable wages, must *more* than suffice for his comfortable sustenance as a mere animal. They must enable him to support a family, to supply his own and their social wants as intellectual and moral beings, to discharge his responsibilities as a member of society, and lay up a surplus for the ordinary exigences of the future.

5. The wages of the successful producer of the fruits of the earth, to be equitable, must secure to him, as his possession, a large proportion of those fruits. On a plantation, or in a parish, township, or province, in which the men whose labor has built comfortable houses may not live in comfortable houses; whose labor has procured ample supplies of

food, clothing, and family comforts, but may not share in and enjoy those supplies and comforts, (unless squandered by improvidence,) there could not have been an equitable receipt of wages, by the laborer.

By each and all of these definitions and tests of wages, the slave system, the slaveholding "relation," both in theory and practice, stand condemned. They do not and they cannot accord WAGES to the LABORER.

For, in the first place, "the slave can make no contract," and hence he cannot *stipulate* for wages.

2. "The slave can possess nothing," and hence he cannot receive (because he cannot possess, appropriate, or use) wages.

3. The slave is "goods and chattels," and these cannot earn wages. The sustenance of the horse and ox are not wages. The needful repairs of a machine are not wages. Were *all* the slaves as "fat and sleek" as Henry Clay's, their comfortable fare would not be wages. Besides:

4. The cost of sustenance for the slave (were it matter of mutual stipulation) is too trivial to be dignified with the name of *wages!* Look over the preceding chapters. Estimate the labor. Look at its products—houses, equipages, wardrobes, wines, feasts, exports, returns, revenues, banks, cities, navies! Imagine an exodus of the slaves, like that of the Hebrews out of Egypt, and let the wand of their Moses sweep along with them all the products of their labor! What would be left after them? Then

inquire after the compensation that has been paid for this labor. "A peck of corn a week, with a modicum of salt." Say 12½ bushels of corn a year, at 50 cents, is $6.25—the salt, 25 cents, makes $6.50 for a year's board. Then add the wardrobe of John Randolph's "faithful servant Essex"—possibly $10 more. The house-rent, at what the "owner" thinks it worth! Then foot up the sum total—or, take the estimate of slaveholders themselves, in Reports of Committees of Agricultural Societies, published to the world, viz., $15 to $20 per annum, along with the confession of Thomas Clay, Esq., of Georgia: "The present economy of the slave system is, to get ALL YOU CAN from the slave, and give him AS LITTLE as will support him in a *working* condition." It is no counterproof or palliation, that the system is unprofitable. To "use a neighbor's service without wages" has always been profitless, because always wrong, and heaven-abhorred.

The balance between the slave's *earnings* (possessed or squandered by his "owner,") and the cost of the slave's *support*, may tell us whether the slave could "take care of himself" if suffered to receive honest wages.

Again, we say, look at the wealth earned by the slave; then look at the slave, half famished, half naked, without a bed, shivering, sleeping on the bare ground with an old blanket around him, or turned off, perhaps, in decrepid old age, by his "owner," "a gentleman [reputedly] of great benevolence and generosity of character," to beg in the streets of

Charleston, (S. C.,) because "too old to work, and therefore *his allowance was stopped;*"* then learn how "the innocent legal relation" enforces LABOR WITHOUT WAGES.

When we say it is "the legal relation" that does this, we have the testimony of Southern judicial decision to sustain us.

In the case of the State *vs.* Mann, before cited, Judge Ruffin said:

The slave is "doomed, in his own person and his posterity, to live without knowledge, and *without capacity to make any thing his own, and to toil that others may reap the fruits.*" (Wheeler's Law of Slavery, p. 246, copied from 2 Devereaux's North Carolina Rep., 263.)

---

* See Weld's "Slavery as it is," p. 54. Testimony of the daughter of Judge Grimke, of Charleston, (S. C.)

CHAPTER XIII.

PUNISHMENTS OF SLAVES BY THE OWNER AND HIRER.

Being the absolute property of the Owner, the Slave is wholly in his power, without any effectual restraint.

WE have seen that "the legal relation" of slave ownership, being the relation of an owner to his property, invests him with *unlimited power*. We have traced the exercise of that power in a number of directions, and have witnessed at every step, thus far, the express sanction or the silent acquiescence of the slave laws. Or, if limitations to his power have, at some points, and in some of the States, *appeared* to be interposed, it has been found, on a close scrutiny, to be *only* an appearance, and not a reality. In the vitally important matters of absolute purchase, sale, seizure for debt, inheritance, distribution, marriage, (or rather, *no* marriage,) annihilation of family sanctities, incapacity to possess property, to make a contract, or to receive wages in the appointment of labor, supply of food, clothing, and habitations, we have seen the power of the master *every thing*, the rights, the protection, the defense, the redress, and the power of the slave, *nothing!* We come now to inquire whether, in the item of slave *punishments* by the master, there are any available limitations or restrictions of his power. In other words, whether, in "the legal relation" of slave owner and slave, the "owner" be, in reality, at this vital point, *amenable to law;* or whether here, as at all the preceding points, he rises *above* law, making it the *instrument* of his will, but not *subjecting himself* to its authority.

If there *be* any such limitation, it must be, thus far, an inroad upon *the principle* of human chattelhood, denying its claims, and thwarting the exercise of the "rights of property" involved in it. The rights of property in brute animals might be limited at this point, without danger to the *tenure* of such property. The *brute* could take no advantage of such lenity, to throw off the yoke of dominion and outgrow its chattelhood. Not so with chattels endued with thought and reason. To be held and used as chattels at all, they must be taught (as before quoted from Prince's Digest, 450) that "the life of the slave must be in his master's keeping," or, as Judge Ruffin expressed it, "the slave must be sensible that there is no appeal from his master." The old Romans understood this necessity, when they engrafted the same maxims into their civil code: the slaves "are not capable of being injured"—they may be "punished at the discretion of their lord, or even put to death by his authority." The people of the South, their courts, and their jurists, understand this, when they "generally refer" (as Stroud says they do) to the Roman civil code, "as containing the true principles of their institution," "except where modified by statutes, or by usages which have acquired the force of law." Those statutes and usages (on this point) we are now to inquire after. If it be found that Judge Ruffin, and that Mr. Prince, in his Digest, have rightly represented them, the apologists of the "innocent legal relation" must not too severely or too exclusively arraign *their* barbarism for expounding (not enacting) the law of the "relation."

It could hardly be supposed that, in any civilized country, the Legislature would, by express statute, *authorize* the master to commit cruel outrages upon the persons of his slaves, or murder them; nor that, in the present age of the world, a civil government would openly proclaim impunity to any persons beforehand, in the commission of such crimes. If it were desired and intended by the Legislature to produce such a result, the more feasible and effectual means of doing this (especially in an elective government) would be to make a show of prohibiting and punishing the crimes, but under circumstances and arrangements so contrived as to render the execution of the law or the conviction of the offenders impracticable.

Laws and courts of justice are chiefly needed for the protection of the weak and the defenseless. That class in any community that, from these causes, is most exposed to violence and outrage, is the class in respect to which the Legislature, *if it intends to protect them at all*, will most solicitously seek methods of doing it effectually. If *any* distinctions are made between the subjects of the government, it will be made in *their favor.* Whenever an *opposite* policy is witnessed, especially when this is carried so far that the exposed class are not allowed to bring a *complaint* against one of the class to whose aggressions they are most exposed, or even to bear *testimony* against them, we may be certain that no protection of them was *intended;* but that, on the other hand, the powerful party was intended to be countenanced in their injurious aggressions. And this would be doubly confirmed, if none but the same powerful party administered the law, or had any share in the government, or participation in the immunities or privileges enjoyed under it. Let such be the case between Catholics and Protestants, Normans and Anglo-Saxons, or Turks and Greeks, and no reader of history would hesitate in making such a decision. This is the precise fact in respect to American slaveholders and slaves. No principle in the slave code is more firmly established than this: that a slave can bring no suit against his master, unless it be a suit for his freedom. Even the minor female slave who is to be free at the age of twenty-one can have no suit brought by a free parent for her relief from ill treatment. Such was the decision (before alluded to) of Judge Martin, in the case of Dorothee *vs.* Coquillon et al., Jan. Term, 1829. (19 Martin's Louisiana Reports, 350. Wheeler's Law of Slavery, p. 198.)

It must be idle to pretend that any statutes for the

protection of the slave can be of any avail in the presence of such rules, and the following:

"*It is an inflexible and universal rule of slave law*, founded in one or two States upon *usage*, in others sanctioned by *express legislation*, THAT THE TESTIMONY OF A COLORED PERSON, WHETHER BOND OR FREE, CANNOT BE RECEIVED AGAINST A WHITE PERSON." (Stroud's Sketch, p. 27.)

To this feature of slave law we have alluded before, and shall devote to its details a distinct chapter, when we come to treat of the *civil* relations of the slaves. In the mean time, it is a feature of sufficient notoriety to be assumed in this chapter, having been, at one time, enacted in the free State of Ohio, and also incorporated into the ecclesiastical polity of the Methodist Episcopal Church, as administered in those States where it obtains as civil law.

In the presence of such a regulation, very clearly, there can be no adequate protection of the slave under any laws framed for his benefit, however well constructed in other respects. Nevertheless, we will examine them, and notice their spirit, and the kind and degree of protection they appear to contemplate.

SOUTH CAROLINA.—Act of 1740: "In case any person shall wilfully cut out the tongue, put out the eye, castrate, or *cruelly* scald, burn, or deprive any slave of any limb or member, or shall inflict any *other cruel* punishment, OTHER THAN by whipping, or beating with a horsewhip, cowskin, switch, or small stick, *or* by putting irons on, or confining or imprisoning such slave, every such person shall, for every such offense, forfeit the sum of one hundred pounds, current money." (2 Brevard's Digest, 241.)

This law, it is believed, is still on the statute book. We have said, it could hardly be supposed that any legislature, in a civilized country, would, by express statute, authorize the master to commit cruel outrages upon the persons of his slaves. But this is done in the statute just quoted. The expression "*other than*," in its connection, *does expressly* authorize "*cruel* punishment." And it authorizes "cruel punishment" in a number of forms specified, viz: "by whipping or beating with a horsewhip, cowskin, switch, or small stick, or by putting irons on, or confining or imprisoning." "Cruel punishment," if inflicted in either of these ways, is expressly excepted from the "cruel punishments" forbidden. And on inspection it will be found, that the methods of "cruel punishment" forbidden are such, and such only, as diminish the pecuniary value of the slave. The "legal relation" which contemplates the slave only as a chattel, was evidently the presiding genius of this enactment.

The specific prohibitions assure us that certain "persons" (whether owners, overseers, or others) *had committed* outrages of that character, or *such* particular specifications would not have been thought of. Such wanton destruction of "property" was not to be suffered. The heavy pecuniary fine would afford some security to slave "owners" against passionate "overseers" and others. The defenselessness of the slave, and the brutality of those around him, are frightfully depicted in this statute, the like of which was never needed for the security of domestic beasts. Yet no compensation or damages are awarded to the sufferers. The "owner" might be the aggressor, but the slave was not allowed "to go free for his eye's sake," like the Hebrew servant, whose master had thus injured him. (Exodus xxi. 26, 27.) The "cruelty" authorized is a sufficient proof that the Legislature had little or no regard to the suffering or pain endured by the slave, provided the article of "property" were not essentially *damaged.*

LOUISIANA.—"The slave is *entirely* subject to the will of his master, *who may* correct and *chastise* him, though not with *unusual* rigor, nor so as to maim or mutilate him, or to expose him to the danger of loss of life, or so as to cause his death." (Civil Code of Louisiana, Art. 173.)

Here, again, the protection of slave *property*, rather than the prevention of *suffering* by the slave, appears to be the leading object in view. The slave may not be maimed, he may not be mutilated, he may not be killed. Beyond this, there is nothing in the way of *prohibition* that is tangible or definite. *Permission* to the master is far more distinct and prominent. The "master *may* chastise," and he *may* chastise "with *rigor*," (severity; without abatement, relaxation or mitigation. Vide Webster,) but "not with *unusual* rigor." There is something in this singular phraseology that requires study. Such a law, instead of *correcting* prevailing usages, receives its definition *from* them. That which is "*usual*" is *authorized*, whatever it may be, short of maiming mutilation, and murder. And the more rigorous, severe, and cruel may be the prevailing usages of a community, the more rigorous, severe, and cruel they are expressly *authorized* to be. The individual is referred, as a standard of lawful action, to the common practices of his neighbors around him. What is "*usual*" among *them* is lawful for *him*. If it is "*usual*" to "chastise" a slave by inflicting on him a hundred lashes, it is *lawful* to do so. If it is "*usual*" to add five hundred lashes more, it is equally *lawful!* In short, the current *usages* of the fraternity of slaveholders (with the exceptions specified) are proclaimed, by the Civil Code of Louisiana, to constitute *the law*. This approximates closely to the abrogation of law, so far as slaveholders are concerned, or the abdication of supremacy by the civil government in their favor. The condition of this great nation of twenty millions of people, controlled by a little more than one hundred thousand slaveholders, seem but an expansion of this idea.

"*Unusual* rigor" must be defined in the light of what is *usual*. And we may learn something of what was then considered *usual* rigor in Louisiana, by the fact that the provisions of the law of South Carolina, before cited, *with exception of its prohibition of mutilation*, had been substantially in force there, up to the time this new Civil Code was adopted. We may infer, therefore, that "cruel punishment" by "whipping or beating with a horsewhip, cowskin, switch, or small stick, or by putting irons on, or confining or imprisoning," was not "unusual," and consequently not forbidden, by the new Civil Code.

In 1819, the Legislature of Louisiana recognized the lawfulness of putting iron chains and collars upon slaves, to prevent them from running away, as follows:

"If any person or persons, &c., shall cut or break any iron collar which any master of slaves shall have used in order to prevent the running away or escape of any such slave or slaves, such persons so offending shall, on conviction, be fined not less than two hundred dollars, nor exceeding one thousand dollars; and suffer imprisonment for a term not exceeding two years, nor less than six months." (Act of Assembly of March 6, 1819. Pamphlet, p. 64.)

Compare this penalty with that imposed by the Legislature of the same State for cruelties committed on slaves, viz: "not more than five hundred dollars nor less than two hundred," (1 Martin's Digest, 654,) and it will appear that the *releasing* of a slave from the "usual" punishment of the "iron chain or collar" is regarded a more aggravated crime than *inflicting* upon him the "unusual punishment," whatever it may be, prohibited by law! For the act of mercy, the offender may be fined $1000 and imprisoned two years; for the act of atrocious cruelty, he may be fined $500, but without imprisonment. Thus it is that the Legislature of Louisiana discountenances cruelty.

MISSISSIPPI.—The Constitution *empowers* the Legislature to make laws to oblige the owners of slaves to treat them with humanity—to abstain from all injuries to them extending to *life* and *limb*, and in case of their refusal or neglect to comply with the directions of such laws, to have such slave or slaves sold, for the benefit of the owner or owners. (Const. Mississippi, title slaves, Sect. 1. Rev. Code, 554.)

The Legislature, so far as appears, have taken no action under the powers granted in this last clause for the sale of maltreated slaves.* Under the former clause the action of the Legislature is as follows:

"No cruel or *unusual* punishment shall be inflicted on any slave in this State. And any master or other person entitled to the service of any slave, who shall inflict such cruel or unusual punishment, or shall authorize or permit the same to be inflicted, shall, on conviction, &c., be fined according to the magnitude of the offense, at the discretion of the

* No such provision appears to exist in any of the States, except, perhaps, in Louisiana; and this constitutes another harsh feature of modern American slavery, as contrasted with the ancient. Nothing can be more manifest than that no laws against the cruelty of masters and overseers can be of much benefit to the slave, if he is still to remain in the hands of a master whose tyranny had already demanded legal interference, and who would, in most cases, be exasperated against the slave on whose behalf the interference had been made. Judge Ruffin, if we rightly understand him, in the case of "the State *vs.* Mann," adduces this as a reason why the master must not be indictable for a battery on his slave. It would only prompt him to "bloody vengeance, generally practised with impunity, by reason of its privacy." (Wheeler's Law of Slavery, p. 247.)

Court, in any sum not exceeding five hundred dollars," &c. (Rev. Code, 379; Act of June 18, 1822.)

Here, again, no satisfaction or remuneration is awarded to the *slave*, for "a slave is not capable of being injured;" he is a "chattel"—a "thing"—not a person. And it is only an "*unusual*" punishment that is forbidden! The masters and overseers have only to repeat their excessive punishments so frequently that they become "*usual*," and the statute does not apply to them! In this view it holds out an inducement to render the most cruel inflictions *usual*. Besides all this, the slave can bring no suit. He can enter no complaint. He can bear no testimony. No other slave or free colored person can bear testimony against a *white* person; and the law is administered by slaveholders. It is incredible that owners and overseers should be much restrained by the provisions of this act.

ALABAMA—has a statute similar to that of Mississippi, except that the fine imposed is only *one* hundred dollars, instead of *five* hundred. (Toulman's Digest, 631.)

MISSOURI.—The Constitution not only *empowers* the Legislature "to oblige the owners of slaves to treat them with humanity, and to abstain from all injuries to them extending to *life* or *limb*," (Art. 3, Sec. 26, last clause, 1 Missouri Laws, 48,) but it is also made its DUTY to pass such laws as may be necessary for this purpose.

Here, as before, the "life and limb"—the pecuniary value of the "property"—appears the prominent idea. Owners of property may not wantonly destroy it, to the public detriment, at the risk of their families and creditors. Owners of this refractory species of property, being "nursed and daily exercised in tyranny," are under special temptations. "To treat them [the slaves] with humanity" is an indefinite expression. Rightly construed, it would restore to them the right of testimony—the rights of human beings. But this was not the design, nor is it the practical construction of the instrument. So far as is known, (or previously to 1827, the latest dates in our possession,) "*no* law has been enacted on the authority of this article in the Constitution." (Vide Stroud's Sketch, p. 43.)

The following, however, is found on the statute book:

"If any slave resist his or her master, mistress, overseer, or employer, *or refuse* to obey his or her lawful commands, it shall be lawful for such master, &c., to commit such slave to the common jail of the county, there to remain *at the pleasure* of the master, &c.; and the sheriff shall receive such slave and keep him, &c., in confinement, at the expense of the person committing him or her." (1 Missouri Laws, 309.)

"*Lawful commands*"—But what if the commands are *not* lawful? And who is to decide, and by what testimony? The slave can bear no testimony—can enter no complaint—can set up no plea in arrest of proceedings. The "innocent legal relation," being a mere relation of owner and property, would not permit this. A legal process between owner and chattel would be an absurdity, and the statute, accordingly, prescribes none. The *master* simply "commits" his slave to the "sheriff," and it is the business of that public functionary to "receive" him. The insertion of the word "lawful" was a mere farce. It might be the "command" of the "owner" to a slave wife or virgin to submit to his embraces. Worse punishments than imprisonment are known to be in use in such cases, and are believed to be not "*unusual.*" This law has its counterpart or emendation in the municipal regulations of slave cities, where house servants (in the absence of any plantation overseer) are summarily sent to a public officer to be *whipped* a specified number of lashes, without any mention of the offense.

So far from any *limitation* of the "owner's" authority and power, we here find it enlarged. The public arm, instead of protecting the slave against the mas ter, *assists* the master in the exercise of his irresponsible despotism over the slave.

And in doing this the slave owner is invested with a dignity not conferred on any other class of citizens. He becomes *ex officio*, in virtue of his being a slaveholder, a judicial functionary himself, with the powers of a court of justice to award sentence, and order a public officer to put it in execution—a court in which the prosecutor is judge, and without even the forms of trial, or permitting the adverse party a hearing, gives verdict and sentence in his own case!

This feature of the Southern Slave Code was extended over all the United States by the decision of the U. S. Supreme Court, Prigg *vs.* Pennsylvania, in which it was laid down that the slave owner himself has authority to arrest his alleged fugitive without a warrant from a magistrate. The same principle is also contained in the Fugitive Slave Bill, enacted by the Federal Congress in 1852.

From the acts of the Legislatures we now turn to the decisions of the Courts, to learn the *practical value* of the protection provided by the statutes for the slave.

The State *vs.* Maner, 2 Hill's S. C. Rep. 453.

S. P. Hilton *vs.* Caston, 2 Bay's Rep. 98.

White *vs.* Chambers, 2 Bay's Rep. 70.

State *vs.* Cheatwood, Hill's Rep. 459.

"*Per Cur., O'Neill, J.*—The criminal offense of assault and battery *cannot*, at common law, *be committed on the person of a slave.* For, notwithstanding for some purposes a slave is regarded in law as a person, yet generally he is a mere chattel personal, and his right of personal protection belongs to *his master*, who can maintain an action of trespass for the battery of his slave.

"*There can therefore be no offense against the State* for a *mere beating* of a slave, unaccompanied by any circumstances of cruelty, or an attempt to kill and murder. *The peace of the State is not thereby broken*, for a slave is not generally regarded as legally capable of being within the peace of the State. He is to not a citizen, and is not, in that character, entitled her protection." (Wheeler's Law of Slavery, p. 243.)

It may be thought that this case is not in point, in discussing, as we here do, the liabilities of *masters* for maltreating their slaves, as this was *not* the case of a slave master. Our argument is this: If the Courts decide that white persons, *not* the owners of the slave thus abused, cannot be punished for assault and battery, it is very evident that the *owners* cannot be.

And this is distinctly laid down in the case that next follows, where, although the defendant was only *the hirer* and not the *owner*, the Court laid down the rule of law for an *owner*, and then applied it to the *hirer*, which (with the preceding) covers the whole ground, and shows that *the slave* has no legal remedy or protection in the Criminal Code against assault and battery, *from any person whatever!* The right of *the master* to maintain an action against the assailant of his slave property for pecuniary damages, is altogether another question.

"*The master is not liable to an indictment for a battery committed* UPON *his slave.*" (Wheeler's Law of Slavery, p. 244.)

This statement is the Reporter's (or Mr. Wheeler's) marginal title to the case of "The State *vs.* Mann, Dec. 7, 1829. 2 Devereaux's North Carolina Rep. 263."

"The defendant was indicted for an assault and battery upon *Lydia*, the servant of one *Elizabeth Jones*. On the trial it appeared that the defendant had hired the slave for a year; that during the term the slave had committed some small offense, for which the defendant undertook to chastise her; that while in the act of so doing, the slave ran off, whereupon the defendant called upon her to stop, which being refused, he shot at and wounded her. The Judge in the Court below charged the jury that if they believed the punishment inflicted by the defendant was cruel and unwarrantable, and disproportionate to the offense committed by the slave, that in law the defendant was guilty, *as he had only a special property in the slave.* A verdict was returned for the State, and the defendant appealed.

"*Per Cur.*, *Ruffin*, *J.*—A Judge cannot but lament, when such cases as the present are brought into judgment. It is impossible that the reasons on which they go can be appreciated but where institutions similar to our own exist, and are thoroughly understood. The struggle, too, in the Judge's own breast between the feelings of the man and the duty of the magistrate, is a severe one, presenting strong temptation to put aside such questions, if it be possible. It is useless, however, to complain of things in our political state. And it is criminal in a Court to avoid any responsibility which the laws impose. With whatever reluctance, therefore, it is done, the Court is compelled to express an opinion upon the extent of the dominion of the master over the slave in North Carolina." "*The inquiry here is, whether a cruel and unreasonable battery upon a slave, by the hirer, is indictable.* The Judge below instructed the jury that it is. He seems to have put it upon the ground that *the defendant had but a special property.* Our laws uniformly treat the master or other person having the possession and command of the slave, as entitled to the same extent of authority. The object is the same—the service of the slave; and the same powers must be confided. In a criminal proceeding, and indeed in reference to all other persons but the general owner, the hirer and possessor of the slave, in relation to both rights and duties, *is*, for the time being, the owner. This opinion would, perhaps, dispose of this particular case, because the indictment which charges a battery upon the slave of Elizabeth Jones is not supported by proof of a battery upon defendant's own slave; since different justifications may be applicable to the two cases. But upon the general question whether the owner is answerable, *criminalter*, for a battery upon his own slave, or *other* exercise of *authority or force*, not forbidden by statute, the Court entertains but little doubt. *That he* IS *so liable has never been decided, nor, as far as is known, been hitherto contended.* THERE HAS [have] BEEN NO PROSECUTIONS OF THE SORT.* THE ESTABLISHED AND UNIFORM PRACTICE OF THE COUNTRY *in this*

---

* This testimony tells us how much those statutes are worth that pretend to limit the amount of punishment that an owner may inflict on his slave. It may indeed be said that although a master is *not* indictable in general terms for an assault and battery, yet he *may* be indicted for violations of specific provisions of a statute. But if this be so, why was not the defendant, in this case, indicted for the *shooting* of Lydia, if there *existed* any statute forbidding such an outrage? And if *not*, where is the protection?

respect is the best evidence of the portion of power DEEMED BY THE WHOLE COMMUNITY REQUISITE TO THE PRESERVATION OF THE MASTER'S DOMINION. If we thought differently, we could not set our notions in array against the judgment of *every body else*, and say that this or that authority may be safely lopped off. This has indeed been assimilated, at the bar, to the other domestic relation," &c., &c.*

Having answered this plea by showing the *contrast* between such domestic relations and those between master and slave, and the consequent degradation of "the subject," his Honor proceeds:

"What MORAL considerations shall be addressed to such a being, to convince him, what it is *impossible* but that the most stupid must feel and know *can never be true*, that he is thus to labor upon a principle of natural duty, or for the sake of his own personal happiness? Such services can only be expected from one who has no will of his own; who surrenders his will in implicit obedience to that of another. Such obedience is the consequence only of *uncontrolled authority over the body.* There is nothing else which can operate to produce the effect. *The power of the master must be absolute, to render the submission of the slave perfect.* I most freely confess my sense of the harshness of the proposition. I feel it as

* The answer of Judge Ruffin to this plea, we have already copied, in our definition of Slavery in Chapter I., and need not repeat it here.

deeply as any man can. And, as a principle of *moral right*, every person in his retirement must repudiate it. But in the actual condition of things it must be so. *There is no remedy. This discipline belongs to the state of slavery. They cannot be disunited, without abrogating at once the rights of the master, and absolving the slave from his subjection.* It constitutes the curse of slavery to both the bond and the free portions of our population. BUT IT IS INHERENT IN THE RELATION OF MASTER AND SLAVE. That there may be particular instances of cruelty and deliberate barbarity where in conscience the law *might* properly interfere, is most probable.

"The difficulty is to determine where *a Court* may properly begin. Merely in the abstract, it may well be asked, WHICH power of the master accords with RIGHT? *The answer will probably sweep away all of them.* But we cannot look at the matter in that light. The truth is, that we are forbidden to enter upon a train of general reasoning on the subject. *We cannot allow the right of the master to be brought into discussion in the Courts of justice. The slave, to remain a slave, must be made sensible that there is no appeal from his master; that his person is in no instance usurped,* but is conferred by the laws of man at least, if not by the law of God. The danger would be great indeed, if the tribunals of justice should be called on to graduate the punishment appropriate to every temper and every dereliction of menial duty. No man can anticipate the many and aggravated provocations of the master, which the slave would be constantly stimulated, by his own passions or the instigations of others, to give; or the consequent wrath of the master, prompting him to bloody vengeance upon the turbulent traitor; A VENGEANCE GENERALLY PRACTISED WITH IMPUNITY, BY REASON OF ITS PRIVACY. The Court, therefore, disclaims the power of CHANGING THE RELATION in which these parts of our people stand to each other." "I repeat that I would gladly have avoided this ungrateful question; but being brought to it, the Court is compelled to declare, that *while slavery exists among us in its present state*, or until it shall seem fit to the Legislature to interpose express enactments to the contrary, it will be the imperative duty of the Judges to recognize the full dominion of the owner over the slave, except where the exercise of it is forbidden by the statute. And this we do on the ground, that *this dominion is essential to the value of slaves as property*, to the security of the master, and the public tranquillity, greatly dependent upon their subordination; and, in fine, as most effectually securing the general protection and comfort of the slaves themselves. Judgment below reversed, and judgment entered for the defendant." (Wheeler's Law of Slavery, pp. 244–8.")

Here is a document that will repay profound study. The moral wrong of slavery is distinctly and repeatedly admitted, along with the most resolute determination to support it, *by not allowing the rights of the master to come under judicial investigation*, betraying a consciousness that they would not abide the test of the first principles of legal science. The struggle between the *man* and the *magistrate*, implying that slavery requires of its magistrates to trample upon their own manhood; the cool and deliberate decision to do this, and to elevate the law of slavery above the law of nature and of nature's God, are painful but instructive features of the exhibition. And so is the incidental testimony to the frequency of bloody outrages, "generally practised with impunity, by reason of their privacy."

But, in *this* chapter, we are chiefly concerned with this judicial decision that "a cruel and unreasonable battery on a slave by a hirer is not indictable," because such battery by an owner would not be; the testimony that the opposite doctrine has never been held by the Courts; "that he [the master] is so liable has never been decided, nor, so far as known, contended for;" that "*there has been no prosecutions of the sort;*" that "the established habits and uniform practice of the country" prove that the whole community deem this power of the master "requisite to the preservation of his dominion," and that this *must* be so, while the slave system continues. The arguments of Judge Ruffin in proof of this, we deem impregnable. And it deserves notice that this decision, made in 1829, before there was any excitement raised on the slave question, was virtually endorsed in the midst of the anti-slavery agitation, in 1837, by Judge Hitchcock of Alabama, (through his recommendation of the volume for the use of the "Southern bar,") as containing the true Southern doctrine.

All this should be borne in mind, in the discussions of the next chapter. In order to understand, correctly and fully, any one phase or feature of the slave system, it must be studied in its natural and necessary connection with the other features of the system most nearly related to it, and, indeed, with *all* its features; for they are all mutually dependent upon and defined by each other.

CHAPTER XIV.

OF LAWS CONCERNING THE MURDER AND KILLING OF SLAVES.

The structure of the Laws, and the condition of the Slaves, render adequate protection impossible.

WE come now to consider the laws purporting to restrain and punish the murderers of slaves.

The revelations of the last chapter establish clearly the *principle* and the *fact* that the authority of the master is unlimited, and that he is not indictable, and *never has been* indicted and punished for the "cruel and unreasonable battery of his slave." It seems difficult to conceive how, in such a condition of the statute book, the judiciary, and the community, there *could* be any effectual restraints upon the murderers of slaves, or how they could be convicted and punished, at least where the offenders were owners or hirers of the slaves they had murdered. If a man is not protected from cruel and unreasonable battery at the pleasure of his assailant, how can he be protected from the liability to be *killed* by such battery? And if the law permits the optional battery of a

8*

man, what power can it retain to punish him for the natural effects of such battery? Will the law allow one man to beat another as much as he pleases, or *shoot* him, (as in the case last cited,) and then punish him because the man is thus killed?

In former times, the murder of a slave in most, if not all the slaveholding regions of this country, was, by law, punishable by a pecuniary fine only. At present, the wilful, malicious, and deliberate murder of a slave, by whomsoever perpetrated, is *declared* to be punishable with death, in every State. (See Stroud's Sketch, p. 36.) The exclusion of all testimony of *colored* persons, bond or free, is a feature sufficient, of itself, to render these laws nugatory. The "owner" or "overseer" may command the slave to attend him to any secret spot, and there murder him with impunity. Or he may do it openly, (it has often been done,) in the sight of many *colored* persons, with *equal* impunity. But let us examine some of these laws.

South Carolina, 1740.—The Act, in its preamble, sets forth that "cruelty is not only highly unbecoming those who profess themselves Christians, but is odious in the sight of all men who have any sense of virtue or humanity." [Therefore:] "To restrain and prevent barbarity being exercised towards slaves, Be it enacted, that if any person shall *wilfully murder* his own slave, or the slaves of any other person, every such person [i. e., the offender] shall, upon conviction thereof, forfeit and pay the sum of seven hundred pounds, current money, and shall be rendered for ever incapable of holding, exercising, &c., any office, &c. And in case any such person shall not be able to pay the penalty and forfeiture hereby inflicted and imposed, every such person shall be sent to any of the frontier garrisons of the Province, or committed to the workhouse in Charleston for the space of seven years, &c., &c., at hard labor." (2 Brevard's Digest, 241.)

Another provision of the same Act is as follows: "If any person shall, on a sudden heat or passion, OR by *undue correction*, kill HIS OWN SLAVE, or the slave of any other person, he shall forfeit the sum of three hundred and fifty pounds, current money." (Ib., 241.)

For this latter offense there seems to have been no incapacity to hold office.

The greater part of cases, especially in the absence of colored testimony, would come under this latter provision. To shoot down a slave deliberately *would incur* the heavier fine, and the civil disability. To beat out his brains with a club, or whip him to death, would cost £350; that is, if any *free* WHITE person should witness the act, and see fit to institute proceedings.

This Act continued in force till 1821, when the *wilful* murder of a slave was made punishable with death, without benefit of clergy; while the penalty for killing in "sudden heat," or "undue correction," was *reduced* to *five hundred dollars*, but *authorizing* an imprisonment for six months. This latter sum, therefore, in South Carolina, may be considered the price at which a slave owner is licensed to kill a slave, in the prescribed manner, as above; with some hazard, perhaps, of six months' confinement--both contingent upon the testimony of a free WHITE person!

NORTH CAROLINA.—Act of 1798, section 3: "Whereas, by Act of another Assembly, passed in the year 1774, the killing of a slave, however wanton, cruel, and deliberate, is only punishable, in the first instance, by imprisonment, and *paying the value thereof to the* OWNER, which distinction of criminality between the murder of a white person and one who is equally a human creature, but merely of a different complexion, is disgraceful to humanity, and degrading in the highest degree to the laws and principles of a free, Christian, and enlightened country; Be it enacted, &c., that if any person hereafter be guilty of maliciously killing a slave, such offender shall, on the first conviction thereof, be adjudged guilty of murder, and shall suffer the same punishment as if he had killed a free man: *Provided* always, this act shall not extend to any person killing a slave *outlawed* by virtue of any Act of Assembly of this State, *or* to *any* slave in the act of *resistance* to his lawful owner or master, *or* to any slave DYING UNDER MODERATE CORRECTION!" (Hayward's Manual, 530.)

What a contrast between the preamble and the details of the Act! Disgraceful to make a distinction between white and colored persons, yet still keeping up the disgraceful distinction. The "wilful and malicious murder" of the slave to be punished, "*provided*" said "wilful and malicious murder" be not thus and thus committed, &c.; implying impunity to *other* forms of such murder.

Notice the exceptions provided against.

1. "Wilful and malicious killing a slave" is to be punished, "*provided*" it be not "the killing of a slave *outlawed*," &c.

The meaning of this appears in the fact, that a proclamation of *outlawry* against a slave is authorized by statute, whenever he *runs away* from his master, *conceals* himself in some obscure retreat, and, *to sustain life*, "kills *a hog*, or some animal of the cattle kind." (See Hayward's Manual, 521. Act of 1741, ch. 24, sect. 45. Stroud, p. 38.)

2. Another exception is the case of "any slave in the act of resistance to his lawful owner or master." The Courts have determined that this proviso renders it lawful to kill a slave "resisting or *offering* to resist his master by force." (2 Hayward's Reports, p. 54.)

No matter what the occasion or the necessity of resistance may be—whether to ward off murderous attacks, or (in the case of females) outrages worse than murder, the first motion or preparation for self-defense is the signal for lawful slaughter, on the spot, *according to statute!* This, in an Act ostensibly for the slave's protection. Bearing in mind that the master's account* of the matter (in the absence of

* At Alexandria, (D. C.,) in 1823, a slave owner chased his female slave, whip in hand, in open daylight, before multitudes, to the end of a wharf, where she jumped in and was drowned. Verdict of the coroner's inquest: "Death by suicide to escape deserved punishment." The term "*deserved*" being inserted by testimony of the "owner," without even a statement of the offense.

white witnesses) cannot be questioned in Court, we have the doctrine of Judge Ruffin and of Prince's Digest sustained. "The slave must be taught that there is no appeal from his master." "His life must be in his master's keeping."

3. The third exception is the case of a slave *dying under moderate correction!!!* This gives us a legislative definition of "moderate correction." It is such as may be apprehended or supposed to endanger and even take away the life of the slave. In the light of this, we may understand also the prohibition of "*unusual* punishment." It does not always reach the case of those who die under the lash, for even this may be "moderate correction," and consequently not "unusual."

The sum of the matter is, then, this: In North Carolina, the "wilful and malicious killing of a slave," if proved by WHITE witnesses, is to be punished by death, "*provided*" the said slave, being "in pursuit of" "liberty and happiness," does not hold his "right to life" more sacred than the life of "a hog, or some animal of the cattle kind!" Provided, also, that, in self-defense, she or he never offers to lift a finger to avert rape or murder; and provided, finally, that he is not killed "under moderate correction!"

TENNESSEE.—Act of October 23, 1799; similar to the Act of North Carolina, and with a like proviso. (Laws of Tennessee.)

The outlawry of slaves is a very common occurrence in the slave States.

GEORGIA.—Constitution, art. 4, sect. 12: "Any

person who shall maliciously *dismember* or deprive a slave of *life*, shall suffer such punishment as would be inflicted in case the like offense had been committed upon a free white person, and on like proof,* except in case of insurrection of said slave, and unless SUCH DEATH SHOULD HAPPEN BY ACCIDENT, IN GIVING SUCH SLAVE MODERATE CORRECTION." (Prince's Digest, 559.)

One question presents itself in a review of such enactments. *What definite objects were* INTENDED *to be reached by them?* A decent respect for the intellects and the common sense of Southern legislators forbids the supposition that they could have been seriously intended for the protection of the slave. The uniform exclusion of *colored* witnesses is conclusive of this. When, in a distinct chapter, we shall consider that feature of the Slave Code, this conclusion will, perhaps, be more deeply impressed. The preambles quoted from the Acts of North and South Carolina betray a consciousness that the sterner features of the Slave Code are "odious," "disgraceful," and "degrading" to a "free, Christian, and enlightened country." Philanthropic men at the South, more or less distinctly dissatisfied with the Slave Code, might be also appeased by some apparent relaxations. Attempts by some members of the Legislatures to

* It must not be inferred that this provision restores the testimony of colored witnesses. It only reminds us that such witnesses cannot be summoned to attest the murder of one white person by another, thus weakening the arm of civil protection in general, throughout the entire South.

introduce reforms would be likely to be marred and rendered abortive by incongruous provisos, engrafted by the majority upon bills proposed by them. In these ways, we may readily account for the absurd and confused legislation recorded in this and the preceding chapters.

We turn next to the reported cases in Wheeler's Law of Slavery, for any additional light on the subject of this chapter, and of the preceding one. One division of his book, numbered XIV., on page 200, is headed thus: "MASTERS' AND OTHERS' LIABILITIES FOR MALTREATING THEIR SLAVES." If any materials are to be found "in all the decisions made on that subject [of Slavery] in the several Courts of the United States and State Courts,"* of which Mr. Wheeler's work is "a compilation," which could show that adequate legal protection against outrage and murder is extended to the slave, we have certainly a right to look for it under this appropriate head. Especially might it be reasonably expected, after such a note by the author or compiler as the following, which is appended to the title of this same division or chapter, at the foot of page 200, viz:

"It is stated in Stroud's Sketch of the Laws relating to Slavery, p. 35, '*that the master may, at his pleasure, inflict any species of punishment upon the person of his slave.*' This proposition, so repugnant to humanity, is equally opposed to the fact, and also to the law. In those States where there are no enact-

---

* See title-page of Wheeler's Law of Slavery.

ments upon the subject, the common law would be efficient to protect the slave. Our books are full of criminal prosecutions for cruelty to horses and other animals. And the common law remedy is considered effective without any statutory enactment. And if the slave be considered an *animal*, still he is under the protection of the law, and acts of inhumanity and cruelty to him is a public misdemeanor, and the person guilty may be indicted and punished."

On this note of Mr. Wheeler we remark:

1. It is undoubtedly true that the common law, *if applied* to the slave, would amply protect him from outrage and murder. It would also protect him in his right to his earnings and to the disposal of the products of his industry, to exemption from seizure and sale: in a word, the common law, if applied to the slave, would emancipate him; for every body knows, and the Louisiana and Kentucky Courts have decided, that the slave becomes free the moment he comes under the jurisdiction of common law, by being carried by consent of his master out of the jurisdiction of the *municipal* law which alone binds him. There is no such municipal law against "horses and other animals," removing them from the protection of the common law. Mr. Wheeler does not appeal to the municipal law, as existing either in statutes or in the judicial decisions with which he is so conversant, to prove that the slave enjoys effective protection. It is this municipal law, and *not* the common law, that defines the condition of the slave.

2. Judge Stroud had explained and vindicated his

statement by the following explanation, of which Mr. Wheeler takes no notice:

"From the laws which I shall now cite, it will fully appear that, *so far as regards the pages of the statute book*, the *life*, at least, of the slave is safe from the *authorized* violence of the master. The evil is *not* that laws are wanting, but that they cannot be enforced; not that they sanction crime, but that they do not punish it. And this arises chiefly, if not *solely*, from the cause that has been more than once mentioned—the exclusion of the testimony, on the trial of a *white* person, of all who are *not* white."

If the reader will examine the laws against the murder of slaves which we have already quoted, he will probably agree with us that Judge Stroud has conceded quite enough in their favor.

3. On a candid review of *all* the slave laws we shall have collected in this book, with the judicial decisions we shall have quoted from Wheeler's Law of Slavery, let the reader judge what benefit the slave derives from the existence either of common law, or of statutes, or of decisions of Courts.

4. "Our books," says Mr. Wheeler, "are full of criminal prosecutions for cruelty to *horses and other animals!*" This is undoubtedly true. But this is not pertinent to the question at issue. Mr. Wheeler, in order to have met the statement of Judge Stroud, should have been able to say, "Our books abound in criminal prosecutions for *cruelty to slaves.*" But this he has *not said.*

5. And this brings us back to the observation

before made, that if the Courts *have* extended to the slave effective protection against outrages and murders, especially by their owners, we have a right to expect the *reported cases and instances*, in this division of Wheeler's "compilation of all the decisions," &c., &c., which is headed, "MASTERS' AND OTHERS' LIABILITIES FOR MALTREATING THEIR SLAVES."

Let us, then, see what this division of the work contains, and notice whether it "is full of criminal prosecutions for cruelty to" SLAVES, and notice, too, the amount of protection thus afforded to them.

The reported cases under this head occupy less than five pages, and are only seven in number. *Two* only of these were "*criminal prosecutions*" in the name of "THE STATE." The remaining five are suits at law between one white citizen and another, respecting this peculiar kind of *property*.

1. "Markham *vs.* Close, Sept. 1831. 2 Louisiana Rep., 581.—Held by the Court, *Porter*, *J.*, that the infliction of cruel punishment on a slave by his master is a criminal offense, and must be punished by a *criminal* prosecution, and not before a *civil* tribunal. And after conviction, the fine is to be levied on the offender by the Court before whom the conviction takes place." (Wheeler's Law of Slavery, p. 200.)

The decision seems at variance with that of Judge Ruffin before quoted, but the real object and the *effects* of the decision do not clearly appear. If, as seems implied, the *defendant* was the owner of the slave he abused, the right of the *plaintiff* to bring a suit against him is not apparent. And the decision would seem to have dismissed the proceedings on the ground that there was no foundation for a private litigation. Whether any "criminal prosecution" was ever brought against the offender, we do not learn. Very probably the effect of the decision was to quash the proceedings and hush up the matter entirely, while the marginal title reads, "Master *may be* convicted and fined for maltreating his slave." We get no evidence that he *was* thus convicted and fined.

2. "Allan *vs.* Young, Jan. T., 1821. 9 Martin's Louisiana Rep., 221.—*Matthews, J.:* "This is a case in which the plaintiff seeks to *recover damages* to the value of a slave, alleged to have been killed by the defendant." The decision is thus stated in the margin: "If a slave of a bad character is pursued on suspicion of felony, attempt to seize a gun, flies and is killed in the pursuit, the Supreme Court will not disturb *a verdict for the defendant who killed him.*"

Of *what* felony the slave was "*suspected*," or in what respects he sustained "a bad character," we are not informed. He may have ventured to take a tithe of his own earnings—he may have harbored a fugitive slave—he may have attempted to escape, himself, into freedom—he may have been in the habit of absenting himself to visit his wife—he may have attempted to teach or to learn the alphabet. Or he may have been "*suspected*" of some of these crimes!

3. "Jennings *vs.* Furderburg, Jan. T., 1827. 4 McCord's S. C. Rep., 161.—Trespass for killing the

plaintiff's slave. The defendant, with others, being in search of runaway negroes, surprised them in their camp, and fired his gun towards them as they were running away, to induce them to stop. One of the negroes was, however, killed by a random shot. Decision: "The firing of the defendant in the manner stated was rash and incautious." Hence the *rule,* as in the margin: "To excuse a trespass for killing a slave, on the ground of accident, it must appear to have been done without the least fault on the part of the person killing." (Ib., p. 201.)

4. "Richardson *vs.* Dukes, Jan. T., 1827. 4 McCord's S. C. Rep., 156.—Trespass for killing the plaintiff's slave. It appeared that the slave was stealing potatoes from a bank near the defendant's house. The defendant fired on him with a gun loaded with buck-shot, and killed him. The jury found a verdict for plaintiff for one dollar. Motion for a new trial—which was granted. The point of law established, as stated in the margin, was this: *The proper rule of damages for killing a slave, is the value of the slave to the master at the time of his death.*" (Ib., p. 202.)

5. "Westell *vs.* Earnest and Parker, Jan. T., 1818. 1 Nott and McCord's S. C. Rep., 182." This was another suit for damages in killing a runaway slave by shooting him, as he ran towards a swamp. Verdict for the defendants. Motion to set it aside, which motion prevailed. Judge Colcock said: "If the slave assaults a *white* person, he may be killed; but a slave merely flying away cannot be killed;"

to which it is added in the margin, "and if he be, *the owner may recover compensation for the loss.*" (Wheeler, 202–3.)

6. "The State *vs.* E. Smith and R. Smith, Nov. T., 1817. 1 Nott and McCord's S. C. Rep., 13.—The defendants were convicted of killing a negro, under the Act of 1740." "Sentence was pronounced by the Judge upon the defendants, that they pay three hundred and fifty pounds, old currency." They paid the sum and took the Clerk's receipt. Afterwards the sentence was amended by fining *each* of the defendants £350. On an appeal, before Judge Colcock, the emendation was sustained. (Wheeler, p. 203.)

7. "The State *vs.* Raines, May T., 1826. 3 McCord's S. C. Rep., 533.—The prisoner was indicted for murder." "Verdict, guilty of manslaughter, and motion in arrest of judgment." The motion prevailed, on the ground that the charges in the indictment were not sufficiently specific. (Ib., pp. 203–4.)

Whether the defect was intentional cannot be known, but such arts are not uncommon when the guilty are to be shielded.

The reader has now before him all the evidences of protection to the slave, whether by "common law" or otherwise, which Mr. Wheeler has presented under his appropriate division, headed, "Masters' *and others'* liabilities for maltreating *their* slaves"—although, as he says, "Our books are *full* of prosecutions for cruelty to *horses and other animals.*"

Of the seven cases adduced, *not one* of them appears to have resulted in the punishment, in any way, of *a master* for maltreating *his own slave.* Except, perhaps, in the first case, where no conviction was reached, it does not *appear* that either of the defendants were the *owners* of the slaves maltreated or killed. And four of the seven cases were clearly the prosecutions of slave owners against others for the destruction of *their property!*

In the division of the book headed, "*Of the trial and punishment of slaves*," there is a case (that of State *vs.* Reed, June Term, 1823, 2 Hawk's N. C. Rep., 454) which, if it had appeared in the division of "Masters' and others' liabilities," would have seemed a case in point for citation in this discussion. It is *possible* that it was placed, by mistake, under the wrong head, though nothing conclusive appears to show that the prisoner was not a *slave.* He was indicted for the murder of a slave, was found guilty, and a motion for arrest of judgment because of the insufficiency of the indictment was overruled. (Wheeler, p. 210.)

Another case occurs in the division of the book headed, "*Liabilities of others to masters for abusing their slaves*," which *seems* not to have been classified under the appropriate head. It is *not* a suit of the owner for damages, but a criminal prosecution by the State for the "murder of a slave," under the Act of 1821, viz: State *vs.* Cheatwood, 2 Hill's S. C. Reports. The defendant was convicted, and moved in arrest of judgment, on the ground that the indictment did not charge the crime in the words of the statute. The motion was overruled. The Report does not state whether the prisoner was a slave, a free colored man, or a white man. (Wheeler, p. 250.)

A similar instance appears in the case of "State of Mississippi *vs.* Jones, June Term, 1820, Walker's Rep., 83.) "The *question* in this case," said Judge Clarke, "arising in arrest of judgment, transferred *on doubts from Adams Superior Court, is, whether, in this State, murder can be committed on a slave.*" His Honor proceeded to argue that *it could,* and decided accordingly. The color and condition of the prisoner does not appear from the Report.

In the same division is found the case of the State *vs.* Hale, December Term, 1823, 2 Hawk's N. C. Rep., 582, in which it was decided by Judge Taylor, as stated in the marginal note of the Reporter, that "a battery committed on a slave, no justification or circumstances attending it being shown, is an indictable offense." (Wheeler, pp. 239–40.) But this could not have been intended to apply to the case of a slave master abusing *his own* slave, as the case stands under the heading of "Liabilities of others *to* the master for abusing *his* slave." And in giving his opinion, Judge Taylor said: "If such offenses may be committed with impunity, the public peace will not only be rendered extremely insecure, BUT THE VALUE OF SLAVE PROPERTY MUST BE MUCH IMPAIRED, *for the offenders*" [previously described as a low class of persons] "*can seldom make any reparation* IN DAMAGES." "It cannot be disputed that a slave is rendered *less capable of performing his master's service,* when he finds himself exposed by the law to the violence of every turbulent man in the community."

We seem to have, here, a revelation of the existing state of things in *that* community, which compelled the Courts, with the ready assent of the slaveholders, to make use of the *criminal* code *to protect slave property!* And this perhaps explains, further, why it is that we find, in Wheeler's Law of Slavery, under the head of "Liabilities of others *to* the master for abuse of *his* slave," a number of Reports of *criminal* prosecutions, in the name of the *State*, for battery and even for the murder of slaves! What had seemed to *us* an inappropriate classification, is now, perhaps, explained. Irresponsible rowdies, "of dissolute habits," unable to pay "DAMAGES" to the "*owner*" of the slaves whom they may maim and murder, must be restrained and punished by the *criminal code!*

"Hall, J.: I concur in the opinion given. I think it would be *highly improper that* EVERY *assault and battery on a slave should* be considered an indictable offense," &c. "Much depends on the circumstances of the case, when it happens," &c.

Anomalies and self-contradictions may be expected in slave jurisprudence, for slavery is an anomalous thing. The *chattel principle* is, however, the key to its mysteries. An "attempt to kill and murder" a slave is a blow at *slave property.* Even if an *owner* kills his slave, it familiarizes murder, and incites others to similar acts.

In the case of State *vs.* Maner, it was decided that

"an assault with intent to *murder* a slave is indictable." (Wheeler, p. 244.)

"Commonwealth vs. Carver, June T., 1827. 5 Rand's Va. Reports, 600.—The prisoner was indicted for feloniously, maliciously, and unlawfully shooting, with intent to maim, disfigure, disable, and kill a negro man slave, of the name of Armistead, THE PROPERTY *of Andrew Houten*, under the Act of 9th of February, 1819. The Judge DOUBTED whether a negro slave is the subject or person on which the offense created and the penalties prescribed by the Act can be committed or incurred, and *adjourned* the case to the General Court.

"*The Court—Breckenbrough, J.*,—after referring to Dolly Chapple's case, 1 Virg. Cas. 184, declared that the slave *was* a person on whom the offense of stabbing and shooting might be committed; and that the Act was intended to protect slaves as well as free persons from such outrages. It may further be remarked that there appears no reason, arising from the relation of master and slave, why a free person should not be punished as a felon for maiming a slave. *Whatever power our laws may give to the* MASTER *over his slave*, IT IS AS IMPORTANT FOR THE INTEREST OF THE FORMER as for the protection of the latter, that A STRANGER should not be permitted to exercise an UNRESTRAINED authority over him. The opinion of the Court is, that judgment ought not to be arrested." (Wheeler, p. 254.)

The plain implication here is, that the power of the MASTER IS as unrestrained as was represented and decided by Judge Ruffin, as before cited.

And in this case, again, we see the *criminal* law of "the State" wielded as a mere implement for enforcing "the liabilities of *others to* the master, for abusing *his* slave," to the injury of his "interests."

In the case of Fields *vs.* the State of Tennessee, (Jan. T., 1829, 1 Virger's Reports, 156,) on writ of error to arrest judgment against said Fields, on a verdict against him for manslaughter, it was decided that "the felonious slaying of a slave without malice is manslaughter." Judgment affirmed.

We close our examination of Wheeler's Law of Slavery on the topics involved in our present chapter, without having been able to ascertain a single instance in which a slave *owner* has been convicted or even *prosecuted* for the murder of his *own slave;* nor have we found an exception to the statement of Judge Ruffin, before cited, that a "cruel and unreasonable battery on a slave" by his *owner*, or *hirer*, is not an indictable offense, and that "*there have been no prosecutions of this sort.*" Thus far, therefore, the statement of Judge Stroud, that "the master may, at his pleasure, inflict any species of punishment on the person of his slave," though contradicted by Mr. Wheeler, stands unimpeached, so far as we can discover, by any cases he has recorded in his compilation of Reports. Not even the case of Markham *vs.* Close furnishes any such instance, so far as appears from his Report of it.

If it be said that a motive of self-interest in the

master would prevent his inflicting outrages upon his slave, we answer, (1.) That this restraint operates only in those cases where the injury would destroy his property in the slave, or impair his power to labor: it would be no protection against the infliction of any sufferings and indignities which *fall short* of this. (2.) Abundant evidence is at hand to prove that this motive is *not*, in numerous instances, sufficient to restrain the passions of the masters, and prevent the maiming and killing of their own slaves, as will be shown in another chapter. (3.) Were it otherwise, the fact remains that *the law does not* protect the slave against his master. (4.) Anger and malice often act in opposition to self-interest. How comes it that "our books are full of criminal prosecutions for cruelty to horses and other animals," if the interest of the owner is *itself* a security against his abuse of his own property? The malignant passions of the master are far more likely to be excited against his slave, who by a word or a *look* may dispute his authority, defy his power, or withhold the respect he claims, than by a dumb animal, governed only by natural instinct.

CHAPTER XV.

OF THE DELEGATED POWER OF OVERSEERS.

All the Power of the Owner over his Slave is held and exercised also by Overseers and Agents.

WE have, thus far, considered chiefly the power of the slave *owner*. It has been seen, likewise, that essentially the same power is lodged in the *hirer* of a slave. Incidentally, the power of *overseers and agents* has been alluded to. But we must now take a more distinct view of this feature of slavery. It has been expressed thus:

"*All the power of the master over the slave may be exercised, not by himself only, in person, but by any one whom he may depute as his agent.* (Stroud's Sketch, p. 44.)

Considering the judicial authority vested in the slave owner, whoever he may be, (drunk or sober,) and the duty of the "sheriffs" and public negro whippers to execute his decisions, (as already noticed,) this *additional* power of delegating his magisterial dignity and authority to whomsoever (drunk or sober) he may think proper, becomes a very remarkable one. Irresponsible himself, and absolute, he commits the same authority over the slave to a subordinate despot, responsible solely to himself.

LOUISIANA, by express statute, enacts as follows: "The *condition of a slave* BEING MERELY A PASSIVE ONE, his subordination to his master, AND ALL WHO REPRESENT HIM, *is not susceptible of any modification or restriction*, (except in what can excite the slave to the commission of crime,) in such manner that he owes to his master and to *all his family* a respect WITHOUT BOUNDS and an ABSOLUTE OBEDIENCE, and he is consequently to execute all the orders which he receives from him or from them." (1 Martin's Digest, 616.)

Thus does "the innocent legal relation" of slave ownership confer on every slave owner a power which no magistrate or government holds over *him*, or over any subject or citizen; and, not content with this, it clothes him with the prerogative of transferring this authority, not only *by the sale* of the slave, but by verbal commission while he yet owns him. His wife, his housekeeper, his overseer, and even his young children share his unlimited power and authority over the slave, though at the age of three-score! Instead of controlling his own children, the slave is controlled by the children of his master, and by hired overseers.

The *exception*, in the statute just cited, informs us that when the slave is "incited to crime" by the commands of his tyrant, whom he may not resist, he may nevertheless be held responsible for the crime! In its practical bearings, the law can effect nothing else, unless it be the martyrdom of the slave. Whatever crime he may be commanded to commit, he can lodge no information against his master, he can bear no testimony against him. If he persists in refusing to assist in the commission of the crime, his master may lawfully "chastise" him with the "moderate correction" that may cause his death, and then, if he "offers" resistance, he may be lawfully killed!

Louisiana is said to be the only State with an express statute on the topic of the master's delegated authority, but the usage, recognized by the Courts as law, universally exists. "In the other slave States," says Stroud, (p. 44,) "the subjoined extract from Mr. Stephen's delineation of Slavery in the West Indies will, it is believed, accurately express the law and the practice:

"'The slave is liable to be coerced or punished by the whip, *and to be tormented by every species of personal ill-treatment*, subject only to the exceptions already mentioned, (i. e., the deprivation of life and limb,) *by the attorney, manager, overseer, driver, and every other person to whose government and control* the owner may choose to subject him, as fully as by the owner himself. Nor is any special mandate or express general power necessary for this purpose; *it is enough that the inflictor of the violence is set over the slave for the moment, or by the owner or by any of his delegates or sub-delegates, of whatever rank or character.*' (Stephen's Slavery, p. 46.)

"This power of deputation by the master is one of the degrading and distinguishing features of *negro* slavery. It was not permitted by the laws of villeinage." (Stroud, p. 45. See 9 Coke's Reports, 76 A, &c. See Stephen, supra.)

The following description of "*overseers*" is from William Wirt's Life of Patrick Henry: "Last and lowest, (i. e., of the different classes of society in Virginia,) a *feculum* of beings called *overseers*; the most abject, degraded, unprincipled race, always cap in hand to the Dons who employed them, and furnishing materials for the exercise of their pride, insolence, and spirit of domination."

The great majority of slaves, male and female, labor on plantations, under the charge of these "overseers." The "house servants," as already seen by the statute of Louisiana, are under absolute subjection to every member of the family. Slaves hired out, waiters at hotels, &c., are, in this particular, in no better condition. Almost every where, they are controlled by others, in addition to the direct control of their owners.

CHAPTER XVI.

OF THE PROTECTION OF SLAVE PROPERTY FROM DAMAGE BY ASSAULTS FROM OTHER PERSONS THAN THEIR OWNERS.

Slaves are better protected as PROPERTY, than they are as SENTIENT BEINGS.

IT has been represented that the slaves are sufficiently protected from outrage and murder on the part of those who are not their owners, by the fact that slave property is, of course, protected by law from such depredations, and that the interest of the master affords a guaranty for the enforcement of such laws.

In our researches after the legal protection of slaves, in the preceding chapters, a large portion of all the legal proceedings that have come before us have been found to be of this character. Under the head of "*Masters*' and *others*' liabilities for maltreating *their* slaves," we have met, *chiefly*, with suits of masters against the depredators upon their *property!* And what purported to be *criminal prosecutions*, we have found, on inspection, to be *State* actions to prevent "damage" to the slaveholder. But we come

9*

now to consider, directly, the laws avowedly framed for that object.

"Slaves, being objects of property, if injured by third persons, their owners may bring suit and recover damages for the injury. This is a maxim of the common law, in respect to property in general, and it may therefore be assumed to be the law of all the slaveholding States, in regard to slaves also." (Stroud's Sketch, p. 59.)

MARYLAND.—Decision of Supreme Court: "There must be a *loss of service*, or at least a diminution of the *faculty* to labor, to warrant an action by the master." (1 Harris & Johnson's Reports, 4; Cornfute *vs.* Dale. Stroud, p. 59. Wheeler, p. 239.)

SOUTH CAROLINA.—Act of 1740: "If any negro or other slave who shall be employed in the lawful business of his master, owner, overseer, &c., shall be beaten, &c., by any person or persons not having sufficient cause or authority for so doing, and shall be *maimed*, or *disabled* by such beating from performing his or her work, such person or persons, *so offending*, shall forfeit and pay to the owner or owners of such slaves, the sum of *fifteen shillings* current money per diem, for every day of his *lost time*, and also the charge of the cure of such slave." (2 Brevard's Digest, 231–2.)

The workings of this law will appear in the following:

Constitutional Court of Appeals, South Carolina, 1796. Sims White *vs.* James Chambers.—"Special action in the case for beating the plaintiff's negro man." The negro was charged by his master with the care of a fishing-canoe, with strict orders not to let any one have it. The defendant persisted in taking it away, and the negro persisted in forbidding him, "whereupon, defendant struck him a blow with his fist, then *took a paddle, knocked him down, and afterwards beat him severely, which laid him up for several days, before he was able to go about his business again.*" Verdict for the plaintiff. Damages £5, and costs. (2 Bay's Reports, 70.)

A similar law exists in—

LOUISIANA.—(Statute.) "If the slave (*maimed*, &c.) be *for ever rendered unable to work*, the offender shall be compelled to *pay the value of said slave*, according to the appraisement made by two freeholders, appointed by each of the parties; and the slave thus disabled shall for ever be maintained at the expense of the person who shall have thus disabled him, which person shall be compelled to maintain and feed him, agreeably to the duties of masters and slaves, as ordered by this Act." (1 Martin's Digest, 630–2.)

NORTH CAROLINA.—It has been held that patrols are not liable to the master for inflicting punishment on the slave, unless their conduct clearly demonstrates MALICE AGAINST THE MASTER." (1 Hawks' Reports, 418, Tate *vs.* O'Neal.)

VIRGINIA.—Supreme Court of Appeals. May *vs.* Brown and Boisseau. Action of trespass, &c., for breaking into his close, and *beating several of his slaves, so that he was deprived of their services for a long time.*

The defense in mitigation of damages was, that *plaintiff had given a general permission to* BROWN (though not in his employ as overseer) *to* VISIT *his negro quarters, and chastise any of his slaves who might be found acting improperly!* This defense failed, because BOISSEAU, who had inflicted the beating, had received no such permission from the plaintiff. (1 Munford's Reports, 288. Stroud's Sketch, pp. 59–60. Wheeler's Law of Slavery, p. 248.)

The workings of the principle of delegated authority are signally exemplified in this last case.

In Wheeler's Law of Slavery, the division or chapter entitled, "*Of the liability of others to the master for abusing his slave,*" occupies about 27 pages. Some of the cases we have cited already. Under this head are classed several *State* prosecutions for *crime;* viz: State *vs.* Hale, State *vs.* Maner, State *vs.* Mann, (before Judge Ruffin,) State *vs.* Cheatwood, State of Mississippi *vs.* Jones, and Commonwealth of Virginia *vs.* Carver, which we have before cited in our 13th and 14th Chapters. Under this same classification, we found and cited also a number of civil prosecutions for *killing* slaves, some of whom were runaways.

We will here glance hastily at a few other decisions of the same class.

Smith *vs.* Hancock, 4 Bibb's Ky. Rep., 222.—"Held by the Court that in an action of trespass for beating a slave, the property of the plaintiff, *whereby he died*, the defendant may justify by showing that the slave was *at an unlawful assembly*, combining to rebel, and that he refused to surrender, and resisted by force." (Wheeler, p. 239.)

Meetings of slaves for religious worship or mental instruction are "*unlawful assemblies*," as will be shown in the proper place.

In the case of Skidmore *vs.* Smith, *the harboring* of slaves was the ground of complaint. (Wheeler, p. 248.) It will not be claimed that there is any valuable protection to the slave in this.

Crawford *vs.* Cheney, A. D. 1824, 15 Martin's Louisiana Rep., 142, was "an action brought to recover *the price* of a negro whom the plaintiff charges the defendant with having shot and killed." The testimony, it was argued, was weak. Judge Porter said: "*The act charged here is one rarely committed in the presence of witnesses;*" (owing, he might have added, to the law excluding *colored* witnesses.) He therefore allowed "presumptive evidence to support the verdict." (Weeeler, p. 249.)

Jourdan *vs.* Patten, 1818; 5 Martin's Louisiana Rep., 615.—A suit for damages by injuring a slave, who was made blind by the assault. The defendant was adjudged to *pay the price* of the slave, and to *take possession* of him, as his property. Marginal note, (as a rule of law established:) "If, on an injury to his slave, the plaintiff recovers his full value, *the property is transferred to the defendant*, on payment of the judgment." (Wheeler, p. 249.) And so the disabled slave is "transferred" from perhaps a kind master or mistress, and from the presence of his wife and children, and the scenes of his childhood, and turned over to the tender mercies of his persecutor, rendered the more bitter against him for the losses sustained in the transaction, and the prospect of receiving no valuable service from him! And this is *the protection* (in this exigency) afforded to the *slave* by *his master's* right of prosecuting his assailant!

The Court, it seems, were not unaware of the effects of this decision. In making it, Judge Matthews said: "The principle of *humanity*, which would lead us to suppose that the mistress, whom he had so long served, would treat her miserable blind slave with more kindness than the defendant, to whom the judgment ought to transfer him, *cannot be taken into consideration*, in deciding the case." And so the judgment of the "Parish Court" (which had decreed the payment of the price of the slave, with an additional annuity for his sustenance, and *to remain with the plaintiff*) was reversed. (Ib.)

The benefit *to the slave* of this protection of slave *property* is sufficiently apparent. It is the *master* that is protected in his *property*, not the *slave* in his right to *security*. The award is to his *master*, not to *him*. It is for the "loss of service" or "capacity to labor," not for indignities and sufferings endured; it is for the injury of a working *beast*, not of a *man;* for in this the maxim of the civil law holds good—"the slave is not capable of being injured!" Property damaged, or "malice against the *master*," constitute the offense—compensation to the *master* is the redress! The "legal relation" of owner and property is worthily honored and expressed in all this. Incidentally and remotely, the slave, it may be, in some instances, is protected by this from injuries that would otherwise cripple or kill him. The dread of the bill of "damages" may be some restraint. Slender as it is, it is the *best*, if not the *only* protection afforded to him by the law.

In one important and comprehensive view, this incidental and dubious *protection*, if it *be* such, is an injury to the slave in the long run, and on the whole. It not only certifies and sanctions his degradation to the condition of a brute, but, in so doing, it stands in the way of any *suitable* legislative and judicial protection. It is regarded as a substitute or equivalent for it. It not only prevents proper enactments and processes, but it vitiates those in existence and in use. We have seen how it confounds the *criminal* with the *civil* prosecutions for maltreating slaves, classifies indictments for *murder* under the head of "liabilities of others *to the master* for abusing his slave;" makes the *penal code* the instrument of the slave owner, and seduces even the better portion of the judges, as in the case of "the State *vs.* Hale," (Wheeler, pp. 239–43,) while making the most favorable and merciful decisions known to slave jurisprudence, into the lamentable expedient of grounding their decisions upon "*the interests*" *of the owner*, and "*the value of slave property*," instead of the majesty of violated law, and the sacredness of human life; or, perhaps, commingling incongruously the two classes of considerations!

As a matter-of-fact result of all this, we may well be assured that a judiciary and a community accustomed to award "*damages*" to a slave owner for the maiming and killing of his slave, will not long continue to prosecute with efficiency *any other*—any *criminal* processes for the same acts. *One* punishment for one misdemeanor will be accounted sufficient. If the one is inflicted, the other will, as a general if not a universal fact, be withheld or evaded. On the first announcement of a barbarous or murderous outrage upon a slave, human nature even among slaveholders will gush forth, in demands for justice upon the perpetrator. An indictment for murder may be talked of, or even resorted to. In the mean time comes the "*owner*" with his suit for damages *for loss of property!* All eyes are directed to watch the result. The high tone of *moral* indignation gives place to an anxiety for the pending issue of *dollars and cents!* If the defendant loses his case and pays the equivalent, the public feeling is appeased or modified. Perhaps a sympathy is got up in the defendant's favor. The indictment for murder slumbers, or results in an acquittal or a pardon. *The man is not to be fined five hundred dollars and then hanged!* And in a community wherein slaveholders administer the law, the prosecution for *damages* will be deemed of paramount importance.

CHAPTER XVII.

FACTS ILLUSTRATING THE KIND AND DEGREE OF PROTECTION EXTENDED TO SLAVES.

The extent, the atrocity, the frequency, and the impunity of barbarous outrages upon Slaves, show that the Laws afford them little or no protection.

WE have occupied so much space with the *laws* on the subject of the protection of slaves, that we can spare little room for the abundant *facts* which correspond with and illustrate them.

In respect to the murdering of slaves by white men, with general impunity, two propositions, if sustained, will settle the question. *First*, the murdering of slaves by white men has all along been, and still is, notoriously frequent. Not a few of these murdered their own slaves. *Second*, upon the most diligent inquiry and public challenge, for fifteen or twenty years past, not one single case has yet been *ascertained** in which, either during that time or pre-

---

* We say "*ascertained*." We have already alluded to some few cases in Wheeler's Law of Slavery, which *may have been* of that character, though the result does not appear clearly, which is the more remarkable, as the compiler had called in question the state-

viously, a master killing his slave, or indeed any other white man, has suffered the penalty of death for the murder of a slave. These two general facts, if they *are* facts, tell the whole story, so far as the *protection of the lives* of slaves is concerned.

At a time of much general excitement on this very question, during the period just now mentioned, (1839,) a case occurred which, it was generally supposed on all hands at the North, *would* prove an exception. A Court in South Carolina convicted a white man of having murdered a slave, and sentenced him to death. Governor Butler declined to comply with an application for his pardon, assigning, as a reason, that the eyes of the civilized world were upon them, and that the reputation of the State was at stake. This appeal, it was supposed, would be sufficient, but it only added fuel to the general excitement occasioned by the unusual if not unprecedented sentence of the Court. The whole State was in a ferment. The Court and the Governor were denounced. The press fulminated its anathemas; and before the day of execution arrived, the community were quieted with the announcement that the prisoner had escaped! Whether the locks were opened with keys, or the bolts broken; whether the walls were pierced or the windows opened; or whether the higher or lower authorities connived, the great public never heard! The Southern papers

ment of Stroud. There may have been convictions, and sentences of death may have been passed, and the criminals permitted to escape, or pardoned.

were watched for announcements of executive offers of reward for the prisoner's apprehension, but none ever appeared. The fugitive was not a fugitive *slave.* He might come to the North, if he pleased, without danger that the arm of the Federal Government would molest him! He was not guilty of rebelling against a slave *owner's* authority. He had *only* murdered a *slave!*

The *frequency* of such murders in South Carolina, so long ago as 1791, was publicly announced in her Courts of law, no one contradicting it. In the case of the State *vs.* McGee, Messrs. Pinkney and Ford, Counsel for the State, said: "*The frequency of the offense* (*wilful* murder of a slave) was owing to the *nature of the punishment*," &c., (i. e., a pecuniary fine.) (1 Bay's Reports, 164. Vide Stroud, p. 39.)

"In 1791, the Grand Jury for the District of Cheraw, (South Carolina,) made a presentment on the same subject, expressing their confidence that the Legislature would provide some other *more effectual* measures to prevent the FREQUENCY of crimes of this nature." (Matthew Carey's American Museum for February, 1791, Appendix, p. 10. Weld's Slavery, &c., p. 155.) Yet thirty more years elapsed before the penalty was changed, and still the law seems as powerless as ever. It is paralyzed by "the innocent legal relation" between an owner and his human chattel!

If any one doubts the frequency and the impunity of such murders, let him con over the attested facts in the book to which we have so frequently referred,

Weld's "Slavery as it is." Take a few specimens. On page 47 are four cases, related by Rev. William T. Allan, son of a slaveholding D.D. in Alabama.

(1.) "A man near Courtland, Ala., of the name of Thompson, recently shot a negro *woman* through the head, and put the pistol so close that her hair was singed. He did it in consequence of some difficulty in his dealings with her as a concubine. He buried her in a log heap; she was discovered by the buzzards gathering around it." (2.) "Two men, of the name of Wilson, found a fine-looking negro man at Dandridge's Quarter, without a pass, and flogged him so that he died in a short time. They were not punished." (3.) "Col. Blocker's overseer attempted to flog a negro. He refused to be flogged, whereupon the overseer seized an axe, and cleft his skull. The Colonel justified it." (4.) "One Jones whipped a woman to death for grabbing a potatoe hill."

Compare these four cases with the slave laws already cited. The second and fourth, being deaths by whipping, would pass, probably, as cases of "death under moderate correction." The third, Col. Blocker's overseer, would be justified by a Court of law as readily as by the Colonel. The slave was "resisting" or "offering to resist" the overseer, and was therefore an outlaw. The first case is not quite as clear. If the concubine "resisted" or "offered to resist" Mr. Thompson's advances, whether revengeful or lustful, she came, plainly, into the same legal predicament, and was lawfully killed! For "the legal relation" must be maintained! But were not these flagrant cases of murder? Take some other facts, furnished also by Mr. Allan on the page previous, (46.)

(1.) Mr. Turner stated that one of his uncles, in Caroline county, Virginia, had killed a woman—broke her skull with an axe-helve: she had insulted her mistress! No notice was taken of the affair. (2.) Mr. T. said that slaves were *frequently murdered.* (3.) In Mississippi a slave chanced to come forward hastily from eating, to hear the 'orders,' with a knife in his hand. The overseer, alarmed, raised his gun and shot him dead. He afterwards saw and confessed his mistake. But "*no* notice was taken" of the killing.

On page 50 will be found, by the testimony of Mrs. Nancy Lowry, a native of Kentucky, three cases of "premature deaths"—"generally believed by the neighbors that extreme whipping was the cause." Mr. Long, the inflictor and owner, was "a strict professor of the Christian religion," and "thought to be a very humane master." The victims, "John, Ned, and James, had wives." They were flogged frequently and "severely." "The *cause* of their flogging was, commonly, *staying, a little over the time, with their wives!*"

On page 97, in the testimony of Rev. Francis Hawley, there is a characteristic case. A son of a slaveholder "took," as was believed, "the wife of one of the negro men. The poor slave felt himself greatly injured, and expostulated with him. The wretch took his gun and deliberately shot him.

Providentially he only wounded him badly." This shows, however, the cause of many murders of slaves.

In South Carolina, a physician whipped his slave to death, "was tried and *acquitted*, and the next year ELECTED TO THE LEGISLATURE!" (Ib., p. 173.)

"I know a local Methodist minister, a man of talents, and popular as a preacher, who took his negro girl into the barn to whip her, *and she was brought out a corpse*." (p. 173.) This is the testimony of Mr. Geo. A. Avery, of Rochester, N. Y., who states further that the friends of the minister seemed to think it of "little importance to his *ministerial standing*." Of course he was not indicted! This was in Virginia.

A minister in South Carolina, a native of the North, had a stated Sabbath appointment to preach, about eight miles from his residence. He was in the habit of riding thither in his gig or sulkey, after a very swift trotting horse, which he always drove briskly. Behind him ran his negro slave on foot, who was required to be at the place of appointment as soon as his master, to take care of his horse. Sometimes he fell behind, and kept his master waiting for him a few minutes, for which he always received a reprimand, and was sometimes punished. On one occasion of this kind, after sermon, the master told the slave that he would take care to have him keep up with him, going home. So he tied him by the wrists, with a halter, to his gig behind, and drove rapidly home. The result was that, about two or three miles from home, the poor fellow's feet and legs failed him, and he was dragged on the ground all the rest of the way, by the wrists! Whether the master knew it or not till he reached home, is not certain; but on alighting and looking round, he exclaimed, "Well! I thought you would keep up with me this time!" so saying, he coolly walked into the house. The servants came out and took up the poor sufferer for dead. After a time he revived a little, lingered for a day or two, *and died!* The facts were known all over the neighborhood, but nothing was done about it! The minister continued preaching as before; and another slave of his, unable to labor or walk, was seen laid under a shed, near the house, where he would have starved, but for the food thrown over the fence to him by some mechanics working near by, and which he devoured ravenously. He was sent off to the plantation, and soon after died. When that minister comes up to our General Assemblies, Annual Conferences, or May Anniversaries, he can doubtless tell us all about the "innocent legal relation" of slave owner, and how kindly the slaves are treated by their masters! We should not publish *this* narrative, which has never before appeared in print, had it not been told to us by an eye-witness, with whom we are well acquainted, and in whose statements we can implicitly confide: Mr. John W. Hill, Green Point, near New-York city. He saw the gig when it came up, with the slave dragging behind, and saw the minister alight and go in.

"I knew a young man" (in Virginia—says Mr.

Geo. A. Avery, of Rochester, N. Y.) "who had been out hunting, and returning, with some of his friends, seeing a negro man in the road, at a little distance, deliberately drew up his rifle, and shot him dead. This was done without the slightest provocation, or a word passing. This young man passed through the *form* of a trial; and although it was not even *pretended* by his counsel that he was not guilty of the act, deliberately and wantonly perpetrated, *he was acquitted.* It was urged by his counsel that he was a *young* man, (about twenty years of age,) had no *malicious* intention, his mother was a widow, &c., &c." (Weld's "Slavery as it is," p. 172.)

The young man or his mother probably paid the "owner" the value of the chattel, (if he *was* a slave,) and he would perhaps be cautious in indulging his propensities as a sportsman, in shooting such expensive game, in future. In a civil suit of the "owner" for "damages," a jury of slaveholders would be less lenient. It would, however, be too much to expect of them that, for the same act, they would first oblige the unfortunate young gentleman to pay the market value of the *commodity*, and then hang him for the murder of the *man*—especially where it is gravely maintained that satisfaction to the *master* is a sufficient protection to the *slave!* The FACTS, as *thus* stated, (the most charitable version that could be made,) present the most favorable illustration of the LAW. It would appear still worse if there was not even the pecuniary forfeiture. The facts and the law combined are the legitimate and natural results of "the legal relation of owner and slave." If the *principle* and the relation are *right*, it might be difficult to show the *practice* to be *wrong*. Communities educated in the former will be sure to become involved in the latter.

Will it be said that these statements are only the fictions or exaggerations of Northerners? Or that they describe only a few isolated cases? Or that they apply only to the lower circles of society at the South? Listen, then, to a Virginian slaveholder, moving in the very highest circles of Southern society—the Hon. John Randolph, of Roanoke:

"Avarice alone can drive, as it does drive, this infernal traffic, and the wretched victims of it, like so many post-horses, WHIPPED TO DEATH in a mail-coach. Ambition has its cover-sluts in the pride, pomp, and circumstance of glorious war; but where are the trophies of avarice? *The handcuff, the manacle, the blood-stained cowhide!* WHAT MAN IS WORSE RECEIVED IN SOCIETY FOR BEING A HARD MASTER? WHO DENIES THE HAND OF A SISTER OR DAUGHTER TO SUCH MONSTERS?" (Speech in Congress.)

Study this picture. Wholesale murder—barbarism—cruelty. The general prevalence of these in the highest circles, and no one regarding the perpetrators the worse for it, or shrinking back from the closest family affinity with "the monsters!"

What Northern pencil has drawn a more frightful picture of the slave States than this? Old Virginia sat for the likeness, drawn by one of her most gifted sons! Was John Randolph a slanderer, a fanatic?

Hear the testimony, then, of another honored son of Virginia, the sage of Monticello.

"When the measure of their *tears* is full; when their GROANS HAVE INVOLVED HEAVEN ITSELF IN DARKNESS, doubtless a God of JUSTICE will listen to their DISTRESS." (Jefferson's Correspondence.)

Recall to mind the wholesale murders of Gen. Wade Hampton, recorded in another connection, (Chap. XI.) Remember the still more extensive and systematic murders of the Louisiana sugar planters, (Chap. V.,) complacently regarded and connived at by pious slave-breeders in Virginia, (Chap. X.,) cold-blooded, calculating, diabolic, like that of pirates; then say whether it be credible that such laws as have been reviewed in this chapter could protect the lives of slaves! Say, rather, what *possible* enactments could avail for them, while the "legal relation" of slave ownership continues?

If any further light is wanted on that feature of the Slave Code that insultingly proffers to the slave its protection from "*unusual*" punishments, the inquirer might see what punishments are "*usual*" by looking over the advertisements and paragraphs of a dozen leading Southern journals, from as many different States, for twelve months. Cut out, arranged, and pasted in a scrap-book, with an index, they would furnish him with a copious and authentic commentary on the slave laws. Every successive year, if he chose to repeat the process, would furnish a new volume. If he would save the labor, and avail himself of a faithfully collated scrap-book, made up to his hand, we refer him to Weld's "Slavery as it is," large portions of which he will find to have been gathered by this process.

He will there find numerous advertisements of runaway slaves, and of jailers' notices of apprehensions and commitments of them, in which the descriptions specify scars from whipping, from iron collars, from gun-shots, from brandings, &c., &c. Many are described as *having on* handcuffs, chains, and iron collars. One is "much marked with the whip"—another "severely bruised"—another, "a great many scars from the lash"—another, "several large scars on his back from *severe* whipping *in early life!*"—another "had a collar on, with one prong turned down"—another "had on a drawing-chain, fastened around his ankle with a house-lock"—another was "much *marked* with irons"—another (negress Fanny) "had an iron band about her neck," &c., &c. All this, as the reader now knows, is *authorized by law*—not prohibited as "*unusual.*"

Then comes another class, which, if not expressly authorized, are found by their *frequency* to be outside of the prohibited pale of "*unusual.*" "Mary has a scar on her back and right arm, caused by *a rifle ball*"—another "*branded* on the left jaw"—"Arthur has a scar across his breast and each arm, made by a knife; loves to talk much of the goodness of God"—"George has a sword-cut, lately received in his left arm"—"Mary has a small scar over her eye, a good many teeth missing, the letter A *branded* on her cheek and forehead." Many others "scarred with the bite of a dog."

"RAN AWAY, a negro woman and two children. A few days before she went off, *I burnt her* with a hot iron on the left side of her face. *I tried* to make the letter M."

Another class are described by mutilations which, though nominally prohibited by law, appear to be far from being "*unusual;*" and neither fear of law nor of public odium prevent the public advertisement of them.

One "has only one eye;" another, "Rachel, has lost all her toes except the large one." "Joshua, his thumb is off, on the left hand." Another, "his right leg broken." "John, left ear *cropt;*" another "has lost one of his ears."

Many pages might be occupied with similar advertisements, which appear in the most respectable Southern journals, with the names of the advertisers, many of them prominent citizens, and sometimes respectable ladies!

One case, on page 15 of Mr. Weld's book, is doubtless a specimen of tens, if not hundreds of thousands; assuredly it does not come under the condemnation of being "*unusual.*" The "owner" of a female slave, who was a Methodist, proposed a criminal intercourse with her: she refused. He sent her to the "overseer" to be flogged. Again he made advances—again she refused, and again she was flogged! Afterwards she yielded to his adulterous wishes! And now, the attentive reader of the preceding pages will have learned that all this was strictly within the protection of the law! Its limitations this monster had not overstepped. At least, there is no adequate law for his punishment—nay, so far as appears, there have been no legislative attempts or even pretensions to provide protection against *such* outrages!

But details of this kind, on this subject, are always set down as *exceptions.* We turn, then, again to a specimen of *general* testimonies.

Rev. GEORGE WHITEFIELD, in his letter to the slaveholders of Maryland, Virginia, the two Carolinas and Georgia, after admitting "particular *exceptions*," charges them, in general, with treating their slaves "worse than if they were brutes." He adds, "The BLOOD of them, SPILT for these many years in your respective provinces, will ascend up to heaven against you."

WILLIAM PINCKNEY, of Maryland, (1789,) calls Maryland "the foster-mother of petty despots, the patron of *wanton oppression!*"

Dr. JONATHAN EDWARDS, of Connecticut, (1791,) says, "The smack of the whip is all day long in the ears of those who are on the plantation, or in the vicinity; and it is used with such dexterity and severity as not only to lacerate the skin, but to tear out small portions of the flesh at almost every stroke. This is THE GENERAL TREATMENT of the slaves. But *many* individuals suffer still more severely. *Many are knocked down; some have their eyes beaten out; some have an arm or a leg broken*, OR CHOPPED OFF; and many, for a very small or for no crime at all, have been BEATEN TO DEATH," &c.

JOHN WOOLMAN, of New-Jersey, (1758:) "Their punishment is often severe, and sometimes desperate." (Journal, &c., p. 74.)

GEORGE BUCHANAN, M. D., of Baltimore, (4th of July Oration, 1791:) "Their situation" [the slaves'] "is *insupportable:* misery inhabits their cabins, and pursues them in the field. Inhumanly beaten, they OFTEN fall sacrifices to the turbulent tempers of their masters. Who is there, unless inured to savage cruelties, that can bear to hear of the INHUMAN PUNISHMENTS DAILY INFLICTED upon the unfortunate blacks, and not feel for them? *Can* a man, who calls himself a Christian, coolly and deliberately tie up, *thumb-screw, torture with pincers,* and beat unmercifully, a poor slave, for, perhaps, a trifling neglect of duty?"

AMERICAN COLONIZATION SOCIETY: "We have never heard of slavery in any country, ancient or modern, Pagan, Mohammedan, or Christian, *so terrible* in its *character, as the slavery which exists in these United States.*" (Seventh Report, 1824.)

The PRESBYTERIAN SYNOD OF KENTUCKY (1834) said, "*Brutal stripes,* and all the *varied* kinds of personal indignities, are not the *only* species of *cruelty* which slavery LICENSES."

"They [the slaves] *suffer* all that can be inflicted by wanton caprice, by grasping avarice, by brutal lust, by malignant spite, and by insane anger. Their happiness is the sport of every whim, the prey of every passion that may occasionally or habitually infest the master's bosom."

Rev. JAMES A. THOME, now of Ohio City, a native of Kentucky, and son of a slaveholder, says, "Slavery is the parent of more suffering than has flowed from any one source since the date of its existence. *Such* sufferings too! Sufferings inconceivable and innumerable; unmingled wretchedness from the ties of nature rudely broken and destroyed; *the acutest bodily tortures*, groans, tears and *blood;* lying for ever in weariness and painfulness, in watchings, in hunger and in thirst, in cold and in nakedness."

We forbear citing further witnesses. It is manifest that *human* chattels *must* be worse treated than brutes, in order to be *kept* in chattelhood. *Other* working animals are not punished as *examples* to their fellows. They are not the objects of suspicion, jealousy, lust, or revenge. They are not hated. They are not threatened. They are not conversed and quarrelled with. They cannot be regarded guilty, or proper subjects of censure or punishment. They have no aspirations above their condition. They have no keen sense of being injured by being imbruted. They can utter no provoking language, nor retort, nor retaliate. All these items are bulwarks of defense to the *brute*, but inlets and avenues of attack upon the slave. The individuals and the classes of men *most wronged*, are proverbially *most hated* by the wrong-*doer*. This is the dreadful doom of the poor negro, and he is completely under the power of his tyrant. As the exercise of despotic power over the defenseless makes men hardhearted and cruel, it is evident that the *more absolute* any despotism becomes, the *more cruel* will the persons become who administer it. And the most absolute form of despotism known among men, is that of human chattelhood in the United States of America, as its code proves.

The unnatural and monstrous "legal relation" of slave ownership, unhumanizing human beings, *insures* cruelties that human language cannot describe, nor human imagination conceive! No pencil can portray them; no statistics exhibit the sum total. The slave code is sufficiently horrible, but every syllable of it can be written, printed, and measured by pages. The practical illustration has no limits; its horrors swell into infinity!

"No people were ever yet found who were better than their" [living and recognized] "laws, though many have been known to be worse."

CHAPTER XVIII.

FUGITIVES FROM SLAVERY.

The Slave, being Property, may be hampered or confined to prevent his escape—may be pursued and reclaimed—must not be aided, or concealed from his Owner—and when too wild or refractory to be USED by his Owner, may be KILLED by him with impunity.

THIS topic is closely connected with those of several of the preceding chapters, and is, in some of its aspects, a branch of them. The laws on this subject are too verbose and various to be transcribed at large, which would swell the volume and weary the reader. We shall present only an abstract of what is characteristic and most important, connected with the usages under them. One design of these laws and usages is to prevent escapes; another, to facilitate recaptures; another, to punish the fugitives and deter others; another, to punish slaves, free colored people, or whites who may entice or aid the fugitives.

Prevention of escapes is sometimes sought by the use of iron collars, chains, handcuffs, locks, &c., as before mentioned, whenever the "owner" or his agent thinks proper; and the law, as has already been seen, authorizes this, and punishes any one who may cut or break them.

Another frequent precaution is the locking up of the slaves at night, and this, too, is within the lawful power of the master, at his own discretion.

In cities, corporate towns, &c., there are regulations forbidding the slaves or free people of color to be in the streets after a specified hour in the evening. At Wilmington, (N. C.,) we knew a case (1821) in which the holding of a Methodist meeting (under charge of white persons) a few minutes too late, occasioned the locking up of one half the worshipping assembly in the watch-house, men, women, and children, till eight or nine o'clock the next morning, church members and all, when the legal forms were gone through with, to effect their release; in which it appeared that a "class-leader" at the meeting had "taken up" five members of his own "class," and all in obedience to "the law!"

A general rule on plantations is, that slaves must not be absent from "quarters" in the evening, nor leave the plantation at any time without a written "pass." In at least *some* of the States, there are laws strictly enforcing this rule. Then, there are "patrols" established in city and country, regulated by law, and clothed with ample powers to arrest whom they please, and see that the existing laws and usages are enforced.

An Act of Maryland, (1715,) chap. 44, sect. 6, "for the better discovery of runaways, &c., requires that "*any person or persons whatsoever*," travelling beyond the limits of the county wherein they reside, shall have "*a pass* under the seal of said county;" otherwise, "if apprehended, not being sufficiently known, nor able to give a good account of themselves," the magistrate, at his discretion, may deal with them as with runaways. (Stroud, p. 83.) This is particularly remarkable as being *without distinction of color*, and so applicable to the class of low *whites*. These, however, were to be released after six months, in distinction from "negroes and mulattoes."

To facilitate recaptures, sect. 7 of the same Act—"for the better encouragement of all persons to seize and take up all runaways *travelling without pass*, as aforesaid"—provides a bounty, in tobacco, (commuted for six dollars,) "to be paid by the owner" of said runaway; "and if such *suspected* runaways be *not* servants, *and refuse to pay the same*, he, she, or they shall MAKE SATISFACTION BY SERVITUDE OR OTHERWISE, &c." In 1719, an additional provision authorized the sheriff, in case of nonpayment of costs, &c., by these wronged and innocent free negroes and mulattoes, to sell them to the highest bidder!!! This monstrous provision was afterwards expunged from the Code of Maryland, but not till after the cession of the Federal District, which therefore remains under the old law. And this furnishes the foundation of those laws of the Corporation of Washington City by which, at the present day, FREE NEGROES OF MULATTOES arrested as fugitive slaves, and not being claimed by any one, are held liable for their jail fees, and, in default of payment, sold into slavery. (Vide Jay's Inquiry, p. 154; and Jay's View, p. 33, &c., where it is shown that such cases frequently occur.)

It is made the official duty of sheriffs and constables to arrest suspected fugitives, and of jailers to commit them to prison. By law of Maryland, (1723,) ch. 15, sect. 2, &c., it is made the *duty* of the constables to repair monthly to all suspected places, and *whip* every negro he finds there without a license!* Owners of plantations, by the same Act, are required to send home to their masters any "strange negroes" on their premises; they are authorized to *whip* them, &c.; and forbidden to harbor or encourage them, on penalty of fine, &c. Same law in Federal District. (Snethen's Dist. Col., p. 13.)

"In Georgia, *any* person may inflict twenty lashes on the bare back of a slave found without license on the plantation, or without the limits of the town to which he belongs. So also in Mississippi, Virginia, and Kentucky, at the discretion of the justice." (Jay's Inquiry, p. 134.)

"In South Carolina and Georgia, *any* person finding more than seven slaves together in the highway without a white person, may give each one twenty

---

* In this aspect, the slave is neither treated as a *man* nor as a *brute*, but worse than either man or beast is treated! A man has the right of locomotion and social intercourse. And when a brute animal leaps his fence in quest of food or company, or to roam at large, no one thinks of treating him as a criminal, of subjecting him to punishment. The power of the State is not in requisition, to send sheriffs and constables after him.

lashes." (Ib.) Similar in Delaware: "more than six slaves." (Delaware Laws, 104. Stroud, p. 102.)

This law has also been introduced into Florida, since its cession to the United States, contrary to the milder code of Spanish slavery. Many of the Indian slaves in East Florida, with most of the free people of color near St. Augustine, transported themselves to Havanna, as soon as they heard of the approach of the American authorities. (Stroud, p. 101.)

"In Kentucky, Virginia, and Missouri, a slave, for keeping a gun, powder, shot, *a club*, or other weapon whatever, offensive or defensive, may be whipped thirty-nine lashes, by order of a justice." (Ib.)

"In North Carolina and Tennessee, a slave travelling without a pass, or being found in another person's negro quarters or *kitchen*, may be whipped *forty lashes*, and *every* slave in whose company the visitor is found, *twenty lashes!*" (Ib.) The visits of parents and children, husbands and wives, may be thus punished.

"In Louisiana, a slave, for being on *horseback*, without the written permission of his master, incurs twenty-five lashes; *for keeping a dog*, a like punishment." (Ib.) Horses and dogs, as well as weapons, might assist their escape.

"By the law of Maryland, for 'rambling, riding, or going abroad in the night, or riding horses in the daytime without leave, a slave may be *whipt*, *cropped*, or *branded* on the cheek with the letter R, or otherwise punished, not extending to life, *or so as to unfit him for labor*.'" (Ib.)

In Georgia and South Carolina, "If any slave shall be out of the house, &c., or off the plantation, &c., of his master, &c., and shall refuse to submit to an examination by *any white person*, &c., such white person may apprehend and *moderately correct* him; and if he shall assault or strike such white person, he may be *lawfully killed*." (2 Brevard's Digest, 231. Prince's Digest, 447. Sect. 5 of Act of 1770, and page 348, No. 43; title, Penal Laws. Stroud's Sketch, p. 101.) The reader will recollect here that "moderate correction," as legally defined, is such as *may* cause death! And the slave not submitting quietly to this may be lawfully killed!"

"If any slave shall presume to come upon the plantation without leave *in writing* from his master, employer, &c., not being *sent* on lawful business, the owner of the plantation may inflict ten lashes for every such offense." (1 Virg. Rev. Code of 1819, 422–3. Mississippi Rev. Code, 371. 2 Littel and Suigert's Digest, 1150. 2 Missouri Laws, 741, sect. 3. Maryland Laws, Act of 1723, chap. 15, sects. 1 and 5.)

North Carolina.—"*Any person* may lawfully kill a slave *who has been outlawed* for running away and lurking in swamps," &c. (Act of 1741. Haywood's Manual, 521–2. Stroud, 103.) Similar in Tennessee.

In Maryland and District of Columbia, "If any negro or other slaves, absenting themselves from their master's service, running out into the woods and there remaining, killing and destroying hogs and cattle belonging to the people of this province, shall refuse to surrender themselves, and make resistance against such persons as pursue to apprehend and take them up, being thereunto legally empowered, it shall be lawful for such pursuers, when such resistance is made, to shoot, kill, and destroy such negroes or other slaves." (Laws of Maryland, 1723, chap. 15, sect. 7. Snethen's Dist. Col.)

In North Carolina, (as cited in the chapter previous,) a *proclamation* of outlawry against a slave is authorized whenever he runs away from his master, conceals himself in some obscure retreat, and, to sustain life, "kills a hog, or some animal of the cattle kind." (See Haywood's Manual, 521. Act of 1741, chap. 24, sect. 45. Stroud, p. 38.) The same or similar in Tennessee.

In Virginia, "in 1705, two justices of the peace were authorized, by proclamation, *to outlaw runaways*, who might thereafter be *killed* and destroyed by *any* person whatsoever, *by such ways and means as he may think fit*, without accusation or impeachment of any crime for so doing." (Stroud's Sketch, p. 103.) This Act was, however, repealed in 1792. (Ib.)

From an article in the Norfolk (Va.) *Herald* of Feb., 1837, it however appears that a case of slave hunting and shooting had just occurred "near New Point Comfort." "It was not until a musket was fired at them, [the slaves,] and one of them slightly wounded, that they surrendered." (Weld's "Slavery as it is," p. 160.)

The customary usages of the South in general, on this subject, are such as to supersede the necessity of any formal *proclamation* of outlawry by the magistrates. The more *general* laws, as in South Carolina, Georgia, Maryland, and District of Columbia, just now cited, sufficiently answer the same purpose.

In South Carolina, "a slave endeavoring to entice another slave to run away, if provisions, &c., be prepared, for the purpose of aiding such running away, shall be punished with DEATH." (2 Brevard's Dig., 233, 244.) "And a slave who shall aid and abet the slave so endeavoring to entice another slave to run away shall also suffer DEATH." (Ibid.) An equivocal and unimportant modification of this Act was afterwards made. (Stroud, p. 104.) The "owner" of slaves sentenced to death is probably remunerated out of the public treasury. This is the law of Maryland. (Laws of Maryland of 1737, chap. 2, and of 1751, chap. 14. Vide Snethen's Dist. Col., p. 16.)

"If a slave harbor, conceal, or *entertain* another slave, being a runaway, in South Carolina and Georgia, he is subjected to corporal punishment to any extent, not affecting life and limb." (2 Brevard's Digest, 237. Prince's Digest, 452.) In Maryland, thirty-nine stripes is the penalty for harboring *one hour*. (Act of 1748, chap. 19, sect. 4.)

In South Carolina, "if a FREE negro harbor, conceal, or *entertain* a runaway slave," he is fined ten pounds for the first day, and twenty shillings for every succeeding day; and if unable to pay the fines and charges, he may be SOLD at public outcry, and the overplus, if any, paid into the hands of the public Treasurer." (2 Brevard's Dig., Act of 1740.)

In August, 1827, the Charleston Court passed sentence, according to this law, against Hannah Elliott, a free black woman, her daughter Judy, and her sons Simon and Sam, and they were sold into slavery. (Stroud's Sketch, p. 17.) Yet Judge Stroud is of opinion that that section of the Act of 1740 had been repealed. (Ib.) The law of 1821 provides "corporal punishment, not extending to life or limb." (Ib.)

White as well as colored persons are forbidden, under heavy penalties, to entice, transport, or secretly carry away slaves. (Laws of Maryland of 1715, chap. 19, sect. 4. Snethen's Dist. Col., p. 12.) Also, forbidden to entertain slaves unlawfully absent. (Laws of Maryland, 1748, chap. 19, sect. 2, &c. Snethen, p. 17.) Also, masters of vessels to conceal slaves on board. (Laws of Maryland, 1753, chap. 9, sect. 3. Snethen, p. 19.)

"By Aiken's Alabama Digest, p. 109, it is declared that '*any* person or persons, being convicted of harboring or concealing any negro or negroes belonging to any other person or persons whatsoever, or suffering the same to be done with his consent or knowledge, shall *be fined* in a sum not exceeding seven hundred dollars, and shall *be imprisoned* not less than one calendar month, nor exceeding six calendar months; and shall be *liable in damages* to the party injured, to be recovered by action on the case before any tribunal having competent jurisdiction.' And similar enactments are to be found in the statute books of the other States." (Wheeler's Law of Slavery, note, pp. 264–5.)

Giving passes to slaves is prohibited in Maryland by Act of 1796, chap. 67, sect. 20. (Snethen, p. 29.)

And "free negroes or mulattoes" who may sell or give away their "certificates of freedom," may be fined $300, which, if not paid, may be raised by the *sale* of such *free* persons into *slavery!* (Laws of Maryland, 1796, chap. 67, sect. 18. Snethen, pp. 28–9.)

By Act of Congress of 1852, heavy penalties are imposed upon all persons who knowingly entertain or aid fugitive slaves; and it is made the duty of United States Commissioners, Marshals, and "all good citizens," to assist in returning them.

In our examination "of the laws concerning the murder and killing of slaves," (Chap. XIV.,) we had occasion to cite some cases from Wheeler's Law of Slavery, by which it would appear that the Courts are quite familiar with such occurrences as the shooting and killing of fugitive slaves, since the owners often bring suits against the "hunters" for damages in killing them! And these suits are as coolly argued and disposed of as if it were a question of the shooting of a mad bull. Sometimes, where the shooting appeared to have been needless, "rash, and incautious," the plaintiff recovered damages. Other cases conclude with "judgment for the defendant."

The subject of "Runaway or fugitive slaves" occupies a distinct division or chapter, of above a dozen pages, in Mr. Wheeler's Compilation of Reported Cases. The decisions of the Courts are in harmony with the statutes already cited, and show that they are not a dead letter. We refer to a few cases. The first case introduces us to Slave Law as expounded in the State of New-York:

Glen *vs.* Hodges, Jan. T., 1812; John's New-York Reports, 67. Trespass for taking the plaintiff's slave. The fugitive had been seized by his master in Vermont. The defendant, who had a claim on the negro for debt, pursued him, and, with a writ of attachment, took him from the plaintiff's possession, and imprisoned him for debt. It was decided that the contract with a slave was void, and therefore the defendant had no right to take him. (Wheeler, pp. 266–7.)

Hutchins *vs.* Lee, Dec. T., 1827; Walker's Miss. Reports, 293. In this case it was decided that in the sale of a fugitive slave by a sheriff, "if the slave sell for less money because of any neglect in the sheriff to perform his duty, the remedy is by an action against the sheriff for damages." (Ib., p. 270.)

Labranche *vs.* Watkins, June T., 1816; 4 Martin's Louisiana Reports, 391. This was a litigation between a slave owner and the sheriff, who had had him in custody as a runaway. The sheriff sold the slave, then bought him back of the purchaser. The Court decided the act of the sheriff to be fraudulent, and that "a runaway slave cannot be sold by the sheriff till he had been advertised two years." (Wheeler, pp. 275–6.)

Under the head of "harboring slaves," in Wheeler's Law of Slavery, a number of cases are put down, *e. g.:*

Scidmore *vs.* Smith. The Court decided that "the penalty for harboring slaves is cumulative, and does not destroy the common law remedy." (p. 442.) That is, the penalty for the criminal act is in *addition* to the *damages* that may be claimed by the master in a civil suit.

We need occupy little space with proofs that the part of the Slave Code contained in *this* chapter, frightful as it is, is not a dead letter! Slave hunts, with muskets and bloodhounds, are too horribly frequent, by the testimony of the Southern journals, to admit of any doubt on this subject. And so are advertisements of runaway slaves by their owners, with offers of reward for them, "*dead or alive*"*!* or "for killing them," or for "evidence of their being killed!" Of such slave hunts the inquirer may find ample details in Weld's "Slavery as it is," pp. 21, 97, 102, 108, 155, 160. Specimens of such advertisements may be found on page 156 of that book, together with a proclamation of outlawry, and an announcement of the consequent "killing" of a negro.

The following advertisement is from the *Ouachita Register*, a newspaper dated "Monroe, La., Tuesday evening, June 1, 1852":

"NEGRO DOGS.

"The undersigned would respectfully inform the citizens of Ouachita and adjacent parishes, that he has located about 2½ miles east of John White's, on the road leading from Monroe to Bastrop, and that he has a fine pack of Dogs for catching negroes. Persons wishing negroes caught will do well to give him a call. He can always be found at his stand when not engaged in hunting, and even then information of his whereabouts can always be had of some one on the premises.

Terms.—Five dollars per day and found, when there is no track pointed out. When the track is shown, twenty-five dollars will be charged for catching the negro.

Monroe, Feb. 17, 1852. M. C. GOFF."

With a full knowledge of these laws and of these facts, nay, under the hardening effects of familiarity with them, our leading statesmen and religious teachers will affect to believe that the slaves are contented and happy in their present condition. In almost the same breath they will exhort us to the patriotic and Christian duty of enforcing the infamous Fugitive Slave Bill; quote the Bible and the Constitution to sustain their exhortations; and then complain of being slandered, if accounted pro-slavery!

"No people were ever yet found who were better than their [recognized and living] laws, though many have been known to be worse."

Judge Tucker, Professor of Law in the University of William and Mary, Virginia, speaking of this law of "outlawry" of runaways, and others of a similar nature, said: "Such are the cruelties to which SLAVERY *gives birth;* such the horrors to which the human mind is capable of being reconciled by *its adoption*." (Stroud, p. 103.)

The tree is known by its fruit. The laws on this subject, State and national, are but the natural progeny, as they are also the indispensable defenses of "the innocent legal relation." Repeal them, and slave "property" takes to itself legs, and runs away. To recognize the right of "property" is to recognize the right of reclaiming it, and the duty of its restoration. But it is likewise to reverse the divine law: "Thou shalt *not* deliver unto his master the servant which is escaped from his master unto thee: He shall dwell with thee, even among you, in that place which he shall choose, in one of thy gates, where it liketh him best: thou shalt not oppress him." (Deut. xxiii. 15, 16.)

CHAPTER XIX.

THE SLAVE CANNOT SUE HIS MASTER.

Slave Property cannot litigate with its Owner!

THE slave is a "chattel;" his master is his "owner." This "legal relation" precludes the idea of a suit at law between them, especially a suit in which the chattel should be plaintiff! As a horse or an ox cannot sue his owner, so neither can a slave; for "slaves shall be deemed, sold, taken, reputed and adjudged in law to be chattels personal, &c., &c., *to all intents, constructions, and purposes whatsoever.*" "A slave is one who is in the power of his master, to whom he *belongs.*" These all-comprehensive definitions are not a dead letter, and they accordingly settle, at every step, every question that can be raised concerning the condition of the slave. This is "the legal relation," and the whole of it. If this be tolerated, all the rest of the system, in all its parts, and in all its legitimate and natural workings and results, may be tolerated likewise. The parts, severally, cannot be worse than the whole.

"A slave cannot be a party before a judicial tribunal, in any species of action against his master, no matter how atrocious may have been the injury which he has received from him." (Stroud's Sketch, p. 57.)

We cited this paragraph in our Chapter IX., in proof of the master's "unlimited power." In the chapters succeeding it has been shown that the laws ostensibly framed for the protection and redress of the slave are of no value to him. *And no where have we found any provision for a suit at law by the slave against his master.* If the master assaults his life, if he inflicts torture, if he takes away his wife by force, or ravishes her before his eyes, neither he nor his wife can bring him to trial, nor enter complaint or bear testimony against him. If any instance has occurred, amid the outrages of the last two hundred years, LET IT BE PRODUCED.

"The law is unquestionably as stated above, without any exception or limitation." (Stroud's Sketch, p. 57.) *

The proposition at the head of this chapter, that "*a slave cannot sue his master*," is involved, of necessity, in the still more comprehensive one (which will be established when we come to treat of "the *civil* condition of the slave") that *a slave cannot be a party in any civil suit whatsoever.* It would be absurd to suppose that he could maintain a suit

* The case of an *alleged* slave bringing a suit for his freedom (which will be considered in its place) is not an exception to the above proposition, because the question *whether* the plaintiff *be* a slave is still to be settled, and is not to be taken for granted.

against *his owner*, when he could maintain a suit against *no body else*. And it would be equally absurd to suppose that he who could *possess* nothing, if he should *gain* a suit, could have any power to *bring* a suit before the Courts for so idle a purpose. The testimony of Mr. Wheeler to *this* point, in his "Law of Slavery," p. 197, we reserve for its more appropriate place hereafter, but refer to it here, for the convenience of the inquiring reader.

The following cases, extracted from the same author, will, however, be as appropriately inserted here as elsewhere, though they prove *more* than the mere proposition now before us:

"Berard *vs.* Berard et al., Feb. Term, 1836; 9 Louisiana Rep., 156.

"*Per Cur.*, *Martin, J.:* The plaintiff is a person, and SUES HER AUNT, Marie Louise Berard, for the purpose of establishing her and her children's claim to their freedom. The defendant disavowed any title to the plaintiff, but averred that she belonged to her late sister, Marie Jeane Berard, and that she descended to her sister's *natural children and legal heirs*, Celina and Antoine Garidel. These heirs intervened, and claimed the plaintiff and her children as their property, in the right of their deceased mother. The case was tried by a jury, who found a judgment for the intervening party, and the plaintiff appealed.

"The Court instructed the jury that the interveners *were not bound to show their title.* The plaintiff excepted.

"On a full consideration of the case, this Court is

11

of opinion that the instruction given to the jury by the District Judge was correct. A slave cannot stand in judgment for any other purpose than to *assert his freedom.* He is not even allowed to contest the *title of the person* holding him as a slave." (Wheeler's Law of Slavery, 197–8.)

This decision covers the entire ground of the incapacity of the slave to sue his master, or any other person. And it lifts the curtain from the scenery of society in a slaveholding community. It shows us a niece, suing her aunt for her freedom—the aunt claiming her niece as a slave, not for herself, but on behalf of two other nieces—*those* nieces coming forward to claim their cousin and her children as their slave—the Court and Jury sustaining the claim without calling upon the claimants to show their title—the Supreme Court, "on a full consideration of the case," confirming the decision, and all as coolly as if the claim were for a horse! yet upon a principle by which no horse could be held, without showing a title! This is slavery in the concrete, as actually existing, sanctioned by the Courts, and not merely an abstraction.

The case that follows has been twice alluded to already, and may be referred to again. We give it in full here:

"Dorothee *vs.* Coquillon et al., Jan. T., 1829; 19 Martin's Louisiana Rep., 350.

"Appeal from the Parish Court of the parish and city of New-Orleans.

"*Per Cur., Martin, J.:* The plaintiff, a free woman

of color, complained that her child was directed to be emancipated at the age of twenty-one, by the will of her mistress, who bequeathed her services, in the meanwhile, to defendant's daughter, who is still a minor; that the will requires the child to be educated in such a manner as may enable her to earn her livelihood when free; that *no care of her education is taken, and she is treated cruelly.* The prayer of the petition is, that the child be declared free at twenty-one, and in the meantime hired out by the sheriff. The answer *denies the plaintiff's capacity to sue;* that she has any cause of action; and the general issue is pleaded. *The petition was dismissed*, and the plaintiff appealed. The plaintiff cannot sue for her minor daughter, in a case in which the latter could not sue were she of age. The daughter is a *statu liber*, and as such, a slave till she reaches her twenty-first year. *Clef des loix romaines verbi statu liber.* As a slave, she can have no action except to claim or prove her liberty. (Civil Code, 177.) Her right to her freedom will not begin till she is twenty-one; if in the meantime the legatee fails to perform the conditions of the bequest, and the heirs of the testatrix have the legacy annulled therefor, the *statu liber* must continue a slave in the meanwhile, and her services enjoyed by her heir; so that the object of the suit, so far as concerns her, *is relief from ill treatment, which a* SLAVE *cannot sue for.* The plaintiff is without any right of action. Judgment affirmed, with costs." (Wheeler's Law of Slavery, pp. 198–9.)

And so the poor free colored woman loses her

case in behalf of her slave daughter, who is *to be* free at twenty-one, and is saddled with the costs of two Courts, because she did not know better than to suppose that a slave might sustain an action against her master for ill-treatment, and that the conditions of the Will would be enforced by the Courts!

CHAPTER XX.

NO POWER OF SELF-REDEMPTION, OR CHANGE OF MASTERS.

The Slave, being a Chattel, has no power of Self-redemption, nor of an exchange of Owners.

An ox cannot buy himself of his owner, nor transfer himself to the ownership of another. Here again, "to all intents, constructions, and purposes whatsoever," the slave is on a level with other working chattels! This must be his predicament in the very nature of the case, if the principle of *chattelhood* is to be consistently maintained.

"Slaves cannot redeem themselves, nor obtain a change of masters, though cruel treatment may have rendered such a change necessary for their personal safety." (Stroud's Sketch, pp. 57–8.)

It is of American slavery in the nineteenth century of the Christian era, and among a people boasting their pure religion and their free institutions, that this is affirmed. Among ancient heathen nations were found laws providing that slaves abused by their masters might apply to the magistrates, who would order them to be sold to a new master.

In Mississippi, as before noticed, the Constitution has *empowered* the Legislature to enact such a law, but the Legislature have not seen fit to exercise the power.

In Louisiana, the new Civil Code contains a regulation looking apparently in that direction, but difficult, if not impossible, to be made effective. It is as follows:

"No master shall be compelled to sell his slave, but in one of two cases, to wit: the first, when, being only co-proprietor of the slave, his co-proprietor demands the sale, in order to make a partition of the property; *second*, when the master shall be CONVICTED of cruel treatment of his slave, *and the Judge shall deem it proper* to pronounce, besides the penalty established for such cases, that the slave shall be sold at public auction, in order to place him out of the reach of the power which his master has abused." (Art. 192.)

It is to be noticed here, that the Judge is only *empowered*, not *directed*, to make such a decree. He *may* apply merely the *other* penalties alluded to, and which have already been examined, (Chap. XIII.) The master must be CONVICTED of cruelty by "WHITE" testimony, by a Court and jury of slaveholders, and amid legal rules and usages that expressly authorize chastisement with rigor, provided it be not "*unusual*," nor "so as to maim or mutilate," or endanger life. (Civil Code of Louisiana, before cited, Chap. XIII.)

It is not known that this law of Louisiana has

ever been enforced, and no other slave State in the Union, so far as we know, has any similar provision, though they are careful to provide, in this particular, for the security of *indented apprentices.* Without a *change of masters*, it is evident that no *other* laws against cruelty would be of any value. To punish an owner or overseer for abusing a slave, (even if it ever were done,) and then send the slave back again to be under the power of the same tyrant, (enraged, as he would be, at his punishment,) would only be to secure fresh injuries in secret.

As to the slave's power of self-redemption, there is no legal provision for it in any of our American slave States. Under the Spanish laws—as, for example, in Cuba—a slave may apply to the proper magistrates and be appraised. If, within a specified period, by the assistance of friends, or by a customary if not prescribed arrangement with the master, and by his own extra exertions, the amount of the appraisal can be raised, he becomes free. In this way many emancipations take place, as was also the fact among the ancient heathen. Our Christian and *Protestant* slavery knows no relaxation of the kind! The late U. S. Senator, James D'Wolfe, of Rhode Island, who owned a slave plantation in Cuba, and who was, in early life, a captain or supercargo of a slaver to Africa, was wont to dwell with satisfaction on this feature of *Cuban* slavery, and to congratulate himself that *he* was not a slaveholder under our *American* Code, which allowed no opportunity to an industrious and enterprising slave to become free.

CHAPTER XXI.

THE RELATION HEREDITARY AND PERPETUAL.

Slaves being held as Property, like other domestic animals, their Offspring are held as Property, in perpetuity, in the same manner.

"THE law of South Carolina says of slaves, 'All their issue and their offspring, born or *to be* born, shall be, and are hereby declared to be, and remain FOR EVER HEREAFTER, absolute slaves, and shall follow the condition of *the mother*." (Jay's Inquiry, p. 129. See Act of 1740. 2 Brevard's Digest, 229.)

In Maryland, "All negroes and other slaves, already imported or hereafter to be imported into this province, and *all children, now born or hereafter to be born of such negroes and slaves, shall be slaves during their natural lives*." (Act of 1715, chap. 44, sect. 22. Stroud's Sketch, p. 11.)

Similar in Georgia. (Prince's Dig., 446. Act of 1770.) And in Mississippi. (Revised Code of 1823, p. 369.) And in Virginia. (Revised Code of 1819, p. 421.) And in Kentucky. (Littell and Swigert's Digest, 1149–50.) And in Louisiana. (Civil Code, art. 183.) In all these laws it is laid down that the *child* follows the condition of *the mother*, whoever the *father* may be! The same usage, whether with or without written law, prevails in all our slave States; and under its sanction, the slave "owner" very frequently holds and sells his own children as "property," though sometimes as white as himself.

"That IS property which the law declares TO BE property. Two hundred years of legislation have sanctified and sanctioned negro slaves as property." (HENRY CLAY; Speech, U. S. Senate, 1839.)

So also Mr. Gholson, in the Legislature of Virginia: "The owner of land has a reasonable right to its annual produce, the owner of brood mares to their products, and the owner of female slaves to their increase."

Thus the perpetuity of slavery grows out of its hereditary transmission, and this again comes from its tenure of chattelhood. If the "legal relation" be valid and innocent, there can be no argument admitted against the right of its perpetuity; and slave property may be held so long as other property is held. The duty of a future liberation would imply the unlawfulness of present possession. Intelligent slaveholders, perceiving this, are careful to fortify their *present* claims upon human chattels, by enactments seeking the perpetuity of the system.

In Jamaica, before emancipation, the mixed breed, at the fourth degree of distance from the negro ancestor, were liberated by express law. In the other British West India Islands, a similar custom prevailed. (See Stephen's West India Slavery, p. 27, and Edwards' West Indies, book 4, chap. 1.) In the

Spanish and Portuguese colonies, (probably, also, in the French,) a similar usage is believed to prevail. (Vide Stroud's Sketch, p. 14.) Not so in our North American slave States, where biblical defenses of slavery, on the pretended foundation of Hebrew servitude, forget to define it by the Hebrew usages, and are resorted to in defense against the proclamation of the Hebrew Jubilee! By this process, and by defenses of or apologies for "the legal relation" of slave ownership, the idea of "rights of property" is sustained, which includes the right of perpetuity, of course, and makes it a work of supererogation to emancipate. Refusing to do so, the citizen remains as good as the laws; and the Christian (so he is taught) as good as the apostles and Moses, so far as the slave question is concerned. With "fanatics" he leaves it to attempt being better. Hence, the people (with few exceptions) are "no better than their laws" in *this* matter.

CHAPTER XXII.

RIGHT TO EDUCATION—RELIGIOUS LIBERTY—RIGHTS OF CONSCIENCE.

The Slave, being held as a Chattel, is held by a tenure which excludes any legal recognition of his rights as a thinking and religious being.

WE are not now speaking of laws or of usages that directly infringe such rights and prohibit their exercise. *There are such laws*, and we shall give some specimens of them, when we come to inquire after the condition of the slave in relation to *civil society.** At present, we are only unfolding to view "*the legal relation of master and slave.*" We affirm that a recognition of the validity or lawfulness of that relation is equivalent to a denial of the literary and religious *rights* of the slave. And if that relation be an innocent one, then the denial and the withholding of those rights, AS RIGHTS, are innocent likewise. The mere bestowal of *privileges*, with the *permission* to enjoy them, is not the recognition of *rights;* it is rather an implied denial of their existence. Men do not grant *permission* nor confer privileges where

---

*Chapters VI. and VII., Part II.

they recognize *rights.* The power to *permit* and to *confer*, carries with it the power to *refuse* and to *withhold.* Both the master and the slave understand this, where permissions are most frequently given. It is injurious to confer, as it is degrading to accept as a boon, what belongs to every man AS man, by absolute and inherent RIGHT. The rights of investigation, of free speech, of mental culture, of religious liberty, and of conscience, are of this class. Man may no more affect to *confer* them or *permit* their exercise, than he may presume to take them away.

The statement, then, is *not* that slave masters do not educate nor permit the education of their slaves, nor allow nor furnish them the benefits of religious instruction and social worship. As a general statement, with particular and local exceptions, it *might* be made and sustained, as will appear in its allotted place. But we waive and pass by all this, for the present, to affirm distinctly that "the legal relation" of slave ownership, in America, as defined by the code that upholds it, is a relation that cannot and does not consist with the recognition (either in theory or practice) of the intellectual and religious RIGHTS of the slave.

The slave "is a chattel." But chattels have no literary or religious rights. He is a chattel "to all intents, constructions, and *purposes* whatsoever." He is "in the power of a master, to whom he belongs"—"entirely subject to the will of his master"—"not ranked among *sentient beings*, but among *things.*" It would be an absurdity for *such* a code to recognize the slave as possessing religious rights. It is free from any such absurdity.

Except the provisions, in some of the States, for the "*baptism*" of slaves, and for their "spiritual assistance when *sick*," (see Chap. VII., Part II.,) we have found no recognition of their religious wants, their religious natures, or immortal destinies. Even *here* they seem to be considered passive beings, whose salvation is to be bestowed by their masters. The American Slave Code, from beginning to end, knows no rights of conscience in its subjects. The master is to be implicitly obeyed. His will is to be law. The slave is allowed no self-direction, no sacred marriage, no family relation, no marital rights—none that may not be taken away by his master.

Religion and its duties are based on human relations, including family relations. *These* relations, the "relation of slave ownership" and chattelhood abrogates. Religion requires and cherishes self-control; but the "owner's" authority supersedes and prohibits self-control. Religion implies free agency; but "the slave is *not* a free agent." His "condition is merely a passive one." So says the Slave Code, and so says ecclesiastical law, and therefore releases him from the obligations of the seventh commandment. Witness the decision of the Savannah River Baptist Association, while allowing its slave members, without censure, to take second or third companions, in obedience to their masters, by whom their original connections had been severed!

Rights of conscience require, and therefore *au-*

thorize a man to choose his own place of worship, and not "forsake the assembling together;" nay, to choose and follow the avocation, and select the residence and the associates where, *in his own judgment*, he can best serve God, fit his own soul for heaven, and lead his fellow-men to the Saviour. It commands and authorizes him to "search the Scriptures," and train up his family "in the nurture and admonition of the Lord." The master emancipates his slave, and ceases to be his "owner" when he fully accords to him, *in practice* and in theory, these Heaven-conferred RIGHTS. It is useless to attempt evading this, by adducing the case of children and minors. The slave, at maturity, is entitled to the rights and responsibilities of *a man*, and without them he is despoiled of his religious rights.

The slave master *may* withhold education and the Bible; he *may* forbid religious instruction, and access to public worship. He *may* enforce upon the slave and his family a religious worship and a religious teaching which he disapproves. In all this, as completely as in secular matters, he is "entirely subject to the will of a master, *to whom he belongs*." The claim of chattelhood extends to the soul as well as to the body, for the body cannot be otherwise held and controlled.

There is no other religious despotism on the face of the earth so absolute, so irresponsible, so soul-crushing as this. It is not subjection to an ecclesiastical body or functionary of any description; a presbytery, a conference, a bishop, a prelate, a pope, who may be supposed to be sensible, in some sort, of their sacred and responsible charge! The free *white* American exults in his exemption from the jurisdiction of these, except during his own free consent. He would freely part with his life's blood, in martyrdom or in war, rather than relinquish or compromise this right! But he thinks it a light matter (if he thinks of it at all) that three millions of his countrymen are in a worse spiritual thraldom than this, under bishops that regard and treat them as "chattels personal!" a bishopric entailed by descent, or conferred by the hammer of the auctioneer, the writ of the sheriff, or the chances of the billiard-table, and transferable in the same manner! nay, exercised by deputation every day, by the brutal overseer, the ignorant housekeeper, the spoiled child; a bishopric, Christian or infidel, drunken or sober, chaste or lewd, as the chances may happen! *Who thinks of it*, that the religious RIGHTS of *immortal men* are thus trampled in the dust in this country; that their religious *privileges* are in such keeping? How is it that Christian ministers, "sons of the Pilgrims," can overlook all this, as they do, when they speak of the "innocent legal relation" that involves, of necessity, all this? The absolute power of the Pope, though conferred, as it once was, by the almost unanimous consent of all Christendom, they can denounce as "THE Antichrist," forgetful of the *more* absolute power of every "owner" of an American slave! The doom of the former they read in the Apocalypse; the latter they deem Heaven-sanctioned and approved, blaming only *its abuse!* Why may not *Papal* power have the benefit of the same apology? Whence comes it that the absolute religious despotism (for such it is) of the slave owner is so much more sacred and unapproachable than that of the Protestant or Catholic Church?

A single incident—we hope it is an uncommon one—will illustrate this absolute power of the slave-holder. At a planter's dinner-table, one day, (perhaps over the wine,) a guest remarked upon the hypocrisy of all religious slaves. The planter dissented. He was the owner of one who would rather die than deny his Redeemer. This was ridiculed. The slave was brought and put to the test. He was ordered to deny his belief in the Lord Jesus Christ. He refused; was terribly whipped; retained his integrity; the whipping was repeated, and "he died in consequence of this severe infliction." This was in South Carolina. The facts were related to Miss Sarah M. Grimke, daughter of Judge Grimke, of Charleston, by an intimate friend, the wife of a slave-holder. The particulars, over the signature of Miss Grimke, are inserted in Weld's "Slavery as it is," p. 24.

There is *no adequate legal protection* against such outrages, nor *can* there be, consistently with the "legal relation" of slave ownership. There was probably no legal investigation of this case. *If* there had been, and if "white" witnesses had attested the fact, the verdict, in conformity with the laws of the State, would probably have been, "*death by moderate correction!*" Into the *causes* or *reasons* of chastisement, the Slave Code does not inquire! It is sufficient that the slave *disobeys* his "owner," "overseer, or agent!"

We have made no quotations from the statutes or judicial decisions of the slave States, on the subject of this chapter directly, *because we have found none!* Neither Stroud nor Wheeler, nor any other compiler of slave laws and decisions that we know of, appear to have discovered any provisions for the education and religious liberties of slaves! The eloquent silence of these significant blanks in the statute book and judicial reports of the slave States, is sufficient to certify the facts of the case. Whoever has read the preceding enactments and decisions well knows how to interpret such silence.

CHAPTER XXIII.

ORIGIN OF THE "RELATION," AND ITS SUBJECTS.

The so-called "legal relation" of slave ownership of Negroes originated in that African Slave-Trade which our laws now punish as piracy; but Slavery is, in general, extended over all classes whom the slaveholders have been able to seize upon and retain; over Indians, free persons of color, and whites.

SIR JOHN HAWKINS obtained leave of Queen Elizabeth, in the year 1562, to transport Africans into the American Colonies *with their own free consent*, a condition with which he promised to comply. But he forfeited his word, and forced them on board his ships by acts of devastation and slaughter. For this he was denominated a murderer and a robber, even by the historian Edwards, an advocate of the slave-trade. (Vide Clarkson's History, p. 30; and Edwards' Hist. W. Indies, vol. 2, pp. 43–4.) This was the beginning of the slave-trade by Englishmen.

By Act of 23 George II., the "trade to Africa" was "regulated," including a strict prohibition, under penalties, of the taking on board or carrying away any African "*by force, fraud, or violence.*" (Vide Clarkson, p. 314. See also Spooner's Unconstitutionality of Slavery.)

Under no other legal sanction than *this*, the forcible and fraudulent seizure and transportation of slaves from Africa to the British-American Colonies was carried on till the West India and North American Colonies were stocked with slaves, and many were introduced into England, held as slaves there, and the tenure accounted legal!

But in 1772 it was decided by Lord Mansfield, in the case of James Somerset, a slave, that the whole process and tenure were *illegal;* that there was not, and *never had been*, any legal slavery in England. This decision was understood by Granville Sharpe, the chief agent in procuring it, to be applicable to the *British Colonies*, as well as to the mother-country, and undoubtedly it was so. The United States were then Colonies of Great Britain. But the slaves in the Colonies had no Granville Sharpe to bring their cause into the Courts, and the Courts were composed of slaveholders.

In the great struggle, afterwards, in the British Parliament for abolishing the African slave-trade, William Pitt cited the Act of 23 George II., (which we have already mentioned,) and declared that instead of authorizing the slave-trade, as was pretended, it was a direct prohibition of the whole process, as it had actually been carried on by fraud, force, and violence. An elaborate investigation by Parliament sustained the statement; and, after a long struggle, the doctrine prevailed, and the traffic was expressly and solemnly abolished, though it has been secretly carried on to the present day, and is prosecuted still. There is reason to believe that great numbers are still smuggled annually into the United States, as it is known that numerous plantations in the States bordering on the Gulf of Mexico are stocked with slaves, evidently African, and unable to speak English.* *The whole process is, and has been, illegal, from beginning to end.*

The first introduction of slaves into Georgia was in direct violation of express statutes of the Colony itself, until slaveholders gained the ascendency and repealed the laws. Into the other Colonies slaves were introduced a long time before there were any colonial enactments authorizing it, and consequently without any show of legal sanction. When statutes *were* enacted, they did not pretend to create or originate the relation. Nor did they define, with exactness, who were slaves and who were not slaves. They only *assumed* or took for granted the existence

* See Weld's Slavery as it is, (p. 139, &c.,) for important facts on this subject, among which are the following: The President's Message, in 1837, stated that a naval force had been employed in preventing the importation of slaves. Mr. Middleton, of South Carolina, in 1819, declared, in a speech in Congress, that "*thirteen thousand* Africans are annually smuggled into the Southern States." Mr. Mercer, of Virginia, in a speech in Congress, declared that "cargoes" of African slaves were smuggled into the South, to a deplorable extent. Mr. Wright, of Maryland, in a speech in Congress, estimated the "number imported annually at *fifteen thousand.*" Particulars are also given of the importation of a cargo of five hundred from Guinea and Congo, into Savannah, the capture, the sham trial of the importers, their acquittal, and the distribution of the slaves among the planters! New-Orleans papers, in 1839, recorded the fact of frequent and extensive smuggling.

of slave property, and made laws for its security and regulation. The consequence is, that no slaveholder can now prove that the particular slaves claimed by him were ever made slaves *according to law*, or that their ancestors were thus enslaved! And there are no statute laws in either of the States, by which it can be legally proved by the common rules and usages of Courts, as applied to other subjects, that *slavery legally exists there.* This was avowed by Mr. Mason, of Virginia, in the Senate of the United States, when the Fugitive Slave Bill was pending. He objected to the proposed "trial by jury" that it would bring up the question of the legality of slavery in the States, which, said he, *it would be impossible to prove.* Mr. Bayly, member of Congress from Virginia, took the same ground. So Congress struck out the jury trial, because slaveholders avowed their inability to prove the legality of slavery in a Court of law!

It may be proper to explain, that while these gentlemen admit that there are no express statutes of the States that are adequate to the legalization of slavery, they nevertheless affect to believe that it is legalized by the *common law!* It is not strange that they are unwilling to go with *that* plea into the Courts! The Courts of *Louisiana, Mississippi, and Kentucky* have already set it aside. (See the case of Marie Louise *vs.* Mariott et al., May Term, 1836; 8 Louisiana Reports, 475. Wheeler's Law of Slavery, 348–9. Also, same principle in Rankin *vs.* Lydia, Fall Term, 1820; 2 Marshall's Kentucky Rep., 467. Wheeler, p. 339. Also in Lunsford *vs.* Coquillon,

May Term, 1824; 14 Martin's Louisiana Rep., 401. Wheeler, p. 335. See also Harvy and others *vs.* Decker and Hopkins, June Term, 1818; Walker's Miss. Rep., 36. Wheeler, pp. 340–6. See also Commonwealth of Massachusetts *vs.* Thomas Aves, Aug., 1836. Wheeler, p. 368, and Story's Conflict of Laws, 92–97.)*

All these affirm that slavery, being without foundation in nature, is the creature of municipal law, and exists only under its jurisdiction. In the case first mentioned, (Marie Louise *vs.* Mariott et al.,) in which the slave had been taken to France by her master, and brought back to Louisiana, Judge Matthews said: "*Being free for one moment in France, it was not in the power of her former owner to reduce her again to slavery.*" (Wheeler, p. 349.)

The absence, therefore, of municipal law, is fatal to the legality of the claims of the slaveholder, even by the Slave Code. In the case of Lunsford *vs.* Coquillon, above mentioned, Judge Martin said: "*The relation of owner and slave is, in the States of this Union in which it has a* LEGAL *existence, the creature of municipal law.*" (Wheeler, p. 335.)

In Wheeler's Law of Slavery, pp. 8–11, there is a brief account of the origin of slavery, which in no essential particular conflicts with the account we have here given of it, and in some of the most im-

* While these statements were in the hands of the printer, a gentleman of the city of New-York, who, for several years, was a practising lawyer in *Georgia*, informed the author that there had been similar judicial decisions in that State.

portant particulars is coincident with it. The same remarks will apply to the statements cited from Judge Matthews, of Louisiana, pp. 15, 16.

"It is an admitted principle, that slavery has been permitted and *tolerated* in all the colonies established in America by the mother-country. Not only of Africans, but also of Indians. NO LEGISLATIVE ACT OF THE COLONIES CAN BE FOUND IN RELATION TO IT." (Wheeler, pp. 8, 9.)

In other words, the practice had no municipal law to sanction it. It was barely "*tolerated;*" that is, it was not suppressed. This is a very different thing from saying that it was LEGAL, which could not be without local enactment, even according to the lowest definition of legality. No lawyer ever speaks of the holding of property in horses (which is a natural right) as being "*tolerated!*" Again,

"Hudgins *vs.* Wright, Nov. T., 1806; 1 Hen. and Munf., Va. Rep., 139.

"Per Cur.: The slavery of the African negro has existed from the time of bringing them into the Colony. In many of the States express enactments have been made declaring them slaves, *and in others they are slaves by* CUSTOM." (Wheeler, p. 12.)

It would have been interesting to have learned from the Court in *which* of the colonies, and *when* and *how* "express enactments" were made. It would then have confirmed fully the statement before quoted, that "*no* legislative enactments" *originating* slavery can be found. Again,

In the case of Seville *vs.* Chretien, Sept. T., 1817;

5 Martin's Louisiana Reports, 275, Judge Matthews admits, and labors to account for, "*the absence of any legislative act of European powers for the introduction of slavery into their American dominions.*" (Wheeler, p. 15.)

So that American slavery owes its *origin* neither to American nor European legislation. The Courts, indeed, whenever they approach the subject, appear to be perplexed with the problem of its legal origin. As for example,

Hall *vs.* Mullen, June T., 1821; 5 Har. and John's Md. Rep., 190.—Judge Johnson said: "But the condition and rights of slaves in this State depend not exclusively either on the civil or feudal law, but may, *perhaps*, rest in part on both; subject, nevertheless, to such changes in their condition," &c., "as the laws of the State may prescribe." (Wheeler, pp. 10, 11.)

By what authority, when, and how, the feudal law or the Roman civil law became established in the American States, we are not informed; nor is it very important, since the Courts at the South will be careful not to allow the feudal law to define slavery, as indeed appears by the preceding.

Whence, then, is the original of slavery? And how does it appear to *have been or to be* legalized? In the case of

Harvey and others *vs.* Decker and Hopkins, June T., Walker's Miss. Rep., 36, the Court said: "*Slavery is condemned by reason and the laws of nature. It exists, and can* ONLY *exist, through municipal regulations.*" (Wheeler, pp. 340–6.)

But the "municipal regulations" (so far as ORIGINATING the "legal relation" is concerned) appear, as has been seen, to be missing! They "cannot be found" on the statute book!

The New-Jersey Judge who frankly confessed that he *could not tell and did not care* how the legal right to enslave the *Indians* originated, took the most prudent course, and should be imitated by all pro-slavery Judges who are so unfortunate as to stumble upon "the delicate question" of the origin of legalized *negro* slavery.

"The State *vs.* Waggoner, April T., 1797; 1 Halstead's N. J. Rep., 374–476.

"They" [Indians] "have so long been recognized as slaves in our law, that it would be as great a violation of the rights of property to establish a contrary decision at the present day, as it would in the case of the Africans, and as useless to investigate the manner in which they originally lost their freedom." (Wheeler, p. 18.)

And yet, in Wheeler's Law of Slavery, we find cases in which even Southern Judges (to their honor be it recorded) have awarded freedom to persons enslaved, upon the opposite principle, that "prescription is never pleadable to a claim of freedom." This is the marginal note to the case of

"Delphene *vs.* Devise, 14 Martin's Louisiana Rep. 650:

"*Per Cur.*, *Porter*, *J.:* The plaintiff urges she is descended from one Marie Catherene, a negro woman now deceased, who was the slave of a certain Marie

Durse, and that the said Marie emancipated and set free Catherene and her children, Florence, Luce, and Catherene, the mother of the petitioner." "The defendant pleaded the general issue, *and prescription.* We shall, before entering upon the merits, dispose of the exception which forms the second ground of defense in the defendant's answer. We do so by referring to the third partida, title twenty-nine, law twenty-four, in which we find it provided that, *if a man be* FREE, *no matter how long he may have been* HELD by another AS A SLAVE, *his state or condition cannot be thereby changed, nor can he be reduced to slavery in any manner whatever, on account of* THE TIME *he may have been held in servitude.*" "The plaintiff is entitled to her freedom." (Wheeler, p. 101.)

Same principle in case of Metayer *vs.* Metayer, Jan. T., 1819; 6 Martin's Louisiana Rep. 16. (Wheeler, p. 103.) Also in Vaughan *vs.* Phebe, Jan. T., 1827; Martin and Yerger's Tenn. Rep. 1. (Wheeler, pp. 395–404.) Judge Crabb said: "*The act of limitations would be no bar.*" (p. 399.)

Neither by *statute*, therefore, nor by the *common law*, nor yet by *prescription*, are the negroes in America LEGALLY held in bondage.

But it is time now, in further confirmation of this, to cite more fully the language held by Judge Matthews, of Louisiana, in the case of Seville *vs.* Chretien, before mentioned.

Having alluded to "*the absence of any legislative act of the European powers for the introduction of slavery into their American dominions*, Judge Matthews adds:

"*If the record of any such act exists, we have not been able to find any trace of it.* It is true that Charles the Fifth, in the first part of the sixteenth century, granted a patent to one of his Flemish subjects for the privilege of importing four thousand negroes into America, which was purchased by some Genoese merchants, who were the first who brought into any regular form the commerce for slaves between Africa and America. A few years before, a small number of negroes had been introduced by order of Ferdinand. But the privilege granted by the Emperor, so far from being the first introduction of slavery into the New World, *was intended as a means of enabling the planters to dispense with the slavery of the Indians by their European conquerors.* A full account of these transactions may be seen in Robertson's History of America." (Wheeler, p. 15.)

It will not, probably, be contended that the enslavement of the Indians, here mentioned, was under sanction of law. But let us hear Judge Matthews further:

"On turning our attention to the first settlement of the British Colonies in America, we find that the introduction of negro slaves into one of the most important, was accidental. In the year 1616, as stated by Robertson, and 1620 by Judge Marshall, in his Life of Washington, a Dutch ship from the coast of Guinea sold a part of her cargo of negroes to the planters on James River. *This is the first origin of the slavery of the blacks in the British-American provinces. About twenty years after, slaves were intro-*

duced into New-England, and it is believed that Indians were at the same time, or before, held in bondage. THE ABSENCE OF ANY ACT OR INSTRUMENT OF GOVERNMENT UNDER WHICH THEIR SLAVERY ORIGINATED IS NOT A MATTER OF GREATER SURPRISE THAN THAT THERE SHOULD HAVE BEEN NONE FOUND AUTHORIZING THE SLAVERY OF THE BLACKS. *The first Act of the Legislature of the Province of Virginia on the subject of the slavery of the Indians was passed in* 1670, and one of its provisions, according to Judge Tucker, prohibits free or manumitted Indians from purchasing Christian servants. The words *free or manumitted* are useless and absurd, if there did not exist Indians who had been slaves and had been manumitted, before and at the time this Act was passed." (Wheeler, pp. 15, 16.)

Thus full and explicit is the testimony of Judge Matthews, of Louisiana, (and in the very act of making a decision against the claims of an Indian "to recover his liberty,") to the fact that both Indians and negroes were originally enslaved in this country, in the absence of either European or colonial legislation to sanction or create the relation of owner and slave.

Put this by the side of the Southern decisions, before cited, that slavery can have no legal existence in the absence of municipal law, and we have the result that slavery in this country had *no legal origin*, and has continued to exist *without* law; since (by the same testimony) "no legislative act of the Colonies can be found in relation to it."

The reader may be curious to know *on what ground* Judge Matthews, of Louisiana, in the case already cited, could maintain the legality of American slavery. It is this:

"However, *we are of opinion* that it *may be* laid down as a legal axiom, that in all governments in which the municipal regulations are not absolutely *opposed* to slavery, persons *already* reduced to that state may be *held* in it; and we also assume it as a first principle that slavery has been permitted and *tolerated* in all the colonies established in America by European powers, most clearly as relates to the blacks and Africans, and also in relation to Indians, in the first periods of conquest and colonization." (Wheeler, p. 15.)

According to this "legal axiom," *any person* in a State where there are no express statutes *forbidding* slavery, (as perhaps in Massachusetts and Maine,) may seize *any other* person and enslave him! And *having* done this, he may *continue* to "hold" him *legally*, because the laws have not forbidden it! By the same or a similar "legal axiom," it would follow that in a State where no express statutes had been enacted against such *minor* injuries as assault, battery, and maiming, such practices might be considered *legal!* Thus the "axiom" ignores the existence of natural law and common law!

Another important circumstance is, that the colonial charters, which were their constitutions of government, expressly provided that the Colonies should enact no laws contrary to the common law, the Constitution and the fundamental laws of Great Britain. But *these* (as decided by Lord Mansfield, and as attested by Coke, Fortescue, and Blackstone) are incompatible with the existence of slavery.

Another fact is, that the thirteen United States, on the fourth of July, 1776, declared that "all men are created equal, and are endowed by their Creator with certain inalienable rights, among which are life, liberty, and the pursuit of happiness." Similar declarations were incorporated into the original Constitutions of the several States, and the Courts in *Massachusetts* decided that this was equivalent to an act abolishing slavery.*

Such was the *origin*, and such are the *legal foundations* of the "legal relation of master and slave" in this country; just as "legal" now, and no more so—

---

* The historical facts hastily hinted at in this chapter, are detailed at length in Goodell's "History of Slavery and Anti-slavery." Since that work was issued, and since this book has been in the hands of the printer, the author has received additional information from John Scoble, late Secretary of the British and Foreign Anti-slavery Society, London. In consequence of atrocities committed by a West India slaveholder of eminence, a legal investigation took place, which resulted in the discovery and announcement that there was no legalized slavery in the British Colonies. This was made public in England previous to the Act of Parliament terminating the practice of slaveholding. The Act, accordingly, does not repeal or assume to repeal any existing laws, either colonial or British. It only provides for the suppression of an unlawful custom or practice. Intelligent Englishmen do not now speak of British West Indian slavery as having ever been *legal*. This accords with the maxim of James Madison and of Lord Brougham that man *cannot* hold property in man.

just as "innocent" now, and no more so, than in the person of John Hawkins, when he first forced a band of naked Africans on board his slave-ship, on the coast of Africa, or when he first offered them for sale in the Colonies; quite as cruel, Heaven-defying, and murderous *now* as it was *then*, and involving its present perpetrators in the same condemnation with John Hawkins, at the bar of an impartial posterity, and at the bar of God. "Where the *foundation* is weak," says the common law, "the *structure* falls." "What is invalid *from the beginning*, cannot be made valid by length of time." (Noyes' Maxims.) "He that stealeth a man and selleth him," says Moses, "or if he be found in his hand, he shall surely be put to death." "The law was made for men-stealers," says Paul. "Stealers of men," said the Presbyterian General Assembly of 1794, "are those who bring off slaves or freemen, and *keep*, sell, *or* buy them." "Those are man-stealers," says Grotius, "who abduct, *keep*, sell, or buy slaves or freemen." "To hold a man in a state of slavery," said Dr. Jonathan Edwards, "is to be, *every day*, guilty of robbing him of his liberty, or of *man-stealing*." "Men-buyers," said John Wesley, "are exactly on a level with men-stealers." We might quote similar language from Dr. Porteus, Bishop of London, Bishop Warburton, Macknight, Abraham Booth, and other eminent writers.

This is the pretended "legal relation" of master and slave in America. Let us now see who are its subjects.

1. The *descendants* of all who were stolen by John Hawkins and others on the coast of Africa! The law of hereditary slavery, as defended by Henry Clay and Mr. Gholson, and as practised by the entire community of slaveholders, *identifies their* slaveholding with the slaveholding of *John Hawkins*, and bases *their* claim of property upon *his!* If this is not so, then they are guilty of commencing the process *de novo*, and of kidnapping the innocent, helpless infant "upon their own hook!" This is called being "born to a slave inheritance!" This is the "innocent legal relation!" The slave law *enables* the heir to seize upon the slaves of his father or their offspring; and he is under the unfortunate necessity of seizing upon all within his grasp—not unfrequently his own *father's* daughters and sons! Were they his own *mother's* daughters and sons too, and if he had the power, it would be the same thing! Equally "legal"—equally "innocent!"

And here is the evidence:

Hudgins *vs.* Wrights, Nov. T., 1806; 1 Hen. and Munf., Va. Rep., 134. *Per Cur.*, Tucker, J.: "From the first settlement of the colony of Virginia to the year 1788, October Session, all negroes, Moors, and mulattoes, except Turks and Moors in amity with Great Britain, brought into this country, by sea or land, were slaves; and, by the uniform declaration of our laws, the descendants of *females* remain slaves to this day, unless they can prove a right to freedom by actual emancipation, or by descent in maternal

nal line from an emancipated slave." (Wheeler, p. 3.)

Hudgins *vs.* Wrights, (same case.) "Held by the Court, *Green*, *J.*, that, to solve all doubts, the Act of 1662 was passed, which declared that all children born in this country shall be bond or free, *according to the condition of the mother.* It is the rule of the civil law. By that law the state of the child was determined by that of the mother at the time of its birth." (Ib., p. 3.) "The rule is universally followed." (Ib., p. 34.)

"The code of the civil law prevails in all the States," (says Mr. Wheeler, in a note on the preceding,) "and in many of them, statutes have been enacted on the subject." (Ib. See also Stroud's Sketch, p. 11.)

By Act of Maryland, 1663, chap. 30, we are informed (in the preamble) that "divers free-born English women," &c., "do intermarry with negro slaves, by which also divers suits may arise touching the issue of such women," &c.; whereupon it was enacted that, in such cases, the *woman* shall also serve the master of her husband during his life, and their children "shall *be slaves, as their* FATHERS *were.*" But in 1770 this law was repealed, and it was enacted that the child should follow the condition of the *mother* instead of the father. (Stroud's Sketch, pp. 8–10.)

As mulattoes, with few exceptions, were the offspring of white fathers by slave mothers, this law, *as was intended*, secured to the father the right of ownership over his own children—a very common and extensive manifestation of "the innocent legal relation." As this law obtains in all the slave States, a large and increasing proportion of the slaves are held in slavery under its operation. If the child followed the condition of the *father*, the system would rapidly run itself out.

2. *Free* people of color *may* be and continually *are* brought into slavery, in this country, in a variety of ways. Some of these ways have been already specified, incidentally, while treating of other topics. Some will be specified hereafter. And they will be clustered together and adverted to again, in a chapter on "The Liberties of the Free People of Color." In the mean time, the topic demands attention here, in our inquiry concerning the *subjects of slavery*, and we shall cite *some particulars* which need not be repeated again.

The *general fact* of the enslavement of the free colored people, of the facility with which it is done, and of the indifference, not to say the *connivance*, of the Southern Courts, will appear from the following:

Davis *vs.* Sandford, Spring Term, 1815; 6 Littell's Ky. Rep., 206.

"The appellant sold to the appellee a slave. The deed of bargain and warranty certified that the negro was *born a slave.* It appeared that the negro had been in Ohio, and had, by the Courts of that State, been declared free, *which fact was known to both parties*—the seller alleging that the judgment declaring the slave free had no force or effect upon his rights, as he was not made a party. The Court, *Ch. J. Boyle*, held that the warranty was not broken, it not being alleged or proved that the negro was *not* born a slave; and the *justice* of the case was with the seller—the buyer purchasing with a knowledge of all the facts, which was properly shown by parol evidence." (Wheeler, p. 121.)

But we must proceed to classify some of the principal methods of reducing free people of color to slavery.

(*a*) Slaves made free by the voluntary act of their masters may be re-enslaved in various ways. A failure of conformity, in every minute particular, to the enactments regulating emancipations, (however vexatious and unreasonable,) will work the forfeiture of liberty to the emancipated.

In cases where infant children of slaves were made free by the will of their "owners," but *inadvertently* the *precise time* of their becoming free failed to be specified, *such* "shall be esteemed *slaves for life!*" (Maryland Laws, Act of 1809, chap. 71. Stroud's Sketch, p. 151. See chapter on Legislative and Judicial Obstructions to Emancipation.)

(*b*) A full and exact compliance with the legal regulations, in emancipating slaves, does not always secure their freedom. The Legislature of North Carolina set aside the decisions of the Courts, and re-enslaved large numbers who had been legally set free. (See chapter just mentioned.)

In Virginia, "if any emancipated slave (infants excepted) shall remain in the State more than twelve months after his or her right to freedom shall have accrued, he or she shall *forfeit* all such right, and may be *apprehended and sold* by the overseers of the poor, &c., for the benefit of the Literary Fund!!!" (1 Revised Code of 1819, 436.)

President Jefferson, in his will, having emancipated *five* of his slaves, adds: "I humbly and earnestly request of the Legislature of Virginia a confirmation of the bequests to these servants, with leave to remain in the State, where their families and connections are," &c.

(*c*) Colored persons who *cannot prove* their freedom may be enslaved. In Mississippi, "every negro or mulatto found within the State, and *not having the ability* to show himself entitled to freedom, may be sold, by order of the Court, as a slave." (Mississippi Revised Code, 389.) And no negro or mulatto can be a witness to prove his freedom!

In North Carolina, by decision of the Courts, this rule is limited to *negroes*, and the *mixed* race is exempted. It is by this unrighteous presumption against color that suspected fugitives, though unclaimed, are sold for the payment of their jail fees in Washington City. In South Carolina, by Act of 1740, the doctrine is affirmed, both in respect to negroes and the mixed races. The same in Georgia by Act of 1770. Also in Mississippi, Revised Code, 389. In Virginia, there is no statute, but the Courts have affirmed the doctrine, except where Indians or *white* persons are claimed as slaves. (See Stroud's Sketch, p. 19; also, pp. 76–88, including Notes.)

"*Every negro is presumed to be a slave.*"—"This is the general doctrine in all the States, and the application of a different rule is only in cases where the person is a mulatto, or some other grade approximating to a white person." (Wheeler, p. 5.)

"*Or person of color.*"—"*Color* and long possession are such presumptive evidence of slavery as to throw the burden of proof on the party claiming his freedom." (Ib., pp. 5, 6; case of Davis, a man of color, *vs.* Curry, Fall T., 1810; 2 Bibb's Ky. Rep., 238.)

And who *is* a "person of color?"

"When there is a distinct and visible admixture of African blood, the person is to be denominated a mulatto, or person of color." (State *vs.* Davis and Hanna, Dec. T., 1831; 2 Bailey's S. C. Rep., 558. Wheeler, p. 4.)

And the fact of color "may be known by inspection." (Wheeler, p. 5; also p. 22.)

(*d*) Free negroes may be enslaved for "entertaining" a runaway slave, and for nonpayment of the fine thus incurred! (See law of South Carolina before cited, and the consequent sentence of the Court of Charleston in the case of "Hannah Elliott, a free black woman, with her daughter Judy, and sons Simon and Sam." Stroud's Sketch, pp. 16, 17.)

(*e*) Also, for selling or giving away to a slave their certificates of freedom, as before mentioned. (Laws of Maryland, 1796, chap. 67, sect. 18. Snethen's Dist. Col., pp. 28–9.)

(*f*) Also, free negroes and mulattoes, arrested on suspicion of being fugitives, but *not claimed* by any one, and unable to pay their *jail fees*, are sold by the sheriff! (Jay's Inquiry, p. 154, and Jay's View, p. 33, &c.)

(*g*) "Where a *white* woman intermarries with a slave, *the issue are slaves;* though the Act subjecting such issue to slavery was repealed, if the *marriage* took place before the repeal of the Act." (Butler *vs.* Boardman, Sept. T., 1770; 1 Har. and M'Hen. Md. Rep., 371. Wheeler, p. 21.)

(*h*) "The issue of slaves entitled to liberty at a future day, if born before the day, are slaves." (Maria *vs.* Surbaugh, Feb. T., 1824; 2 Rand's Va. Rep., and other cases. Wheeler, p. 32.)

(*i*) "Children born during a qualified manumission of their mothers, are born slaves." (McCutchen et al. *vs.* Marshall et al., Jan. T.; 8 Peters' U. S. Rep., 220, and another case. Wheeler, p. 35.)

(*j*) Intermarriages with whites are punished by enslavement. (Maryland, Act of 1717, chap. 13, sect. 5.) "If any *free* negro or mulatto *intermarry* with any *white* woman; or if any *white* man shall intermarry with any negro or mulatto woman, such negro or mulatto shall become *a slave during life*, except mulattoes born of white women, &c., who shall become servants for seven years." (Stroud, p. 19.) For "a white man" to live in adulterous concubinage with his slave woman, incurs no penalty at all. Adulterers are entitled Honorable, but marriage is punished by the Judge!

(*k*) Innumerable free persons of color are kidnapped and sold by the operation of the laws excluding colored witnesses, and forbidding *colored* persons to resist *white* persons. In Philadelphia, *within two years, more than thirty persons, mostly children, known to be free*, were kidnapped and carried away, and *only five* of them, with great difficulty and expense, were reclaimed. (Stroud's Sketch, p. 74.)

This process of kidnapping is facilitated by the fact that such vast numbers of slaves are carried from State to State, not only by the removal of "owners," but by the inter-State slave-trade. The kidnapper of *free* colored persons readily passes for a removing owner, or for a dealer in slaves; and, in fact, many of the dealers are themselves kidnappers of free negroes and mulattoes. Persons ostensibly or in reality employed to arrest fugitives are known frequently to practise the same villany even in the free States, and under this cover they are generally secure. The colored person seized cannot testify in a slave State, and no colored person can testify for him. At the South, very few white persons would pay the least attention to their protestations of being free. It would seldom or never embarrass the auctioneer, or diminish the number and amount of the bids. This is evident from the fact that "hundreds of advertisements in the Southern papers" of sales of negroes at auction, and of runaways, *describe* them as *claiming to be free!* See Weld's "Slavery as it is," pp. 162–3, where specimens of such advertisements may be found, one of them describing a negro "*who was originally from New-York.*"

(*l*) Free people of color, by passing out of a free

State into a slave State, (where by the Federal Constitution they are entitled to all the rights of free citizens,) incur penalties of fines for so doing, which, if unable to pay, they may be *enslaved!* (Jay's Inquiry, p. 24. See chapter on "Liberties of Free People of Color.")

(*m*) Negroes unlawfully imported from Africa are enslaved, not only when clandestinely smuggled, (which is done to a great extent,) but, strange to tell, when brought into port by capture of naval officers! A case occurring at Savannah, and before alluded to, is narrated circumstantially in Weld's "Slavery as it is," pp. 139–40. So openly and systematically has this been done, that the States of Louisiana, Georgia, and Alabama, have enacted statutes for the express purpose of having the slaves sold for the benefit of the State Treasury! A law of Congress, conferring power on the State Legislatures to dispose of the slaves illegally imported, was not repealed until 1819. And the law of Alabama (of 1823) is still more recent, and in open defiance of the laws of the United States abolishing the African slave-trade! (See Stroud's Sketch, pp. 158–164.)

And the Courts have accordingly laid down the principle, that "a slave does not become free on his being illegally imported into the State." Such is the marginal note to the case of "Gomez *vs.* Bonneval, June T., 1819; 6 Martin's Lou. Rep. 656.—*Per Cur.*, *Derbigny, J.:* The petitioner is a negro in actual state of slavery: he claims his freedom, *and is bound to prove it.* In his attempt, however, to prove that he was free before he was introduced into this country, he has failed, so that his claim now rests entirely on the laws prohibiting the introduction of slaves in the United States. That the plaintiff was imported since that prohibition does exist, is a fact sufficiently established by the evidence. What right he has acquired under the laws prohibiting such importation is the only question which we have to examine. Formerly, while the Act dividing Louisiana into two Territories was in force in this country, slaves introduced here in contravention of it were freed by the operation of that law; but that Act was merged in the legislative provisions which were subsequently enacted on the subject of the importation of slaves into the United States generally. Under *the now existing laws*, the individuals thus imported acquire no personal rights. They are mere passive beings, who are disposed of according to the will of the different Legislatures. *In this country they are to remain slaves, and to be sold for the benefit of the State.* The plaintiff, therefore, has nothing to claim as a freeman; and as to a mere change of master, should such be his wish, he cannot be listened to in a Court of justice." (Wheeler, pp. 380–1.)

2. But the descendants of Africans are not the only subjects of American slavery. The *native Indians* have also been enslaved, and *their* descendants are still in slavery. In South Carolina, by Act of 1740, "All negroes, *Indians*, (free Indians in

amity with this Government, and negroes, mulattoes, and mestizoes who are now free, excepted,) mulattoes and mestizoes who now are or shall hereafter be in this province, and all their issue and offspring born or to be born, shall be and are hereby declared to be and to remain for ever hereafter, absolute slaves, and shall *follow the condition of the mother*." (2 Brevard's Digest, 229.) Similar in Georgia. (Prince's Dig., 446, Act of 1770.) And in Mississippi. (Rev. Code Miss. of 1823, p. 369.) And in Virginia. (1 Rev. Code of 1819.) And in Kentucky. (2 Littell and Swigert's Dig., 1149–50.) And in Louisiana. (Civil Code Lou., art. 183. Stroud's Sketch, pp. 11, 12–15.) *Same in New-Jersey*, by decision of Supreme Court, 1797. (Stroud, p. 16.)

And finally,

3. *Whites* are enslaved. Several known instances have occurred already of the successful kidnapping of *free* whites, without a drop of negro or Indian blood in their veins! And the process of intermixture of the races is now so far advanced, and is so rapidly going forward, that a "perfectly white complexion, light blue eyes, and flaxen hair," are scarcely a presumptive evidence of freedom. Persons thus described are advertised as runaway slaves; are liable to be pursued with muskets and bloodhounds, shot, maimed, captured, brought before United States Marshals, sworn to be slaves, given up and sent to the rice and cotton and sugar plantations of the South, *without trial by jury*, and by a "summary" process that precludes any thing deserving the

name of an investigation. Sometimes, under a peremptory refusal to wait a few hours for witnesses. Yet the people imagine themselves free, and their liberties secure under this enactment, (the Fugitive Slave Bill of 1850,) which, *while it makes no distinction of color*, forbids them, under pains and penalties, to "harbor" and "entertain" each other when thus pursued! By the estimate of Henry Clay, (speech in Senate, 1839,) one hundred and fifty years will obliterate the distinctions of race and color in this country, but without abolishing slavery! Reposing, as it does, by his showing, upon the "rights of property," and "sanctified and sanctioned" already "by two centuries of legislation," its conservators look for its perpetuity, as they do for the perpetuity of property in "brood mares and their increase." For "that *is* property which the law declares *to be* property." The blacks will not be the slaves of the whites, but the poorer will be the slaves of the wealthier; and the most they can hope for is that, *perhaps*, they will be kept "fat and sleek!" Their idolized statesmen, their venerated religious teachers, can promise them nothing better. Nor do they seem to desire it! The "innocent legal relation" of slave ownership conducts us to this result, and it leaves us here.

In our chapter concerning "Fugitives from Slavery," it was shown that the State of Maryland, at an early date, (1715,) enacted laws by which *all* persons, *irrespective of color*, were forbidden to travel out of their own county without an official pass;

and "if apprehended, not being sufficiently known, nor able to give a good account of themselves," the magistrates might deal with them as with runaways, and sell them temporarily, to pay their fines. Our Fugitive Slave Bill of 1850, in like manner, *knows nothing of color;* and its provisions are more stringent and humiliating than the *old law of Maryland!*

The reader is referred to Jay's View, pp. 83–87, for a number of advertisements of runaway slaves, in which they are described as being *white.*

As for example—

"$100 Reward.—The above reward will be paid for the apprehension of my man William. He is a very bright mulatto, *straight yellowish hair.* I have no doubt he will change his name, and try to pass himself for a *white* man, which he may be able to do, unless to a close observer.—T. S. Pitchard."

"$100 Reward.—Ran away from James Hyhart, Paris, Ky., &c., the mulatto boy Norton, &c. Would be taken for a *white* boy, if not closely examined. His hair is black and straight, &c."—*New-Orleans Free American*, 11th Aug. 1836.

Anderson Bowles advertises, in the *Richmond Whig*, 6th Jan. 1836, his "*negro!*" who has "straight hair," and is "nearly white;" so that "a stranger" would suppose there was "*no African blood in him.*" "He was with my boy Dick a short time since at Norfolk, *and offered to sell him*, but escaped, under pretense of being a WHITE MAN."

In the *Newbern Spectator*, 13th March, 1837, John T. Lane advertises "William, about 19 years old, *quite white*, and would not readily be taken for a slave."

Edwin Peck, Mobile, April 22, 1837, offers $100 reward for a slave named Sam, "*light sandy hair, blue eyes, ruddy complexion;* is so *white* as very easily to pass for a *white man*."

In the *New-Orleans Bee* of June 22, 1831, P. Balie advertises as a runaway, "Maria, *with a clear white complexion*."

"Mr. Paxton, a Virginia writer, tells us in his work on Slavery, that 'the best blood of Virginia runs in the veins of slaves.'" (Jay's View, p. 85.)

"Dr. Torrey, in his work on Domestic Slavery in the United States, p. 14," relates, that "not far from Fredericktown there was a slave estate, on which there were several *white females*, of as fair and elegant appearance as white ladies in general, held in legal bondage as slaves." (Ib., pp. 85–6.)

"White lady fugitives" have been hunted in the State of New-York, and have taken refuge in Canada. (Vide Utica "*Friend of Man*," and the Syracuse papers.)

"A Missouri paper, reporting the trial of a slave boy, says, 'All the physiological marks of distinction which characterize the African descent had disappeared.'" (Jay's View, p. 86.)

Mr. Niles, in his Register, tells us that John C. Calhoun related a similar instance. (Ib., pp.86–7.)

"Mary Gillmore, of Philadelphia, claimed as a runaway slave in 1835, was proved to be the child of Irish parents, and had not a single drop of African blood in her veins." (Ib., p. 86.)

PART II.

RELATION OF THE SLAVE TO SOCIETY AND TO CIVIL GOVERNMENT.

CHAPTER I.

OF THE GROUND AND NATURE OF THE SLAVE'S CIVIL CONDITION.

The Civil Condition of the Slave grows out of his relation to his Master as "property," and is determined and defined by it.

IF slaves were "deemed, reputed, and adjudged in law" to be "sentient beings," and not "things," then their relation to society and to civil government would be the relation of HUMAN BEINGS. But this is directly the opposite of the fact. "Slaves" are "deemed, *sold*, taken, and adjudged in law to be *chattels* personal, in the hands of their *owners* and possessors, their administrators and assigns, *to all intents, constructions, and purposes whatsoever.*" Their relation to society and to civil government is, accordingly, the relation of BRUTES.

The only real exception to this, or modification of it, is where the interests of the "owner," the wants of society, or the exigences of the Government require an anomalous departure from the principle of slave chattelhood, by the temporary and partial recognition of their humanity. Such exceptions and modifications are never made for the benefit of the slave. They enable the Government to *punish*, as a human being, the poor creature whom, in *no* other respect, it recognizes as such! The slave is subjected to the *control* of the Government, but is not considered entitled to its *protection.*

The slave cannot be considered by the Government as entitled to its protection while he is not regarded by it as having any rights to be protected. And the Government that recognizes and protects slave chattelhood has already, in that very act, denied to the slave the possession of any rights by denying to him the right of *self-ownership*, which is the foundation and parent stock of all other rights, and without which they cannot exist.

Having no right to himself, to his bones, muscles, and intellect, (being all of them the property of his "owner,") he has no right to his own industry, to its wages or its products; no right to property or capability of possessing it, as already shown. Of course he has no *rights of property* to be protected by the Government, and none of the rights that grow out of them.

Having no recognized right of making any contract, he has no contracts with others to be enforced by the Government, and no one has any legal pecuniary claims upon him to be enforced. He can neither sue nor be sued. This is no arbitrary rule. It is the inevitable result of his chattelhood.

Unable to contract marriage, as already seen, he can bring no action at law against the violator of his bed. Having no marital or parental rights, he has none for the Government to protect.

Not being accounted a person, but a thing, he can have no personal rights to be protected—no rights of reputation or character—no right to education—no rights of conscience—no rights of personal security—no social rights—no political capabilities or rights—not even the right of petition, as the Federal Congress (very consistently with its recognition of legal human chattelhood) have affirmed. It would be an anomaly to receive the testimony of such an one in a Court of law!

It is futile, it is absurd, it is self-contradictory, it is short-sighted and foolish (to say nothing more severe) for any persons to find fault with any of these things while they recognize as innocent and valid "*the legal relation of master and slave*," the relation of *slave ownership*, which includes, implies, and necessitates it all. Such persons should ask themselves seriously what they *would* have?

Would they have the Government stultify itself, and add mockery to injustice by pretending to attempt known impossibilities in the enactment of contradictions? by making a show of civil protection where none is intended, or where they have rendered it impossible? What protection *can* they bestow so long as, by sustaining or even permitting or tolerating human chattelhood, *or failing to suppress it as a crime*, they leave not the slave the possession of one single right of humanity *to be* protected?

Or, suppose the Government to be honest and

successful in its attempts to confer upon the slave *civil rights*, to recognize and treat him as a member and component element of *civil society*. Suppose it *to protect*, instead of denying these rights—rights of conscience--rights of security--rights of reputation--right to education—free speech—parental rights—marital rights—right of testimony—right to sue and be sued—right to make contracts—rights of property—right to his earnings and products. What would become of the right of slave ownership, "the legal relation of master and slave?" Would it not vanish and disappear? Assuredly it would.

These thoughts open a wide field for reflection and remark, if we could spare room.

The Hebrew servitude, so often cited as a precedent for modern slavery, was wanting in its essential element, human chattelhood. Its abundant recognition and guaranty of the *civil rights* of servants affords demonstrative proof of this.

In the Spanish, Portuguese, French, and even the (recent) British West India types of slavery, we see the principle of human chattelhood less perfectly developed than in our own, less consistently enforced. They exhibit faint recognitions of civil rights in the enslaved. They are less inveterate, and hence (under the same appliances) less difficult to be overthrown. In our country, where so much is *said* and *known* of human rights, the slave power has been compelled to fortify and entrench itself in the most unlimited and unmitigated system of despotism ever known or conceived.

In dealing with *such* a type of slavery, it is especially important to remember that nothing is to be accomplished without striking directly at the root. Attempts at ameliorations, restrictions, limitations, and gradual removal, are signally out of place here. *Such* a despotism, under such a form of government, and in such a state of society as ours, and at such a crisis as that which is now reached, must be overwhelmed and uprooted speedily, or it will overwhelm and uproot all that does not harmonize with and uphold it. But we must not enlarge.

The statements made in *this* chapter, like those made in the first chapter of the former series, will be found to contain the key to the chapters that follow. And the present series is the sequel to the former one.

The single idea of human chattelhood, or of slave ownership, carried out in all possible directions, gives us the details of the entire code of slavery. Take away *that*, and they all vanish. Retain it, and they all stand firmly. The Courts in the slave States understand this.

"A slave is in absolute bondage. *He has no civil rights.*" So said Judge Crenshaw, in Brandon et al. *vs.* Planters' and Merchants' Bank of Huntsville, Jan. T., 1838; 1 Stewart's Ala. Rep., 320. Same principle in Bynum *vs.* Bostwick, 4 Desauss., 266. Wheeler, p. 6.

"*Slaves are deprived of all civil rights.*" "*Emancipation gives to the slave his civil rights.*" (Judge Matthews, in Girod *vs.* Lewis, May T., 1819; 6

Martin's Lou. Rep., 559. Wheeler, p. 199.) If this be true in Louisiana, with its relics of the *Code Noir*, we may be well assured that it is true of the codes of the other States.

CHAPTER II.

NO ACCESS OF SLAVES TO THE JUDICIARY, AND NO HONEST PROVISION FOR TESTING THE CLAIMS OF THE ENSLAVED TO FREEDOM.

"A Slave cannot be a party to a civil suit." (Stroud's Sketch, p. 76.)

"A SLAVE cannot be a party to a suit, except in the single case where a negro is held as a slave and he claims to be free." [We omit the references to authorities here cited.] "It would be an idle form and ceremony to make a slave a party to a suit, by the instrumentality of which he could recover nothing; or, if a recovery could be had, the instant it was recovered, would belong to the master. A slave can possess nothing. He can hold nothing. He is therefore not a competent party to a suit. And the same rule prevails wherever slavery is tolerated, whether there be legislative enactments upon the subject or not." (Note to p. 197, in Wheeler's Law of Slavery. Case of Berard *vs.* Berard, before cited.)

We proceed to examine the condition of the slave in reference to suits for freedom.

"In all cases where the slave alleges to be free, he

is of course a party. He may have a *habeas corpus*, and if there be a false return, may sue upon it. Or he may bring a trespass for assault and battery, and false imprisonment, in which action, the defendant, *to justify himself*, must plead that *he is his slave*. In many States he may proceed by petitions for freedom." (Note in Wheeler, p. 197.)

In inquiring after "the origin of the relation and its subjects," (Chapter XXIII. of the former series,) it was ascertained that colored persons who *cannot prove* their freedom may be enslaved; that colored persons, whether negroes or mulattoes, whether bond or free, cannot be admitted as witnesses to prove their freedom, (a free colored mother not being permitted to come into Court to identify, under oath, her own kidnapped free child, torn from her arms the day previous, nor give testimony to the fact, nor identify the kidnapper!) it was ascertained, further, that *color* was held to be presumptive evidence of the condition of slavery. The bearing of all this upon law-suits for the recovery of freedom will be readily appreciated. (Hudgins *vs.* Wrights, 1 Hen. and Munf. Va. Rep., 134.) Judge Roane said: "In the case of a person visibly appearing to be a negro, the presumption is, in this country, that he is a slave, and it is incumbent on him to make out his right to freedom; but in the case of a person visibly appearing to be a *white* man, or an *Indian*, the presumption is that he is free, and it is necessary for his adversary to show that he is a slave." (Wheeler, p. 394.)

The same principle appears in other cases, and seems to be the general rule.

South Carolina.—The act of 1740 provides that "if any negro, Indian, mulatto, or mestizo, claim his or her freedom, it shall be lawful" for such person "to apply to the Judges," &c., who are empowered to appoint for the applicant a guardian, to prosecute in his or her behalf, &c., &c. "And if judgment shall be given for the plaintiff, a special entry shall be made, declaring that the ward of the plaintiff is free, and the jury shall assess damages, with full costs of suit;—*but in case judgment shall be given for the defendant, the said Court is hereby fully empowered to inflict* SUCH CORPORAL PUNISHMENT, NOT EXTENDING TO LIFE OR LIMB, *on the ward of the plaintiff, as they, in their discretion, shall think fit.* Provided that, in any action or suit to be brought in pursuance of the direction in this Act, THE BURTHEN OF THE PROOF SHALL LAY ON THE WARD OF THE PLAINTIFF, *and it shall always be* PRESUMED *that every negro, Indian, mulatto and mestizo is a slave, unless the contrary be made to appear;* (the Indians in amity with the Government excepted, in which case the burthen of proof shall be on the defendant.)" (2 Brevard's Digest, 229–30.)

In Georgia, the Act of May 10, 1770, is almost literally a copy of the preceding. (Prince's Digest, 446.)

The slave, it seems, must first find a white friend willing to incur the expense and trouble of conducting the suit, liable, in case of failure, to lose the costs.

Then he must find *white* witnesses to prove his freedom, instead of demanding that the pretended "owner" (as in the case of other property) prove his right to ownership. And then, for the crime of losing his case in Court, (the fault, perhaps, of Judge and jury, even by their own laws,) he may be subjected, by the *same* Court, to corporal punishment, resulting perhaps, in "*death by moderate correction!!!*" But this is not all.

In South Carolina, by Act of 1802, (by way of progress in sixty-two years!) "*the guardian*" (in a trial for freedom) "of a slave" (who may have been illegally imported into the State, and is, on that account, by the same law, declared to be *free*) "claiming his freedom shall be liable to *double costs* of suit, if his action shall be adjudged groundless; and shall be liable to pay to the bona fide owner of such slave, all such *damages* as shall be assessed by a jury, and adjudged by any Court of Common Pleas." (2 Brevard's Digest, 260.)

In Maryland, *the attorney*, in a trial for freedom, must pay all the costs, unless the Court shall be of opinion that there was probable cause for supposing that the petitioner had a right to freedom." (Act of 1796, chap. 67, sect. 25.) And on such a trial, the master (the defendant) is allowed twelve peremptory challenges as to the jurors. (Ib., sect. 24.)

In Virginia, "for *aiding and abetting* a slave, in a trial for freedom, if the claimant fail in his suit, a fine of one hundred dollars is imposed." And this is by the "REVISED Code" (of 1819), 482.

Missouri mercifully allows the slave, on permission of Court, to "sue as a poor person." So far, the law appears praiseworthy. Yet "it is made to depend upon the arbitrament of the Court, or even of a single Judge, whether the petitioner shall be heard by a jury at all." (Stroud, p. 78.)

In Alabama, the objectionable parts of the Missouri law are *retained*, and the beneficial provisions *omitted!* (Ib. Toulmin's Digest, 632.)

It is evident that very few of the thousands of free colored persons kidnapped into slavery, or otherwise held, contrary to even the Southern laws, will ever be able to institute a suit at law for their freedom; and it is equally evident that very few of those who may get their cases into Court will ever derive any benefit from the process, but only secure to themselves a terrible punishment in the first instance, and worse treatment from their masters afterwards. The spirit of these laws warrants us to say this.

CHAPTER III.

REJECTION OF TESTIMONY OF SLAVES AND FREE COLORED PERSONS.

Slavery is upheld by suppressing the testimony of its Victims.

"A SLAVE cannot be a witness against a white person, either in a civil or criminal cause." (Stroud's Sketch, p. 65.)

"It is an inflexible and universal rule of slave law, founded in one or two States upon *usage*, in others sanctioned by *express legislation*, THAT THE TESTIMONY OF A COLORED PERSON, WHETHER BOND OR FREE, CANNOT BE RECEIVED AGAINST A WHITE PERSON. (Ib., p. 27. Same in Wheeler's Law of Slavery, 193–5.)

In Virginia, the Act of Assembly is as follows: "Any negro or mulatto, bond or free, shall be a good witness in pleas of the Commonwealth, for or against negroes or mulattoes, bond or free, or in civil pleas where free negroes or mulattoes shall alone be parties, *and in no other cases whatever*." (1 Revised Code, 422.)

Similar in Missouri. (Missouri Laws, 600.) And

in Mississippi. (Revised Code, 372.) And in Kentucky. (2 Littell and Swigert's Digest, 1150.) And in Alabama. (Toulmin's Dig., 627.) And in Maryland. (Maryland Laws, Act of 1717, chap. 13, sects. 2, 3; and Act of 1751, chap. 14, sect. 4.) And in North Carolina and Tennessee. (Act of 1777, chap. 2, sect. 42.) And in the free State of OHIO. (Act of January 25, 1807.)

In South Carolina and in Louisiana there are enactments which, in direct allusion to this feature of *their* laws, and reciting in a preamble, that "*Whereas many cruelties may be committed on slaves because no white person may be present to give evidence of the same, unless some method be provided for the better discovery of the offense*," &c., &c., *Be it enacted*, &c., &c.: The only remedy provided is, that "when no *white* person shall be present," or, being present, shall refuse to testify, "the owner or other person having charge of such slave [who shall have "suffered in life, limb, member," &c.] shall be deemed guilty and punished," "*unless* such owner or other person, &c., can make the contrary appear by good and sufficient evidence, OR SHALL, BY HIS OWN OATH, *clear and exculpate himself;*" and the Court may administer the oath and "*acquit the offender*, if clear proof of the offense be not made by *two* witnesses at least." (2 Brevard's Dig., 242.)

Judge Stroud (in his Sketch, &c., p. 76) considers this "a modification of the former law, not for the protection of the slave, BUT FOR THE ESPECIAL BENEFIT OF A CRUEL MASTER OR OVERSEER."

In most of the slaveholding States, the owners of slaves are required by law "to keep at least one white person on each plantation to which a certain number of slaves is attached." (Stroud, p. 67.) This indicates the previous absence of white persons, and the consequent lack of white witnesses. Whether the law was ostensibly for the remedy of that defect, or whether it was for the greater security against the slaves, does not appear. It is hardly credible that a white person is employed for the *former* object. And as most of the present overseers are whites, it may be inferred that the design was to discountenance the employment of slaves or other colored persons as overseers. Be this as it may, a white overseer answers the requisitions of the law, and he could hardly be a witness *against* himself, though specially authorized to *exculpate* himself by his own oath!

Chief Justice Ottley, of St. Vincent's, in answer to Parliamentary inquiries proposed to him in 1791, said:

"The only instances in which their [the slaves'] persons *appear* to be protected by the *letter* of the law, are in cases of murder, dismemberment, and mutilation; and in these cases, as the evidence of slaves is never admitted against a white man, the difficulty of establishing the facts is so great, that *white men are, in a manner, put beyond the reach of the law.*"

Sir William Young, Governor of Tobago in 1811, and an advocate of slavery, said: "*I think the slaves have no protection.* In this, as I doubt not in every other island, *there are laws* for the protection of the slaves, and *good ones*, but circumstances in the administration of whatever law, render it a dead letter. When the intervention of the law is *most required*, it will have the *least* effect; as, in most cases, where a vindictive and cruel master *has care* to commit the most atrocious cruelties, even to murder his slave, NO FREE PERSON BEING PRESENT TO WITNESS THE ACT," &c., &c.

Many others, holding official stations in the British West Indies during the existence of slavery, have testified to the same general fact, the insufficiency of all laws for the protection of slaves, in consequence of rejecting slave testimony. (Vide Stephen's West Indian Slavery, pp. 168–9.)

The case is too plain to require either testimony or argument. A community or a Government that could tolerate such rejection of testimony—the testimony of the defenseless against those holding and daily exercising despotic power over them—must be resolutely bent on oppressing instead of protecting them.

Yet the reasonableness of the rule is beyond question, if the "innocent legal relation" is to be preserved. It would be an absurdity for chattels to come into Court and bear testimony against their owners! They could not *be* "chattels, to all intents, constructions, and purposes whatsoever." They could not *remain* chattels at all. The power to testify against their owners and overseers would imply the right of protection from assaults by them. "The slave, to REMAIN a slave," said Judge Ruffin, "must be sensible that there is NO APPEAL from his master." Allow slaves to testify, and the hitherto unimagined secrets of the Bastile would explode like an earthquake. Universal humanity would unite in one general crusade, and break down the whole fabric.

CHAPTER IV.

SUBJECTION TO ALL WHITE PERSONS.

" Submission is required of the Slave, not to the will of the Master only, but to the will of all other White Persons." (Stroud's Sketch, pp. 96–7.)

In Georgia it is enacted, that "If any slave shall *presume* to strike *any white person*, such slave, upon trial and conviction before the Justice or Justices, according to the directions of this Act, shall, for the first offense, suffer such punishment as the said Justice or Justices shall, in his or their discretion, think fit, not extending to life or limb; and for the *second* offense, suffer DEATH." "Provided always, that such striking, &c., be not done by the command and in the defense of the OWNER or OTHER PERSON having the care and government of such slave, in which case the slave shall be wholly excused, and the owner or other person, &c., shall be answerable, as if the act had been committed by himself." (Prince's Digest, 450.)

South Carolina has an Act in the same words, except that death is the penalty of the *third* offense, instead of the *second.* (2 Brevard's Digest, 235.)

In Maryland, for this offense, the offender's ears may be cropped, though he be a *free* black. (Act of 1723, chap. 15, sect. 4.)

In Kentucky there is the same prohibition; and, as in Maryland, *free* colored persons are included. Penalty, "thirty lashes on his or *her* bare back, well laid on." (Littell and Swigert's Digest, 1153.)

In Virginia, the same as in Kentucky, from 1680 till 1792, when the following exception was added: "Except in those cases where it shall appear to said Justice that such negro or mulatto was *wantonly assaulted*, and lifted his or her hand in his or her self-defense." (1 Rev. Code, 426–7.)

In Maryland, "If any slave shall *happen* to be slain for refusing to surrender him or herself, contrary to law, or in unlawful resisting any officer, *or other person*, who shall endeavor to apprehend such slave or slaves, &c., such officer or *other person so killing such slave, as aforesaid*, making resistance, shall be and is by this Act *indemnified* from any prosecution for such killing aforesaid," &c. (Maryland Laws, Act of 1751, chap. 14, sect. 9.) This is cited by Judge Stroud as a specimen of the laws of several States, (pp. 98–9.)

South Carolina.—Act of 1740: "If any slave who shall be out of the house or plantation where such slave shall live or shall be usually employed, or without some white person in company with such slave, shall *refuse to submit* to undergo the examination of *any white person*, it shall be lawful for any such white person to pursue, apprehend, and moderately correct such slave; and if such slave shall assault and strike such white person, such slave may be *lawfully killed*"!!! (2 Brevard's Digest, 231.)

It does not appear that any of these laws recognize or contemplate any self-defense by the slave, male or female, from the most villanous assaults of *any white person*, except the Act of Virginia. And as the "negro or mulatto," whether bond or free, cannot lodge a complaint, or even testify, it is not easy to see how the exception can be made available for his or her benefit. Such laws illustrate the general position already laid down, that the Government cannot secure to the master his assumed right of slave ownership, and yet extend to the slave civil protection. If the negro be *a chattel*, he must needs be restrained from straying; he must be held subject, like other domestic animals, to the superior race holding dominion over him. It would be preposterous for the Legislature to attempt doing this by a process which should at the same time provide for his protection as a man! It would be abusive to demand this at their hands, if the "relation" of human chattelhood is to be held legal and innocent!

Yet the existence of such laws renders more than probable, and even certain, the common prevalence of the worst outrages that could be imagined. The best laws cannot fully protect the weaker portion of a community against the stronger. The weak must be left utterly defenseless when all protecting laws are only repealed. But the climax is reached when, *by express statute*, each member of the weaker class is placed under the absolute control of *any one* of the dominant class; when resistance is forbidden on penalty of stripes and cropping by the public authorities, with the liability of being "lawfully killed" by the assailant! If civil government were designed for human demoralization and torture, it is not easy to see how its ends could be more effectually reached.

CHAPTER V.

PENAL LAWS AGAINST SLAVES.

The Laws are unequal—their administration despotic—their execution barbarous. Even this is exceeded by "Lynch Law."

THE slave, who is but "*a chattel*" on all *other* occasions, with not one solitary attribute of personality accorded to him, becomes "*a person*" whenever he is to be *punished!* He is the only being in the universe to whom is denied all self-direction and free agency, but who is, nevertheless, held responsible for his conduct, and amenable to law. Forbidden to *read* the law, and kept as ignorant and as unenlightened as possible, he is nevertheless accounted criminal for acts which are deemed innocent in others, and punished with a severity from which all others are exempted. He is under the *control* of law, though *unprotected by* law, and can know law only as an enemy, and not as a friend.

The following statement is evidently as favorable a one as could be made, yet it attests the main facts of the case; and what seems to have been intended as a palliation is the strongest condemnation of the slave system, especially of this feature of it.

"Much has been said of the disparity of punishment between the white inhabitants and the slaves and negroes of the same State; that slaves are punished with much more severity, for the commission of similar crimes by white persons, than the latter. The charge is undoubtedly true to a considerable extent. It must be remembered that the primary object of the enactment of penal laws is *the protection and security of those who make them.** THE SLAVE HAS NO AGENCY IN MAKING THEM. He is indeed one cause of the apprehended evils to the other class, which those laws are expected to remedy. That he should be held amenable for the violation of those rules established for the security of the other, is the *natural result of the state in which he is placed.* And the severity of those rules will always bear a relation to that danger, real or ideal, of the other class.† It has been so among all nations, *and will ever continue to be so*, while the disparity between bond and free remains. In a practical treatise it would probably be considered out of place to collect the various statutes in relation to whipping and other punishment of slaves, to be found in the *statute books* of the various States." (Note in Wheeler's Law of Slavery, pp. 222–3.)

* The "primary" and *only* object of all *honest* legislation is the protection of the *equal rights of all.*

† From whence comes that "danger, real or ideal," that calls for such severe laws? What but injustice, and a *consciousness* of that injustice, could make the governing party thus apprehensive of "danger?"

The punishment of slaves by their owners has already been examined. Their punishment by civil government, or by society, is the topic now under review. Not a few specimens have fallen under our notice already, as connected with other points of inquiry. We must briefly recall these, and connect them with others of a like character.

We have seen how the "cruel punishments" inflicted by the master are expressly sanctioned by the Legislatures, and how the public arm, with its sheriffs and prisons, is at the beck of the slaveholder, as his agents and instruments, whenever he wishes his slaves punished! We have seen, too, some few specimens of direct penal infliction upon the slave by the Government. For the crime of earning property and making bargains, we have seen his property seized and confiscated for the benefit of the whites, who pretended to doubt whether he could take care of himself! For the misdemeanor of "hiring himself out," even with the consent of his master, we have seen him "apprehended" as a felon. For seeking liberty, and the protection of law, we have seen him proclaimed an outlaw, and "lawfully killed!" For attending a religious meeting in the evening, conducted by *whites*, and staying till the close of the meeting, we have seen him, with his wife and children, locked up in the watch-house till morning, with no bed but the floor. For keeping a weapon or club, we have seen him subjected, by a cowardly code, to public whipping! For being absent without a "pass," to visit a wife or child, we have seen him under the same sentence! For riding on horseback, whipped or *branded.* For losing a cause at Court, when sueing for freedom, any "corporal punishment, not extending to life or limb," with the hazard of "death by moderate correction."

Free negroes, for entertaining or assisting fugitive slaves, or giving or selling certificates of freedom, we have seen subjected to heavy fines; and, in default of payment, *sale into slavery.* For being arrested on *suspicion* of being slaves, we have seen them fined and enslaved. For "*presuming* to strike a white person," punished with whipping or cropping! In the case of *slaves*, for the second or third offense, DEATH!

All these are but specimens of similar legislation. For taking away or loosing a boat, a slave in South Carolina is to receive thirty-nine lashes; "for the second offense, shall *forfeit and have cut off from his head* ONE EAR." (2 Brev. Dig., 228.) So, as to the first offense, in North Carolina and Tennessee. (Haywood's Manual, 78.)

"For having *any article* of property [in Kentucky] without a ticket of permission from his master, *particularly specifying* the same, and authorizing it to be sold by the slave, ten lashes, by order of the captain of the patrollers;" and "if the slave be taken before a magistrate, thirty-nine lashes may be ordered." (Littell and Swigert's Dig., 11.) Also in North Carolina and Tennessee. (Haywood's Manual, 529.) And in Mississippi. (Rev. Code, 390.)

A slave in Kentucky, being at an *unlawful assembly*,* the captain of patrollers may inflict ten lashes upon him. (Littell and Swigert's Dig., 981; also 2 Missouri Laws, 741, sect. 2; and ibid., 614.) If taken before a magistrate, he may direct thirty-nine lashes.

To beat the Patuxent river, (to catch fish,) ten lashes. (Maryland Laws, 1796, chap. 32, sect. 3, &c., &c.)

In North Carolina, a "slave, hunting with dogs in the woods even of his master, is subjected to a whipping of thirty lashes." (Haywood's Manual, 524, Act of 1753.)

We reserve for their appropriate chapters, the penal laws against mental instruction, and assembling together for religious worship, except with white persons.

The reader will have noticed that a large portion of the offenses thus punished are not considered offenses when committed by *white* persons! Another feature deserves notice.

"In Virginia, *by the Revised Code* (of 1819,) there are seventy-one offenses for which the penalty is DEATH when committed by slaves, and imprisonment when committed by whites." (Jay's Inquiry, p. 134.)

In Mississippi there are seventeen offenses punishable with DEATH when committed by slaves, which, if committed by white persons, are either

* Meetings for "mental instruction" and "religious worship" are among the "*unlawful assemblies*" forbidden, as will be seen in another chapter.

punished by fines or imprisonment, or punishment "not provided for by statute," or at "common law." (Stroud's Sketch, p. 110–11.)

"Where human life is so cheap, and human suffering so little regarded, it is not to be expected that the dispensers of slave justice will submit to be troubled with all those forms and ceremonies which the common law has devised for the protection of innocence. We have seen that, in many instances, *any white* person may, instanter, discharge the functions of judge, jury, and executioner. In innumerable instances, all these functions are united in a single justice of the peace; and in South Carolina, Virginia, and Louisiana, LIFE may be taken, according to law, without intervention of grand or petit jurors. In other States a trial by jury is granted in *capital* cases; but in no one State, it is believed, is it thought worth while to trouble a *grand jury* with presenting a slave. In most of the slave States, the ordinary tribunal for slaves charged with offenses not capital, is composed of justices and freeholders, or of justices only. A white man cannot be convicted of misdemeanor, except by the unanimous verdict of twelve of his peers. In Louisiana, if the Court is *equally divided* as to the guilt of a slave, judgment is rendered against him!" (Jay's Inquiry, p. 135.)

The proper idea of trial by jury includes a trial by the "*peers*" or EQUALS of the accused. *There is no such jury trial for the slave!* Trial by jury of slaves would soon upset the "legal relation" of slave owner!

In Tennessee, the *sheriff* is empowered to make *selection* of "*three justices to preside on the trial, and twelve housekeepers being* SLAVEHOLDERS *to serve as a jury*" *!!!* (Tennessee Laws of 1819, chap. 35.) By a modification of this law in 1831, "House-holders *may* serve as jurors, *if slaveholders cannot be had*"*!* (Child's Appeal, p. 70.)

"In 1832, *thirty-five* slaves were executed in Charleston, in pursuance of the sentence of a Court consisting of two justices and five freeholders, on charge of an intended insurrection. No indictments, no summoning of jurors, no challenges for cause or favor, no seclusion of the triers from intercourse with those who might bias their judgment, preceded this unparalleled destruction of human life." (Jay's Inquiry, p. 135.)

Though no *colored* person, bond or free, can testify in any case where any *white* person is concerned, yet the evidence of "*all free Indians without oath, and of any slave without oath,*" *may be taken for or against a slave!* And among the "*meritorious services*" for which freedom is conferred, the most important is "*information of crimes committed by a slave.*" What a temptation for one slave to bear false testimony against another! See Stroud's Sketch, p. 126, where the authorities are cited for several States where this law prevails, viz: South Carolina, Virginia, North Carolina, Tennessee, Kentucky, and Mississippi; with conditions, in Georgia and Louisiana.

The law of South Carolina provides expressly, that slave trials shall proceed "*in the most summary and expeditious manner;*" and also that, in case of conviction, the "Justice shall award such *manner of death*" as will "be most effectual to deter others," &c. (James's Dig., 392–3.) This authorized "the burning of a negro woman to death, as may be found in the daily prints of 1820." (Stroud, p. 124.) Any *other* tortures might be inflicted.

"The last authorized edition of the laws of Maryland" (said Judge Stroud, in 1827) authorizes "to have *the right hand cut off*, to be hanged in the usual manner, *the head severed from the body, the body divided into four quarters, and the head and quarters set up in the most public places of the county where such fact was committed.*" (Stroud, p. 117.)

The burning to death a free colored man near St. Louis, the frequent infliction of murderous outrages by irresponsible "Lynch Committees" all over the South, by the testimony of their own journals, may assure us that, in the public administration of slave punishments, "the people are no better than their laws," but much "worse!"

Communities tolerating such laws must become lawless; must lose the conception and the proper definition of LAW, in its just sense. They must be at once in a condition of despotism and of anarchy. And such is the known state of society at the South.

And yet, *no practical business man*, who looks over, carefully, the whole ground, and knows human nature, and the circumstances of the times, will be likely to conclude that any better or milder code, or method of administration, could preserve "the innocent legal relation of slave ownership!" If THAT is to be tolerated, all the rest is to be left where it is! Indeed, the Note of Mr. Wheeler, already quoted, (Wheeler's Law of Slavery, pp. 222–3,) very nearly expresses this idea; and in looking over his few reported cases on this subject, we find nothing to disparage the conclusion.

We notice the following items, as the most important:

"*A slave* tried for a capital crime may be convicted on *testimony of a slave*, though uncorroborated by pregnant circumstances." (Wheeler, p. 204. Case of the State *vs.* Ben, Dec. T., 1821; 1 Hawks' N. C. Rep., 434. Opinion of Judge Badger, Judge Hall dissenting.)

"A slave on trial for a capital felony is entitled to a jury of slave owners." (Wheeler, p. 212. Case of the State *vs.* Jim, Dec. T., 1826; 1 Devereaux's N. C. Rep., 142.)

"On an indictment of a slave for a capital offense, the master cannot be compelled to testify." (The State *vs.* Charity, Dec. T., 1830; 2 Devereaux's N. C. Rep., 214.) In delivering his opinion, Judge Ruffin said: "The privilege not to testify, on the ground of interest, is that of the *master*, not of the *slave*. It may consequently be waived by the former. He may himself prosecute, and give evidence against his slave." "Could I separate *her* [the slave's] rights from those of the witness, [her master,] I would do so, and let the verdict stand, [a verdict of conviction for murder.] But they are so connected, that justice *cannot* be done to the master without giving to the slave the benefit of it. We cannot restore *him* his PROPERTY, without yielding her another trial for her *life;* nor reverse the judgment for the costs without reversing it altogether. I therefore conclude, though with great hesitation, that, as the master did object to be sworn, there must be a new trial." (Wheeler, pp. 214–15.)

We see here the sacred rights of public justice on the one hand, (where the prisoner was charged with the murder of her own child,) and the sacred rights of the accused to an impartial trial for her life, BOTH treated as inferior and minor interests, which must bend to the slave master's *right of property* in the accused! If she was acquitted, as she probably was, at the new trial, it was *not* as a matter of justice or of mercy towards the accused or the murdered, but as an act of protection to *slave property!*

"Free persons of color are entitled to trial by jury." (Wheeler, p. 222. Bore *vs.* Bush, 18 Martin's Lou. Rep., 1.) A jury, doubtless, of *white* men, NOT "a jury of their peers" or equals! This is no "trial by jury" deserving the name.

CHAPTER VI.

EDUCATION PROHIBITED.

The Slave not being regarded as a member of Society, nor as a human being, the Government, instead of providing for his education, takes care to forbid it, as being inconsistent with the condition of chattelhood.

CHATTELS are not educated! And if human beings are to be held in chattelhood, education must be withheld from them.

South Carolina.—Act of 1740: "Whereas, the having slaves taught to write, or suffering them to be employed in writing, may be attended with *great inconveniences;* Be it enacted, that all and every person and persons whatsoever, who shall hereafter teach or cause any slave or slaves to be taught to write, or shall use or employ any slave as a scribe, in any manner of writing whatsoever, hereafter taught to write, every such person or persons shall, for every such offense, forfeit the sum of one hundred pounds, current money." (2 Brevard's Digest, 243.)

Georgia, similar; penalty, twenty pounds. (Prince's Dig., 445.)

South Carolina.—Another Act in 1800: "That assemblies of slaves, free negroes, mulattoes and mestizoes, whether composed of all or of any of such description of persons, or of all or any of the same, *and of a portion* of white persons met together *for the purpose of* MENTAL INSTRUCTION, in a confined or secret place, &c., &c., are declared to be an unlawful meeting; and magistrates, &c., &c., are hereby required, &c., to enter such confined places, &c., &c., and break doors, if resisted, and to disperse such slaves, free negroes, &c., &c.; and the officers dispersing such unlawful assemblage *may inflict such corporal punishment, not exceeding twenty lashes, upon such slaves, free negroes*, &c., as they may judge necessary for DETERRING THEM FROM SUCH UNLAWFUL ASSEMBLAGE IN FUTURE." "That it shall not be lawful for any number of slaves, free negroes, mulattoes, or mestizoes, *even in company with white persons,* to meet together *for the purpose of* MENTAL INSTRUCTION, either before the rising of the sun, or after the going down of the same." (2 Brevard's Dig., 254–5.)

Virginia.—*Revised Code* of 1819: "That all meetings or assemblages of slaves, or free negroes or mulattoes mixing and associating with such slaves at any *meeting-house* or houses, &c., in the night; *or* at any SCHOOL OR SCHOOLS *for teaching them* READING OR WRITING, *either in the day or night*, under whatsoever pretext, shall be deemed and considered an UNLAWFUL ASSEMBLY; and any justice of a county, &c., wherein such assemblage shall be, either from his own knowledge or the information of others, of such unlawful assemblage, &c., may issue his warrant, directed to any sworn officer or officers, authorizing him or them to enter the house or houses where such unlawful assemblages, &c., may be, for the purpose of *apprehending or dispersing* such slaves, and *to inflict corporal punishment on the offender or offenders*, at the discretion of any justice of the peace, *not exceeding twenty lashes*." (1 Rev. Code, 424–5.)

Besides the State laws, the corporate towns and cities frequently have ordinances on the subject. As for example, in Savannah, in 1818, the public journals announced as follows:

"The City has passed an ordinance by which any person that *teaches any person of color, slave or free*, to *read or write*, or causes such persons to be so taught, is subjected to a fine of thirty dollars for *each* offense; and every person of color who shall keep a school to teach reading or writing is subject to a fine of thirty dollars, or to be imprisoned ten days, and *whipped thirty-nine lashes!*"

"In North Carolina, to teach a slave to *read or write*, or sell or give him *any* book [Bible not excepted] or pamphlet, is punished with *thirty-nine lashes*, or imprisonment, if the offender be a free negro; but if a white, then with a fine of $200. The reason for this law, assigned in its preamble, is, that 'teaching slaves to read and write tends *to dissatisfaction* in their minds, and to produce insurrection and rebellion.'" (Jay's Inquiry, p. 136.) This was enacted in 1831. (Vide Child's Appeal.)

"In Georgia, if a white teach a *free* negro or slave to write, he is fined $500, and imprisoned at the discretion of the Court; if the offender be a *colored* man, bond or free, he may be fined or whipped, at the discretion of the Court. Of course, a father may be flogged for teaching his own child. This barbarous law was enacted in 1829." (Ib.)

"In Louisiana, the penalty for teaching slaves to read and write is one year's imprisonment." (Ib.)

The following statement will be regarded with interest, as being from one of the highest legal authorities:

"In Georgia, by Act of 1829, no person is permitted to teach a slave, negro, or free person of color to read or write. So in Virginia, by statute, in 1830, meetings of free negroes to learn reading and writing are unlawful, and subject them to corporal punishment; and it is unlawful for white persons to assemble with free negroes or slaves, to teach them to read or write. The prohibitory Act of the Legislature of Alabama, passed in the session of 1831–2, relative to instruction to be given to the slave or free colored population, or exhortation or preaching to them, or any mischievous influence attempted to be exerted over them, is sufficiently penal. Laws of similar import are presumed to exist in the other slaveholding States; but in Louisiana, the law is armed with tenfold severity. It not only forbids any person teaching slaves to read or write, but it declares, that any person using language in any public discourse, from the bar, bench, stage, or pulpit, or in any other place, or in any private conversation, or making use of any signs or actions having a tendency to produce discontent among the free colored population, or insubordination among the slaves, or who shall be knowingly instrumental in bringing into the State any paper, book, or pamphlet, having the like tendency, shall, on conviction, be punished with imprisonment or death, at the discretion of the Court." (Kent's Commentaries, vol. ii., part iv., p. 268, note.)

Bible Societies do not distribute the Bible among slaves, because it is prohibited, and because the slaves are unable to read.

John Woolman, of New-Jersey, (1757,) said:—"*Some* of our Society," (Friends,) "and *some* of the Society called New Lights, use some endeavors to instruct those [slaves] they have, in reading; but *in common* this is not only neglected, but disapproved." (Journal of Life, &c., of Woolman, p. 74.)

In the House of Delegates of Virginia, in 1832, Mr. Berry said: "We have, *as far as possible*, closed every avenue by which light might enter their [the slaves'] minds. If we could extinguish the capacity to see the light, our work would be completed; they would then be on a level with the beasts of the field, and we should be safe! I am not certain that we would not do it, if we could find out the process, and that on the plea of necessity."

Kentucky is one of the few slave States (perhaps the only one except Maryland) in which slave education is not expressly prohibited; but the condition of the slave there was thus described by the Presbyterian Synod of Kentucky, in 1834. "Slavery dooms thousands of human beings to *hopeless ignorance.*" "If slaves are educated, it must involve some outlay on the part of the master." "It is inconsistent with our knowledge of human nature to suppose that he will do this for them. The present state of instruction among this race answers exactly to what we might thus naturally anticipate. *Throughout the whole land*, so far as we can learn, there is but *one school* in which, during the week, slaves can be taught. The light of *three or four Sabbath-schools* is seen glimmering through the darkness that covers the black population of a whole State. *Here and there*, a family is found where humanity and religion impel the master, mistress, or children to the laborious task of private instruction." "Nor is it to be expected that this state of things will become better, *unless it is determined that slavery shall cease.*" (Address, &c., p. 8.)

In North Carolina, the "patrols" were ordered to "search every negro house for books or prints of any kind. *Bibles and hymn books* were particularly mentioned." (Weld's "Slavery as it is," p. 51.)

The appeals and statements made by clergymen, missionaries and others, concerning the religious instruction of slaves, are usually guarded from misapprehension by the use of the phrase "*oral instruction*," indicating that *books* are not to be put into their hands! "A Sabbath-school" for colored children at the South, commonly includes nothing more. Forgetful of their anathemas of the Church or Pope of Rome for withholding the Scriptures, most Protestant ministers at the South, and some at the North, insist that mere "oral instruction" will answer very well for the negroes! And this introduces to us the subject of our next chapter.

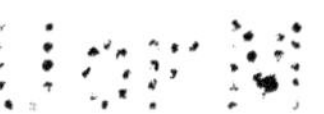

CHAPTER VII.

FREE SOCIAL WORSHIP AND RELIGIOUS INSTRUCTION PROHIBITED.

The Government not only permits the Master to forbid the free Social Worship and Religious Instruction of his Slaves, at his pleasure, but it also steps in with direct prohibitions of its own, which even the Master himself may not relax or abrogate.

It is quite remarkable, that all the *real practical restraints* which the Slave Codes of the South throw around the slave master, are obviously for the purpose of withholding him from some exercise of humanity or of justice towards the slave; not one of them is for the purpose of restraining him from inhumanity and injustice!

From no act of barbarity, cruelty, or even murder, is he in reality restrained. The enactments professing to have that object, we have found to be ineffectual, impossible to execute, deceptive, self-contradictory, and, in fact, *sheer pretense!* We have found no laws that even professed to guard the highest interests of slaves as human beings, family sanctities, female chastity, education, religious de-

velopment. No restraints upon the violation and destruction of these are attempted to be thrown around the slave master. But, on the *other* hand, he *is* restrained, as has been shown, from allowing to his slave (for the mutual benefit of both parties) a *peculium* of property from a tithe of his own earnings, with the benefits of "hiring out" for that purpose! He *is* restrained, as we have seen, from bestowing upon his slave an education that would increase his usefulness, or of *employing* him to do any kind of writing! The slave may be "used" so as to be "*used up*" in seven years; may be used as a "*breeder*," as a prostitute, as a concubine, as a pimp, as a tapster, as an attendant at the gaming-table, as a subject of medical and surgical experiments for the benefit of science, and the Legislature makes no objections against it! But he may *not* be used as *a clerk!* In all *this*, the master's absolute right of ownership is restrained! It is restrained too, as we shall see, by not permitting even the master to allow his slave the privileges of free social worship and religious instruction, well calculated as these privileges may be to increase in him those Christian virtues for which he is sometimes commended in advertisements, to enhance his value in the market! The master's right we shall also find restrained by the laws forbidding him freely, and at self-discretion, to emancipate! The great solicitude of the law seems to be, to prevent the master from being too kind to his slave!

The philosophy of this is readily seen. A minority

of slave owners are deemed exposed to the weakness of exercising some humanity and justice, of manifesting some feeling of responsibility to God in their treatment of their fellow-men! The majority of slaveholders, who make the laws, will not tolerate this! They enter, fully and understandingly, into the spirit of slave ownership. That "legal relation" must be preserved at all hazards; and they know it is endangered by humanity, by justice, by education, and by religion. They know that if others emancipate, their own tenure will be weakened. The rise of an oppressive oligarchy of slave owners begins here. And religious liberty is the very last thing to be tolerated by it. Religious liberty is the precursor of civil and political liberty and enfranchisement, and must be suppressed. The gospel *would indeed* abolish American slavery, (as is often said,) if it could only be introduced among the slaves so far as to confer upon them religious liberty. This our American slaveholders understand, as will now be shown.

In Georgia, by an Act of Dec. 13, 1792, with the title, "To PROTECT religious societies in the exercise of their religious duties," it is required of every justice of the peace, &c., to take into custody any person who shall interrupt or disturb a congregation of WHITE PERSONS, &c., assembled at any church, &c., and to impose a fine on the offender; and in default of payment he may be imprisoned, &c., &c. Yet the *same law* concludes with these words: "No congregation or company of NEGROES shall, *under pretense of divine worship*, assemble themselves, contrary to the Act regulating patrols." (Prince's Digest, 342.)

This Act regulating patrols is understood to be the Act of May 10, 1770, "for ordering and governing slaves," wherein slaves are forbidden to assemble "on pretense of feasting," &c., and "any constable," on direction of a justice, is commanded to *disperse* ANY *assembly or meeting of slaves* which *may* disturb the peace or endanger the safety of his Majesty's subjects; and every slave which may be found at such meeting, as aforesaid, shall and may, by order of such justice, *immediately be corrected*, WITHOUT TRIAL, *by receiving on the bare back twenty-five stripes with a whip*, switch, *or cowskin*," &c. (Prince's Digest, 447.) From the general terms of this Act, there can be no doubt that it was applicable to religious meetings before the Act of 1792 occasioned its reiteration with more distinct specifications.

In South Carolina, in the same Act of 1800, already cited as forbidding "slaves, free negroes, mulattoes, and mestizoes" to assemble for "mental instruction," there is the following additional section:

"It shall not be lawful for any number of slaves, free negroes, mulattoes, or mestizoes, *even in company with white persons*, to meet together and assemble for the purpose of mental instruction *or religious worship*, either before the rising of the sun or after the going down of the same. And all magistrates, sheriffs, *militia officers*, &c., &c., are hereby vested with power, &c., for *dispersing such assemblies*." (2 Brevard's Digest, 254–5.) "Three years afterwards, upon petition, as the Act recites, of certain religious societies, the rigor of the Act of 1800 was slightly abated, by a modification which forbids any person, before nine o'clock in the evening, "to break into a place of meeting wherein shall be assembled the members of any religious society in this State, *provided a majority of them shall be white persons*, or otherwise to disturb their devotion, *unless* such person, &c., so entering said place [of worship] shall first have obtained from some magistrate, &c., a *warrant*, &c., in case a magistrate shall be then actually within a distance of *three miles* from such place of meeting; *otherwise* the provisions, &c., [of the Act of 1800,] to remain in full force." (Brevard's Digest, 261. Stroud's Sketch, pp. 93–4.)

So that, in order to attend a religious meeting securely, the slave must *know beforehand* (1st) that there will be present "a majority of *white* persons; (2d,) that there will be no person there with "*a warrant*" from a justice to apprehend him; and (3d) that a justice will not "*be then*" within three miles' distance! For a mistake in either of these particulars, he (or she) is subjected to the penalty of "twenty-five lashes with the cowskin on the bare back, well laid on!"

"In Virginia, all evening meetings of slaves at any meeting-house are unequivocally forbidden." (Jay's Inquiry, p. 137. See Stroud, p. 94. See also 1 Revised Code (of 1819), 424–5, already cited (Chap. VI.) as prohibiting meetings for promoting education.) The first clause will be found to prohibit "*all* meetings" of slaves, &c., *in the evening*. "Slaves may, however, attend at church on any day of public worship." (Stroud, p. 94.)

Mississippi—same as Virginia, with a proviso that a master *may* permit his slave to attend the preaching of a *white* minister, regularly ordained and licensed, or where at least two *discreet* and respectable *white* persons, *appointed* by some regular church, shall attend. (Mississippi Rev. Code, 390. Stroud's Sketch, p. 94. Jay's Inquiry, p. 137.)

Religious liberty secures the right of the worshippers to choose and arrange *their own* modes and forms of religious worship, and to select their own teachers; *not* the privilege of being permitted to worship when, where, and how the Government or a slaveholder may appoint, and under such religious teachers as they may select. The essence of spiritual despotism and of religious persecution lies in the enforcement of such claims. It is no discredit to the slaves that they have little or no desire to hear religious harangues from their oppressors, or that they loathe the instructions of ministers who preach the rightfulness of slaveholding.

The Southampton slave insurrection of Nat. Turner (once a preacher) may have furnished a pretext for the following:

"The Legislature of Virginia passed a law in 1831, by which any free colored person who undertakes to preach or conduct a religious meeting by day or night may be whipped, not exceeding thirty-nine lashes, at the discretion of *any* justice of the peace; and *any body* may apprehend any such free colored person *without a warrant.* The same penalty, adjudged and executed in the same way, falls on any slave or free colored person who attends such preaching; and any slave who listens to any *white* preacher in the night-time receives the same punishment. The same law prevails in Georgia and Mississippi. A master *may* permit a slave to preach on *his* plantation, to none but *his* slaves." (Child's Appeal, p. 67.)

An early law of Maryland, (Act of 1715, chap. 44, sec. 23,) and a similar one in South Carolina, (in 1711,) permits *the baptism* of slaves, but carefully provides that "such baptism shall not be construed to effect the *emancipation* of any slave." This arose from a contrary apprehension growing out of ancient usages in England, and the opinion of some jurists that *Christians* could not be lawfully enslaved.

In Louisiana the Legislature enacted: "It shall be the duty of every owner to procure his *sick* slaves all kinds of temporal and *spiritual* assistance which their situation may require." (1 Martin's Dig., 610.)

These Maryland and Louisiana privileges of baptism at birth, and of extreme unction on a death-bed, apparently of Roman Catholic origin, were undoubtedly considered great kindnesses; and they constitute, to this day, almost, if not entirely, the sum total of the legal provision for the slave as a religious being.

The prohibitions recorded in this chapter have found their defense or apology in the alleged dangers of insurrection and insubordination! The plea is strongly condemnatory of the system, its apologists, and its administrators! Of no system but an iniquitous one could it be true that religious liberty would array and arm its subjects against its fundamental law! No right-minded person, who was at heart neither a slave nor a tyrant, would ever urge such a plea. And if the slaveholders treated their servants justly and kindly, the danger of insurrection would cease. The plea, if false, should itself be execrated. If founded on a real danger, it reveals the inherent and inexpressible wickedness of slaveholding, and of the so-called "legal relation" that sustains it, and that is itself maintained at such a sacrifice! The "necessity" of such laws, rightly interpreted, resolves itself into the necessity of "immediate and unconditional abolition."

The general condition of the slaves is not better than is indicated by these enactments. We have not room to present a full specimen of Southern testimony on this subject.

The Presbyterian Synod of Kentucky, in 1834, said: "Slavery deprives its subjects, in a great measure, of the privileges of the gospel." "The law, *as it is here*, does not prevent free access to the Scriptures; but ignorance, the natural result of their condition, does. The Bible is before them. But it is, to them, a sealed book. Very few of them enjoy the advantages of a regular gospel ministry."

The Address of the Synod proceeds to say that some have proposed missionaries among slaves, but adds that the "*community*" will never sustain this measure until they are "*ripe for measures for emancipation.*" They add: "It is evident that, as a body, our slaves do not enjoy the public ordinances of religion. Domestic means of grace are still more rare among them."

From a sermon of Bishop Meade, it may be inferred that the religious condition of slaves is not better in Virginia.

The Presbyterian Synod of South Carolina and Georgia, in 1833, published a statement in which they said of the slaves: "There are over TWO MILLIONS of human beings in the condition of heathen, and some of them in a worse condition." "They may justly be considered the HEATHEN of this country, and will bear a comparison with heathen in any country in the world. *The negroes are destitute of the gospel, and ever* WILL BE *under the present state of things.* In the vast field extending from an entire State beyond the Potomac [i. e., Maryland] to the Sabine River, [at that time our South-western boundary,] and from the Atlantic to the Ohio, there are, to the best of our knowledge, *not twelve* men exclusively devoted to the religious instruction of the negroes. In the present state of feeling in the South, a ministry of their own color could neither be obtained NOR TOLERATED. But do not the negroes have access to the gospel through the stated ministry of the whites? We answer, No. The negroes have no regular and efficient ministry: as a matter of course, no churches; neither is there sufficient room in the white churches for their accommodation.

We know of but *five* churches in the slaveholding States, built expressly for their use. These are all in the State of Georgia. We may now inquire whether they enjoy the privileges of the gospel in their own houses, and on our plantations? Again we return a negative answer. They have no Bibles to read by their own firesides. They have no family altars; and when in affliction, sickness, or death, they have no minister to address to them the consolations of the gospel, nor to bury them with appropriate services."

Again, in 1834, the same Synod said:

"The gospel, *as things now are*, can never be preached to the two classes [whites and blacks] successfully in conjunction." "The galleries or back seats on the lower floor of *white* churches are generally appropriated to the negroes, when it can be done without inconvenience to the whites. When it cannot be done conveniently, the negroes must catch the gospel as it escapes through the doors and windows." "If the master is pious, *the house servants alone* attend family worship, and frequently *few or none of them.*" "So far as masters are engaged in the work, [of religious instruction of slaves,] an almost unbroken silence reigns on this vast field."

The *Charleston* (S. C.) *Observer*, and the *Western Luminary*, Lexington, (Ky.,) fully corroborate these statements. So also does Rev. C. C. Jones, of Georgia, who says further: "We cannot cry out against the Papists for withholding the Scriptures from the common people, and keeping them in ignorance of the way of life, for we *withhold* the Bible from our servants, and *keep* them in ignorance of it, while we *will not* use the means to have it read and explained to them."

The North Carolina Baptist Convention adopted a Report concerning the religious instruction of the colored people, with a series of Resolutions, concluding as follows: "*Resolved*, That by religious instruction be understood VERBAL communications on religious subjects!"

But not even verbal instructions, it seems, could be tolerated in South Carolina. In 1838, the Methodist Conference of South Carolina appointed a missionary, Rev. Mr. Turpin, to labor among the colored people, but it was soon suppressed by the principal citizens. The *Greenville* (S. C.) *Mountaineer* of Nov. 2, 1838, contained the particulars. A Committee was appointed, who addressed a note to Mr. Turpin, requesting him to desist. This was backed up by a Remonstrance to the same effect, signed by James S. Pope and 352 others. The document is before us. It argues at length the incompatibility of slavery with the "mental improvement and religious instruction" of slaves. "Verbal instruction," say they, "will increase the desire of the black population to learn. We know of upwards of a dozen negroes in the neighborhood of Cambridge who can *now* read, some of whom are members of your societies at Mount Lebanon and New-Salem. Of course, when they see themselves encouraged, *they will supply themselves with Bibles, hymn books, and Catechisms*"*!* "Open the missionary sluice, and the current will swell in its gradual onward advance. We thus expect that *a progressive system of improvement will be introduced*, or will follow, from the nature and force of circumstances, and, if not checked, (though they may be shrouded in sophistry and disguise,) *will ultimately revolutionize our civil institutions*." "We consider the common adage that 'Knowledge is power,' and as the colored man is enlightened, his condition will be rendered more unhappy and intolerable. *Intelligence and slavery have no affinity with each other*." The document refers to the laws of the State, and hopes that "South Carolina is yet true to her vital interests," &c., &c.

The missionary enterprise was thus suppressed, or was relinquished. The Editor of the *Mountaineer* said: "The opposition to the *late* Home Mission among us comprised the great body of the people."

"*No people are found to be better than their laws*."

"The legal relation" of slave ownership, as understood at the South, *requires all this*. And the Church and ministry there either acquiesce or succumb!

At every point we have found an utter repugnance and opposition between the Slave Code and the Christian religion. And the Slave Code is nothing more nor less than the truthful exponent and the vigilant guardian of the so-called "legal relation of master and slave." While the one remains, the other remains, with all the practical results that naturally grow out of them.

CHAPTER VIII.

LEGISLATIVE, JUDICIAL, AND CONSTITUTIONAL OBSTRUCTIONS TO EMANCIPATION.

The Statutes of the Slave States not only make no provision for a general Emancipation, but they obstruct and prevent Emancipations by the Master. And the Constitutions of some of the States forbid the Legislatures to abolish Slavery.

WE have seen that slavery is hereditary and perpetual in the nature of its tenure, and that the code by which it is defined contemplates no period of its termination, and points out no conditions upon which the slave or his posterity can escape from it. (See Chap. XXI. of the former series.) One avenue of hope only remains for him. The slave master may himself emancipate. In very many instances, slave masters have done so. The hope has been thus inspired of such an increase of manumissions as should weaken and ultimately terminate the whole system.

The hopes of humanity, in this direction, have not outrun the fears of the *majority* of slaveholders, who control the legislation of the slave States. The laws accordingly interpose obstacles to emancipation.

The reasons urged at the South for legislative and

judicial restrictions upon emancipation cannot, perhaps, be more favorably or more forcibly stated than in the following extract from a note by Mr. Wheeler, at the close of his chapter of reported cases concerning "the emancipation of slaves:"

"It will be seen by this chapter that the owner of slaves may emancipate them by deed, will, or contract executed. *But to this* BENEVOLENCE *of the owner there are, in most of the States,* RESTRAINTS *upon the exercise of this power by the owner.* Slaves are recognized, wherever this system is tolerated, as *property*, and are subject to all the rules in the acquisition, possession, and transmission of property. It would seem, therefore, upon a first view of the case, *that the owner should do with his property whatever he pleased*, and should have the privilege of *renouncing his right to it* whenever he pleased, and without being qualified by any public laws or regulations on the subject. Such, however, *is not the fact;* restraints upon this right exist in nearly all the States."

After citing some of the laws on the subject, including those of Tennessee and Alabama, which we shall copy, Mr. Wheeler proceeds:

"When it is considered that slaves are a *peculiar* species of property, it will not excite surprise that laws are necessary for their regulation, and to *protect society from even the benevolence of slave owners*, in throwing upon the community a great number of stupid, ignorant, and vicious persons, to disturb its peace and *endanger its permanency.*

"The right of society to regulate and control the

ownership and control of this kind of property may be justified on the same grounds as some other species of property. No one can doubt the right of individuals to acquire, possess, and sell gunpowder. But if the possessor chooses to take it to his house or store, in a city or populous town, the public become interested, and will restrain him within reasonable and proper limits."* "And the constitutionality of such laws cannot be doubted. So of slaves. The owner may keep as many as he pleases, but if he emancipates them, and turns them loose upon society, they have a right to protect themselves against his improvidence, or even against his benevolence and generosity. They have a right to declare the act illegal, or restrain it within such bounds as shall secure their safety." (Wheeler's Law of Slavery, pp. 386–8.)

In Mr. Wheeler's book we have met with no mention of the laws *forbidding the education of slaves and free colored people, and their free access to the means of religious and moral instruction.* By the side of such laws, the plea for laws restraining emancipation on the ground of the ignorance and vice of the colored people, would have seemed incongruous. It is the intelligence and virtue of the colored race

* To have made the cases parallel, the writer should have adduced laws restraining owners of slaves from having *too many* of them in one place, or else he should have cited laws restraining owners of gunpowder from pouring water upon it, or from transmuting it into articles that could endanger no body! It is *slavery*, and not *liberty*, that is "dangerous."

that constitute the "danger" to be guarded against in this feature of slave legislation and jurisprudence. And the *honesty* and *conscientious misgivings* of repenting slaveholders (quite as truly as their "benevolence and generosity") constitute another danger against which a "society" of slaveholders thus protects itself.

This principle of restriction obtains in the code of *nearly* every one of the slave States, though an express enactment cannot always be cited for it.

In South Carolina, Georgia, Mississippi, and Alabama, the Legislature *only*, by express enactments, have authority to emancipate slaves. (Vide authorities cited by Stroud, p. 147.)

In North Carolina, a slave cannot be emancipated *except for meritorious services*, to be adjudged and allowed of by the Court. (Haywood's Manual, 537, Act of 1796.)

A general principle, pervading the legislation and jurisprudence of the several States, is, that the owner may not emancipate without the consent of his *creditors*. Thus, "in Virginia and Mississippi, an emancipated slave may be taken in execution to satisfy *any debt* contracted by the person emancipating him, previous to such emancipation." (1 Rev. Code of Virginia, 434. Mississippi Rev. Code, 386.)

In Kentucky, the emancipating papers must contain a *saving* of the rights of creditors. (2 Litt. and Swi., 1155.)

In Louisiana, "any enfranchisement made in fraud of creditors is void." (New Civil Code, art. 190.)

In Virginia, Mississippi, and Kentucky, the *widou* of a deceased slaveholder, who may have emancipated a slave, may claim her "*third*" to which the widow is entitled. (1 Rev. Code of Virginia, 435. Mississippi Rev. Code, 386. 2 Litt. and Swi., 1246.) And when *one third part* of an emancipated slave is thus reënslaved, the problem of preserving the remaining *two thirds* of him in a state of freedom would perhaps puzzle his best legal advisers!

In Georgia, "*the attempt*" to set free a slave, otherwise than by application to the Legislature, is punished as an "*offense*"—a fine of two hundred dollars, one half to the informer and the other half to the county; and the manumitted slave is retained in slavery. (Prince's Digest, 457.) And, as if this were not sufficient, an additional Act, in 1818, declares that every last will and testament by which slaves shall be set free, or any such will or *other* "instrument in writing, or by parol," by which slaves shall be allowed the privilege of working for themselves, "to be utterly null and void." And the person executing such writing, or "attempting to give it effect," or "accepting a trust" under it, may be fined "not exceeding one thousand dollars;" and every slave "on whose behalf" such instrument shall be written, "*being thereof convicted,* (*?!*) shall be sold at public outcry, and the proceeds appropriated," &c. (Prince's Digest, 466.)

In Tennessee, the Courts, on petition of the *owner*, and for sufficient *reasons* therein set forth, *may* emancipate a slave! (Tenn. Laws; Act of 1801, chap. 27.)

"Emancipation is guarded in Tennessee by a provision (statute of 1777) that the *State must assent*, or the act of manumission by deed or will is ineffectual; and (as appears in Fisher *vs.* Dabbs, 6 Yerger's Rep., 119,) the emancipated slave must be immediately removed beyond the limits of the United States." (Wheeler's Law of Slavery, p. 387.)

"By statute of Alabama, Aikin's Dig., 647, slaves may be emancipated by the master, on application to the County Court, *and on proof of meritorious services*, but the slave must remove out of the limits of the State." (Ib.)

Mississippi has combined all the obstacles in the laws of all the other States. (Stroud, p. 149.)

Kentucky, Missouri, Virginia, and Maryland, afford greater facilities for emancipation. (Ib.) In Kentucky and Missouri the master may emancipate, "saving the rights of creditors," and by giving bonds for the maintenance of the aged and infirm.

In Virginia the law is similar, only that if the emancipated slave be over twenty-one years of age, he must leave the State in one year, or be reënslaved! (Revised Code, 436.)

Maryland has a proviso that the emancipated slave shall be "of healthy constitution," &c., "capable of labor," and "not exceeding forty-five years of age." (Laws of 1796, chap. 67.)

In Louisiana, "no one can emancipate his slave, unless the slave has attained the age of thirty years, and has behaved well for at least four years preceding his emancipation." But "a slave who has saved the life of his master, his master's wife, or one of his children, *may* be emancipated at any age." (Art. 185, 186.) Also, the child of a deceased slave mother who had acquired the right to freedom at a future time, becomes free *at* that time. (Art. 196.) And a slave entitled to a *future* release is capable of receiving property by testament or donation. (Art. 193.) For these remnants of justice and mercy, humanity is indebted, perhaps, to the former usages of the French and Spaniards, under the *Code Noir*.

From the legislators we now turn to the judges and reporters of judicial decisions.

"With respect to emancipation, it may be stated as a principle without an exception, that, as slaves are considered property upon which *creditors* have a right to look for the payment of their debts due by the owner of slaves, regard must be had to the *rights of the creditor;* and no act of emancipation is valid when these are violated." (Note, in Wheeler's Law of Slavery, p. 310.)

So then the slave, by extraordinary exertions and by agreement with his master, may have obtained emancipation for himself and family, and may have removed with them to a free State. Yet the master's *creditor* may take out an execution, and reënslave them, by the help of the Fugitive Slave Act of Congress. The money paid by the *slave* does not constitute *him* a creditor, in the eye of the law; for it belonged, *in law*, to the master, before it was paid to him!

"Slaves manumitted by Will, where the *personal*

estate is not sufficient to pay the debts of the testator, are not entitled to freedom." This is the marginal note to the case of Negro George et al. *vs.* Corse, Adm'r.; June T., 1827. (2 Harris and Gill's Md. Rep., 1.)

The Will of James Corse, manumitting the slaves, contained the following: "And it is hereby provided that *if my personal estate*, EXCLUSIVE OF NEGROES, should not be sufficient to discharge all my just debts, then my will is that my executor or administrator, as the case may be, may *sell so much of my real estate* as *will pay my debts, so as to have my negroes free,* as before stated."

"It was admitted that the *personal* estate of the testator, either including or excluding the negroes, was not, at the time of his death, or at any time since, sufficient to pay his debts; but that his *real* estate, including his personal property, and excluding the negroes, were, at the time of his death, and still are, sufficient to pay his debts. Verdict for defendants, and petitioners appealed. After argument, the Court, *Dorsey*, *Archer*, and *Earl*, Judges, affirmed the judgment, and that the creditors had a right to their demands out of the *personal* estate." (Wheeler, pp. 327–8.)

Thus the Court annulled the express provisions of the Will, whether with or without authority from the statute, does not appear. And the *principle* established would, in the same manner, set aside a similar Will of a testator who might leave millions in *real* estate, if his *personal* estate, exclusive of negroes, should fall short of paying his debts. The object and spirit of such decisions cannot be hid. The rights of the free as well as of the enslaved are outrageously infringed by such proceedings, in which the death-bed promptings of conscience, repentance, justice, and mercy, are profanely spurned and trampled in the dust.

"Slaves are subject to dower *in all the States.* Not only are they subject to dower, but the widow's interest in them is protected by statutory provisions. If the husband manumits his slaves, whereby creditors and the dower of the widow are affected, the manumission is so far ineffectual that the manumitted slaves may be *sold for a period*, and the proceeds of the sale applied to the creditors of the former owner and his widow." [Numerous authorities cited.] (Wheeler, note to p. 181.)

In *other* circumstances the courts are less regardful of the rights of woman.

"A wife's estate in dower of slaves, by a former husband, on her second marriage, rests in her husband." "*And her right to manumit them is gone.*" (Wheeler, p. 182.)

On the subject of the validity of contracts and promises of masters to manumit, there seems some slight diversity among the judges, as will be seen from the following, in which the general doctrine is apparent:

"A *written* agreement by a master with his slave to manumit him is obligatory; it rests in *benevolence*, not in *contract.*" (Marginal Note.) The Judge said:

"The manumission of a slave does not rest upon the principle of *a contract, depending upon a consideration;* but it is an act of *benevolence sanctioned* by the statute, and made obligatory, *if in writing.*" (Kettletas *vs.* Fleet, Feb. T., 1811; 7 John's *New-York* Rep., 324. Wheeler, p. 232.)

"Chancery cannot enforce *a contract* between master and slave, though the slave perform his part." (Stevenson *vs.* Singleton, Feb. T., 1829; 1 Leigh's Va. Rep., 72. Wheeler, p. 233.)

Same decision in Sawney *vs.* Carter, March Term, 1828; 6 Randolph's Va. Rep., 173. Wheeler, p. 237. Cited in Leigh's Rep. I. 72, Virg., 1829, as follows:

"Application to enforce a contract between master and slave.—*Per Cur.:* In the case of Sawney *vs.* Carter, the Court refused, on great consideration, to enforce a promise by a master to emancipate his slave where the conditions of the promise had been partly complied with by the slave. The Court proceeded on the principle that it is not competent to a Court of Chancery to enforce a contract between master and slave, *even although the contract should be fully complied with on the part of the slave.*"

Fugitive slaves, on arriving at the North, have sometimes exhibited the written agreements of their masters to emancipate them, on condition of their payment of a certain specified amount of money, payable in instalments. Along with these, they have exhibited the receipts of their masters for the several instalments in full. And yet they have been compelled to run away to obtain their hard-earned freedom, with all the hazards of being hunted and re-captured! The writer has seen and examined such documents.

"If an *informal* emancipation takes place, the master *promising* to comply with the legal formalities, his rights are not thereby affected before the formalities be observed." (Bazzy *vs.* Rose and child, May T., 1820; 8 Martin's Louisiana Rep., 149. Wheeler, p. 307.) In this case, the promise, *in writing*, was produced. On a *habeas corpus*, the slaves (Rose and child) had been discharged, as free persons. But the claimant, Bazzi, brought this suit against them, and the Court, *Martin, J.*, decreed them to be slaves of the plaintiff!

"A contract to manumit is obligatory." (Case of Negro Tom, Feb. T., 1810; 5 John's *New-York* Rep., 365. Wheeler, p. 309.)

"*No* declaration or promise made to a *slave* can be enforced in a Court of law." (Marginal note.)

Beall *vs.* Joseph. Trespass to try Joseph's right to freedom. He had been a slave to one Woods, who agreed to let Edwards have him for four years, *after which he was to be free.* Both Woods and Edwards made parol declarations to this effect. But Edwards sold him a slave to Beall. The Judge said, "It is clear that no declaration or promise made to the slave in this State, (Kentucky,) or for his benefit, by the owner or any other person, can be enforced *in a Court of law or equity.* And see Will *vs.* Thompson, in a note at the end of the case, where it was held, that *where a* PURCHASER *in writ-*

ing contracted with the SELLER *to manumit the slave at a specified time, it is not a ground for a suit at common law, but equity will enforce the contract, and give* DAMAGES *for the detention of the negro.*" (Harden's Ky. Rep., 51. Wheeler, p. 331.)

A contrary decision appears in Negro Cato *vs.* Howard. (June T., 1808; 2 Har. and John's Md. Rep., 323. Wheeler, p. 323.)

"Parol evidence of an agreement for the freedom of a slave is inadmissible." (Victoire *vs.* Dussuau, March T., 1816; 4 Martin's Louisiana Rep., 212. Wheeler, p. 334.)

"An *infant* cannot be emancipated," "nor can a slave be set free who is not both under the age of forty-five years, and able to *work*, and *gain* a sufficient maintenance and livelihood, at the time the freedom is intended to commence." (Hamilton *vs.* Cragg, June T., 1823; 6 Har. and John's Md. Rep., 16. Also Hall *vs.* Mullin, 5 Har. and John's Md. Rep., 190. Wheeler, p. 311.)

"A bequest of liberty to slaves, in contravention of the law, is void." (Mary *vs.* Morris et al., Aug. T., 1834; 7 Lou. Rep., 135. Wheeler, p. 311.)

"A deed of emancipation not recorded in the *proper court*, but in some *other*, gives no title to freedom *until properly recorded.*" (Sawney *vs.* Carter, [before cited.] Also Givens *vs.* Mann, 6 Munf., Va. Rep., 191. Also Lewis *vs.* Fullerton, 1 Randolph's Va. Rep., 15. Wheeler, p. 238.)

"Whether a slave, who is directed to be set free by the last will and testament of his master, can have the intervention of a magistrate to prevent his removal out of the State, *quere*." (Marginal note to Moosa *vs.* Allain, 16 Martin's Lou. Rep., 99. Wheeler, p. 317.) The testator, Julien Poydras, directed in his will, that his slaves on his several plantations should each be considered inseparable from the respective plantation on which they were, and that they should, at the end of twenty-five years, be free. The plaintiff was however sold, and taken to another plantation, against his will and consent, and, as he believed, with an intention of carrying him out of the State. He petitioned for a recession of the sale, and to be restored to the plantation where he belonged. There was judgment for the defendant, and the plaintiff appealed. *Judgment affirmed!*

"A slave cannot be emancipated by a nuncupative [verbal, declaratory] will, nor by an executory or conditional instrument in writing." (Cooke [colored] *vs.* Cooke; 3 Littell's Ky. Rep., 236. Wheeler, p. 328.)

Besides these legislative obstructions to emancipation by the masters, there are, in several of the States, constitutional provisions restraining the State Legislatures from abolishing slavery by statute. As the State will not intrust the planters with the power of manumission, so neither will the planters allow the State to hold the power of abolition.

The laws forbidding or obstructing emancipation have been pleaded on behalf of the slaveholders, as an excuse for not emancipating their slaves. But they can be of no avail, except to such as *oppose* those laws. Slaveholders, moreover, might give their slaves "a pass" to the borders of the free States, or accompany them thither. The fact that *others* will reënslave those whom they may emancipate cannot excuse them. They have no right to continue a wicked practice, because others would take it up if they relinquished it!

Concerning the law of Virginia reënslaving the emancipated negro, the Powhatan Colonization Society (addressing the Virginia Legislature) said: "The law was doubtless dictated by *sound policy*, and its repeal would be regarded by none *with more unfeigned regret than by the friends of African colonization. It has restrained many masters from giving freedom to their slaves, and has thereby contributed to check the growth of an already* TOO GREAT AND GROWING EVIL!" (Jay's Inquiry, p. 108.)

It ill befits those who hold and who patronize this language, to cite the laws impeding emancipation, to justify slaveholders in refusing to emancipate! But this incongruity is constantly witnessed! The popularity, at the South and at the North, of those Societies and statesmen and ministers of religion who hold such language and occupy such a position, may assist to throw light on the inquiry, whether, in *this* particular, the people are better than their laws.

And let it be remembered that, in the judgment of those who ought to know, and who are directly interested in the matter, it is only by such laws that "the innocent legal relation" of slave ownership can be sustained.

In Weld's "Slavery as it is," p. 164, may be found the particulars of the reënslavement of one hundred and thirty-four slaves in North Carolina, who had been liberated by the Quakers in 1776. The old law of 1741 could not prevent it. In 1777, *after* the manumissions had taken place, a new law was made prohibiting such procedure, and the County Courts, under this Act, ordered the emancipated slaves to be sold into slavery! The Superior Court, in 1778, reversed the decision, and the negroes were, a second time, set at liberty. But the Legislature, in 1779, *confirmed* the title of the purchasers by a special Act, and they were taken up, and a second time reduced to slavery! A fair illustration of the legality of the "peculiar relation!"

Such are the relations of the slave to civil government and to society; such the protection he receives from them.

PART III.

RELATION OF THE SLAVE CODE TO THE LIBERTIES OF THE FREE.

CHAPTER I.

LIBERTIES OF THE FREE PEOPLE OF COLOR.

The Free People of Color, though not in a condition of Chattelhood, are constantly exposed to it, and at best enjoy only a portion of their rights.

WE have already seen how, in many ways, a free colored person may be enslaved. He may be enslaved for assisting a slave, however nearly related to him, to escape into freedom. He may be enslaved for being *suspected* of being himself a runaway slave; for being thus imprisoned, and unable to pay his jail fees. He may be reënslaved, after having been emancipated, if the process were not in exact accordance with unreasonable and vexatious regulations; or if, however regularly emancipated, he presumes to remain among his friends, and amid the scenes of his childhood. He may be enslaved for incurring fines which he is unable to pay, under unjust and unequal enactments. He may be enslaved for not being able, by *white* witnesses, to prove himself free! Though a Northern man, and always before free, he may be enslaved by entering a slave State, (Georgia or Maryland,) and thus incurring a fine and being unable to pay it. (Jay's Inquiry, 24. Child's Appeal, p. 64.) He may be enslaved, with his children after him, for being married to a slave. He may be enslaved by being unlawfully and piratically imported into a slave State, even though the kidnapper may be arrested and punished! And in none of the free States can any free native colored citizen be safe from the operation of the Federal Fugitive Slave Bill of 1850, and from the clutches of United States Marshals and Commissioners! The law *presumes* him to be a slave unless he can prove himself free. (Wheeler's Law of Slavery, pp. 5, 6.) "In South Carolina, if a free negro cross the line of the State, he can *never* return." (Child's Appeal, p. 68.)

"Mississippi, in 1831, passed a law to expel all [free] colored persons under sixty and over sixteen years of age, within ninety days, unless they could prove good characters, and obtain from the Court a certificate of the same, for which they paid three dollars: these certificates might be revoked at the discretion of the County Courts. If such persons do not quit the State within the time specified, or if they return to it, they may be sold for a term not exceeding five years." (Ib., p. 68.) And persons sold for a term of years seldom regain their freedom, as has been ascertained in the District of Columbia.

In Tennessee, emancipated slaves must leave the State forthwith. (Ib., p. 68.)

While tracing, in the preceding chapters, the legal condition of the *slave*, we have found the "*free* negro, mulatto, or mestizo," associated with him in some of the most painfully humiliating incidents of his degradation. Like the *slave*, the *free* colored person is held incompetent to testify against a white man! Like the slave, he is debarred, to a great extent, from the benefits of education, and from the right of enjoying free social worship and religious instruction! Like the slave, he is required to be passive, without exercising the right of self-defense, under the insults and assaults of the white man! Like the slave, as will be shown, he is denied the ordinary safeguards of an impartial trial by a jury of his peers. Like the slave, he has no vote nor voice in framing the laws under which he is governed. Even in many of the free States he exercises this right only on unequal conditions, or coupled with invidious distinctions! And yet he is complimented with the title of "*free!*" To be a "free *negro*" differs widely, it would seem, from being a free *man!*

For striking a white man, in Maryland, no matter for what cause, a Justice may "direct the offender's *ears* to be cropped, though he be a *free* black." (Stroud, p. 97. Act of 1723, chap. 15.)

In Louisiana it is gravely set forth, by express statute, that "*free* people of *color* ought never to insult or strike *white* people, nor presume to conceive themselves *equal* to the whites; but, on the contrary, they ought to *yield to them on every occasion*, and never speak or answer them but with respect, but, under penalty OF IMPRISONMENT, according to the nature of the offense." (1 Martin's Digest, 640–42.)

"In some of the States, if a free man of color is

accused of crime, he is denied the benefit of those forms of trial which the Common Law has established for the protection of innocence. Thus, in South Carolina, it is thought quite unnecessary to give the Grand and Petit Jury the trouble of inquiring into the case: he can be hung without so much ceremony. But who is a *colored* man? We answer, the *fairest* man in Carolina, if it can be proved that a drop of negro blood flowed in the veins of his mother." (Jay's Inquiry, p. 21–2.) Judge Jay adduces an instance. William Tann, an overseer on a plantation, shot a slave. He was *supposed* to be a *white*, and the customary forms of trial before the COURT OF SESSIONS were in preparation, (before whom, as being a *white* man, he would undoubtedly have been cleared.) But "on an *issue* ordered and tried for ascertaining his *caste*, it was decided that he was of MIXED BLOOD." So he was "turned over by the *Court* to the jurisdiction of magistrates and freeholders, by whom he was sentenced to be hung. The particulars appeared in the *Charleston Courier* in 1835.

"The Corporation of Georgetown, in the District of Columbia, passed an ordinance, making it penal for any free negro to receive from the Post-office, have in his possession, or circulate, any publication or writing of a seditious character." (Jay's Inquiry, p. 23.)

"In North Carolina, the law prohibits a colored man, whatever may be his attainments or ecclesiastical authority, to preach the gospel." (Ib.)

"In Georgia, a WHITE man is liable to a fine of *five hundred dollars* for teaching a FREE negro to read or write. If one free negro teach another, he is fined *and* whipped, at the discretion of the Court! Should a free negro presume to preach to or exhort his companions, he may be seized without warrant, and whipped thirty-nine lashes, and the same number of lashes may be applied to each one of his congregation. (Ib.)

"In some States, free negroes may not assemble in greater number than seven. In North Carolina, free negroes may not trade, buy, or sell, out of the cities wherein they reside, under penalty of forfeiting their goods, and receiving, in lieu thereof, thirty-nine lashes! (Ib.)

"In Ohio, [a free State,] not only are the blacks excluded from the benefit of public schools, but, with a refinement of cruelty unparalleled, they are doomed to idleness and poverty by a law which renders a *white* man who employs a *colored* one to labor for him for one hour, liable for his support through life." (Ib. 24.)

The Ohio law is, we believe, repealed. But in New-York, and some other Northern cities, colored persons are still denied licenses to drive carts, and pursue other similar avocations for a livelihood.

In Indiana, a free State, the testimony of free negroes and mulattoes is not received against a white man. (Child's Appeal, p. 66.)

"By a late law of Maryland, a free negro coming into the State is liable to a fine of *fifty dollars* for every *week* he remains in it! If he cannot pay the fine, he is SOLD!" (Jay's Inquiry, p. 24.)

"Should a colored citizen of Maryland cross its boundary, on business never so urgent to himself and his family, on returning home, more than a month after, he is liable to be seized and SOLD, unless, previous to his departure, he had complied with certain vexatious legal formalities, and which, from ignorance, he would be extremely likely to neglect, or perform imperfectly." (Jay's Inquiry, p. 90.)

"A citizen of New-York, if he happens to be colored, may not visit a dying child in Maryland without incurring a penalty of fifty dollars for every week he remains; and if he is unable to pay the fine, why, then he is to be *sold by the sheriff* at public sale, for such a time as may be necessary to cover the aforesaid penalty. But if a free negro is sold for a limited time, he is in reality sold for life. During the term for which he is sold, he is sold as *a chattel*, and may be transported at the pleasure of his master; and when the expiration of his term finds him in a cotton-field in Missouri, or a sugar-mill in Louisiana, who is to rescue him from interminable bondage?" (Jay's Inquiry, p. 90.)

It is known that such cases have occurred, and that free negroes taken up as fugitives in the Federal District have been sold to the slavetraders and sent to the far South. A case is narrated in a petition to Congress, signed by Judge Cranch and nearly eleven hundred citizens of the Federal District in 1828. And the advertisements of free negroes for sale by the marshal and sheriff, appear frequently in the public journals. Mr. Miner, in the U. S. House of Representatives, in 1829, stated that in 1826–7 no less than *five* persons in the Federal District were thus sold into perpetual bondage for jail fees! (Jay's Inquiry, p. 155.)

"A free colored man living near the line of the District of Columbia, petitioned the House of Delegates of Maryland for leave to bring his grandchild from the city of Washington. The child had probably been left an orphan, and he naturally wished to take it to his own house. The petition was rejected." (Jay's Inquiry, p. 90.)

"In North Carolina, free negroes are whipped, fined, and imprisoned, at the discretion of the Court, for intermarrying with slaves." (Child's Appeal, p. 70.)

In Georgia, "Any person of color, bond or *free*, is forbidden to occupy any tenement except *a kitchen* or *outhouse*, under penalty of from twenty to fifty lashes. Some of these laws are applicable only to particular cities, towns, or counties; others to several counties." (Ib.)

"Emancipated slaves must quit North Carolina in ninety days after their enfranchisement, on pain of being sold for life. Free persons who shall 'migrate into' the State may be seized and sold as runaway slaves; and if they '*migrate out*' of the State for more than ninety days, they can never return, under the same penalty." "A visit to relatives in another State may be called '*migrating;*' being taken up and detained by kidnappers over ninety days may be called '*migrating.*'" (Ib., p. 68.)

In all the seaport cities and towns of the slave States there are regulations forbidding masters of merchant-vessels to land any free colored person. And if any seaman, cook, or steward in such vessel be *colored*, he is immediately seized, (though a citizen of one of the free States,) and kept in jail at the expense of the ship, until she is ready to sail. This is a great grievance, not only to such colored seamen, but to the ship masters and ship owners. It is also a direct and palpable violation of the Constitution of the United States.

The Legislature of South Carolina, in Dec. 1822, by express statute, ordained the enforcement of this usage, by providing that, in case the ship master should refuse paying the expense of the seaman's imprisonment, he may be "indicted and fined not less than one thousand dollars, and imprisoned not less than two months, and such free negroes shall be sold as slaves. The Circuit Court of the United States adjudged the law unconstitutional and void. Yet nearly two years after this decision, four colored seamen were taken out of the English brig Marmion. England made a formal complaint to our Government. Mr. Wirt, the Attorney-general, gave the opinion that the law was unconstitutional. This, as well as the above-mentioned decision, excited strong indignation in South Carolina. Notwithstanding the decision, the law still remains in force." (Child's Appeal, p. 63.)

"North Carolina has made a law, subjecting any vessel with *free* colored persons on board to thirty days' quarantine, as if freedom were as bad as the cholera! Any person of color coming on shore from such vessels is seized and imprisoned till the vessel departs, and the captain is fined five hundred dollars; and if he refuse to take the colored seaman away, and pay the expenses of his imprisonment, he is fined five hundred more. If the sailor do not depart within ten days after the captain's refusal, he must be whipped thirty-nine lashes; and all colored persons, bond or *free*, who *communicate* with him, receive the same." (Ib., p. 69.)

"In Georgia there is a similar enactment. The prohibition is, in both States, confined to *merchant-vessels*; (it would be imprudent to meddle with *vessels-of-war;*) and any person communicating with such seaman is whipped not exceeding *thirty* lashes. If the captain refuse to carry away seamen thus detained, and pay the expenses of their imprisonment, he is fined five hundred dollars, and also imprisoned not exceeding three months." (Ib.)

The State of Massachusetts sent an agent to South Carolina, and another to Louisiana, to see what adjustment could be made of the difficulties growing out of these enactments. But they were both promptly ejected from those States, laden with insults, and gladly hastened their escape, to save their lives!

A most comprehensive class of oppressive enactments against the free people of color, are those designed and operating, directly or indirectly, TO DRIVE THEM OUT OF THE COUNTRY! Some of the enactments mentioned already, particularly those of Maryland, are known to have had this end in view, and to have been instigated by the leading influences seeking their expulsion to Africa!

A favorite scheme of the Virginia slaveholders, at an early day, was to enlist Congress in the enterprise of colonizing the free blacks in Africa, for the better security of the slave system at home. Soon after the alarms of a suspected or attempted insurrection of slaves, the proposition was formally brought forward. It proved a failure; whereupon the leaders of the movement, members of Congress and others, organized the American Colonization Society, which has its auxiliaries in most of the States, North and South. At the North, it has been advocated as an ally of emancipation; at the South, as the grand conservator of the slave system; in both sections, it has infused the sentiment that there must or can be no emancipations, unless connected with transportation to Africa; that it is impossible for the colored race to enjoy the rights of freemen in this country; and that the whites and blacks cannot live together in peace, in the enjoyment of equal rights! Into the history or the merits of this Society we cannot here enter, any further than is necessary in order to understand the State legislation, Southern and Northern, designed to harass and oppress the free blacks, and drive them out of the country. The constitution of the Society restricts it to the colonization of free colored people, with their own free consent. But it is a well-established fact, that many of its leading members have contemplated, whenever practicable, the employment of force. The reader is referred to Jay's "Inquiry" for abundant evidence of this. And the same class of persons have been busily engaged in promoting legislation against the free people of color, both in the slave and the free States. On many occasions, the auxiliary Colonization Societies, their agents and their public speakers, have explicitly justified and sanctioned those oppressive enactments. And the official organ of the Parent Society (the African Repository) has given systematic circulation to those injurious and slanderous aspersions of this much-injured class, upon which the legislative persecution of them has been based. (See Jay's Inquiry, p. 18, &c.) In the preceding chapter, we have quoted an instance of direct approbation of those laws by an auxiliary Society, and will here add one more. The New-York State Colonization Society, in a memorial to the State Legislature, said: "We do not ask that the provisions of our Constitution and Statute Book should be so modified as to RELIEVE AND EXALT the condition of the colored people *whilst they remain with us.* Let these provisions stand, IN ALL THEIR RIGOR, to work out the ultimate and unbounded good of this people!" That is, by compelling them to be colonized, or remain oppressed and degraded!

In Connecticut, in 1833, the leading colonizationists procured a legislative enactment against schools for colored pupils, avowedly for the purpose of breaking up the school of Miss Prudence Crandall, at Canterbury. Under that enactment she was prosecuted, and being unable to procure bail, was committed to prison, but was bailed out the next day. At her trial, before Judge Daggett, a verdict was given against her. "The cause was removed to the Court of Errors, where all the proceedings were set aside on technical grounds." Miss Crandall's school was afterwards broken up by a mob; and the gentleman who had been most active in procuring the passage of the "back act" against the education of free negroes (Mr. A. T. Judson) was appointed agent and orator of the Windham County Colonization Society. We record the facts, in evidence that enactments against the free people of color are not a dead letter, but are procured and sustained by the leading influences in the Church and the State, at the North and the South.

In Philadelphia, in New-York city, and in other places, meetings of the Colonization Society, in which Doctors of Divinity, statesmen, and jurists have declaimed vehemently against the free people of color, denied their right to a home in the land of their birth, and justified the oppressive statutes against them, have been immediately followed by frightful riots against the proscribed class, in which their dwellings have been demolished, their churches broken open and injured, their persons assaulted, and numbers of them, in one instance, killed! And no legal protection nor redress has been extended to them! These scenes have been uniformly followed by special efforts to induce them to be colonized in Liberia "with their own free consent"!!!

The Virginia and Maryland auxiliaries to the American Colonization Society have sought and obtained appropriations from the Legislatures of those States, under circumstances that virtually involved compulsion. The original bill (in the Virginia Legislature) making the appropriation "contained a clause for the compulsory transportation of free blacks." (Jay's Inq., p. 50.) On a motion to strike out the compulsory clause, Mr. Brodnox opposed it, saying: "IT IS IDLE TO TALK OF NOT RESORTING TO FORCE. *Every body must look to the employment* of *force of some kind or other!* If the free negroes are willing to go, they will go. If not willing, *they must be compelled to go.* Some gentlemen think it *politic not now* to insert this feature in the bill, THOUGH THEY PROCLAIM THEIR READINESS TO RESORT TO IT WHEN NECESSARY; they think that for a year or two a sufficient number will consent to go, AND THEN THE REST CAN BE COMPELLED. For my part, I deem it better to approach the question at once, and settle it openly. The intelligent portion of the free negroes know very well what is going on. Will they not see that coercion is ultimately to be resorted to? I have already expressed my opinion that few, very few, will voluntarily consent to emigrate if no compulsory measures be adopted. Without it, you will still, no doubt, have applicants for removal, equal to your means. Yes, Sir. People will not only *consent*, but *beg* you to deport them! But *what sort* of consent? A consent extorted by a species of oppression calculated to render their situation among us insupportable! Many of those who have been already sent off went with their avowed consent, but under the influence of a more decided compulsion than any which this bill holds out. I will not express in its fullest extent the idea I entertain of what has been done, or *what enormities* will be perpetrated to induce this class of persons to leave the State."

Mr. B. proceeded to describe, at length, the process of obtaining "consent" by a series of "flagellations," and then said:

"I have certainly heard (if incorrectly, the gentleman from Southampton will put me right) that all the *large cargo of emigrants* lately transported from that country to Liberia, all of whom professed to be willing to go, were rendered so by some such ministration as I have described." (Jay's Inq., pp. 50–1.)

Mr. Fisher expressed similar sentiments. The compulsory clause was, however, stricken out. The result justified the prediction of Messrs. Brodnax and Fisher.

"I warned the managers against this Virginia business," (said Rev. R. J. Breckenridge,) "and *yet* they sent out two ship-loads of vagabonds, not fit to go to such a place, and that were *coerced* away as truly as if it had been done by a cart-whip." (Speech before the Society. Jay's Inq., p. 51–2.) Dr. Breckenridge, it is believed, has since declared himself openly in favor of compulsory colonization, with a view, perhaps, of avoiding the worse "enormities" described by Mr. Brodnax.

The "Maryland Colonization Society" having, at length, (in 1841,) openly defined its position, we let it speak for itself, in its own language. We have the account from a Baltimore paper. The meeting was held in the Light Street Methodist Episcopal Church, Bishop WAUGH in the chair, and the meeting opened with prayer! The declaration is as follows:

"That while it is most earnestly hoped that the free colored people of Maryland may see that their best and most permanent interests will be consulted by their emigration from this State; and while this Convention would deprecate any departure from the principle which makes colonization dependent upon the voluntary action of the free colored people themselves; yet if, regardless of what has been done to provide them with an asylum, they continue to persist in remaining in Maryland, in the hope of enjoying here an equality of social and political rights, they ought to be solemnly WARNED that, in the opinion of this Convention, a day must arrive when circumstances *that cannot be controlled*, and which are now maturing, WILL DEPRIVE THEM OF THE FREEDOM OF CHOICE, and leave them no alternative but removal."

And this is what is meant by colonizing the free people of color with their own consent! The Maryland Colonization Society, with a Bishop presiding, and with its meeting opened by prayer, have openly taken a position that the Legislature of Virginia, from a remaining sense of decency, could not be persuaded to avow!

A Florida slaveholder wrote "A Treatise on the Patriarchal System of Slavery," in which he says: "Colonization in Africa has been proposed to the free colored people, *to forward* which, a general system of *persecution* against them, upheld from the pulpit, has been *legalized* throughout the Southern States." (Jay's Inq., p. 49.) That "Florida slaveholder" (if we mistake not the person) has good cause to *feel* the injustice he describes. His only heirs are "free people of color," his own children, for whom he has obtained an education among the abolitionists of the North! We see in this, one of the many ways in which the wrongs of the colored race are visited upon their white oppressors.

The constitutions and statutes of free States debarring their free colored citizens from eligibility to office, and from equal access to the ballot-box, are among the most marked and mischievous specimens of injury to the colored race. It is this that sustains the slave States in their oppression of both the bond and the free. And of this iniquitous legislation at the North, the negro pew and the corresponding treatment of negroes in seminaries of learning controlled by the Church are the principal supports. A Legislative Committee, in the State of New-York, alleged *this* as *the* reason why the policy of the State could not be changed. Social customs, placing colored people out of the pale of refined society, come under the same censure. How much better, on the whole, are the PEOPLE than their LAWS, whether at the North or at the South?

The picture presented in this chapter contrasts strikingly with the condition of the free people of color in the British West Indies before emancipation, and at the time it took place. That event, if we are rightly informed, found the free colored people in the enjoyment of civil and political rights, some of them editors of public journals, and holders of municipal office.

But such a condition of things, it may be said, could not consist with the perpetuity of West Indian slavery, and may account for its termination. Be it so. Our slaveholders undoubtedly think so. The whole system of persecuting and of attempting to drive away the free people of color to Africa, has its origin in this apprehension. The main object is the perpetuity of slavery. The fugitive slave bill is chiefly designed and relied upon to *frighten the free colored people of the free States out of the country! This is its chief power!*

The "innocent legal relation of slave ownership" comes in again here, as the responsible parent of all the oppressive enactments recorded in this chapter.

CHAPTER II.

LIBERTIES OF THE WHITE PEOPLE OF THE SLAVEHOLDING STATES.

The White People of the Slaveholding States, whether Slaveholders or Non-slaveholders, are deprived, by the Slave Code, of some of their essential rights, and cannot be regarded as a people in possession of civil, religious, and political Freedom.

THE usages of human chattelhood cannot be tolerated in any community without impairing the freedom and invading the rights of *every member* of that community, whether slaveholder or non-slaveholder. The fact of tolerated human chattelhood is the fact of constantly violated *natural law*, which lies at the basis of *all* law, the guardian of *every* man's rights. In the very act of claiming a slave, a man denies *all* rights of property, by denying the inherent right of self-ownership in all men, upon which right all other rights are based. All rights of *personal security* are denied by the same claim. Wherever "the innocent legal relation" of slave ownership is witnessed and is tolerated, there is witnessed the public and deliberate *denial* of all that which forms the basis of human laws, and upon which all legislative enactments for the protection of human rights must repose.

One necessary consequence must be, that in adjusting the legislation and the jurisprudence of a country to the public recognition of human chattelhood, the adjustment must inevitably trench upon the rights of all *other* men, as well as upon the rights of the enslaved. This may seem to some a mere abstract speculation, but a few familiar instances will make the case clear.

We will take, in the first place, the case of the slaveholder himself. Assuredly, it will be said, the slaveholder is sufficiently free! Let us examine. To be a despot is a very different thing from being free.

Here is a slaveholder who, as a thrifty manager of his own property, wishes to make the best and most economical use of his *slave* property, according to his own best discretion. Can he do so? Here is Tom, a shrewd, intelligent, trustworthy fellow, whom he would gladly make "overseer" of his plantation, as is indeed *sometimes* done. He wishes to send Tom to market frequently with his produce, and to buy goods. It would be very convenient to have Tom read, write, and "cipher," which "the law" will not allow! And here comes the *new* law, requiring each planter to keep "at least one" *white* man on the plantation, (under pretense that a white *witness* must be there.) This *one* white man must, of course, *do something* to pay his way. What can it be but to act as overseer, in which double capacity, if need be, he can bear witness against himself or his employer! So *Tom*, in whom his master reposes more confidence, must sink back into the station of a mere field hand.

Here is a waiting-maid, discreet and pious; or here is a nurse, whom all her owner's children call "Mammy." A little knowledge of letters would qualify one or both of them to teach the little white masters and misses their alphabet. Is it too much to suppose that there is, in all the slaveholding South, *one* "good Christian slaveholder" (so called) who has good sense and humanity enough to desire such an arrangement? [If there is *not*, let "the innocent legal relation" be called to account for it.] If there *be* such an one, where is the legal protection of his right to select a teacher of the alphabet to his own children? In Louisiana, he would be subject to one year's imprisonment for teaching such a slave to read! He enjoys *liberty*, does he?

But here is a master whose aspirations for freedom are less sublimated. He only wishes to make money by slaveholding. And the best way, he thinks—especially as he has not the land for them to cultivate, or does not choose the vexation of attending to that business—is to let them "hire out" in the neighboring borough, where their labor, at various jobs, is much wanted by the *white* citizens. A "peculium" of their earnings would greatly stimulate their exertions. But the Slave Code forbids it! And it forbids the white citizens of the borough, including slave owners, to employ them. This is *liberty for white* people! Forbidden to hire their work done for them! They will be likely, in *such* an exigency, to discover that there is "a *higher law*" than the Slave Code!

Look next at the enactments forbidding emancipation on the soil, or obstructing or forbidding it altogether. Those slaveholding Quakers in North Carolina that emancipated 134 slaves in 1776, only to see them reënslaved!—where were *their* rights? They forfeited them, perhaps, by turning abolitionists.

Look then at the dying Thomas Jefferson, the penman of the declaration that "all men are created equal," now penning a clause of his last will and testament, conferring freedom (as common report says) on his own enslaved offspring, so far as the Slave Code permitted him to do it, supplying the lack of power by "*humbly*" *imploring* the Legislature of Virginia to confirm the bequests, "with permission to remain in the State, where their families and connections are"—then dying, under the uncertainty whether his requests would be granted or his children sold into the rice swamps! One of his daughters, it seems, *was* afterwards sold at auction in New-Orleans, at the *harem price!* And his granddaughter was colonized to Liberia—"coerced" perhaps by the "cart-whip!" A land of liberty for white people—for slaveholders, *is it*—where *a Jefferson* cannot bequeath liberty to his own children! In Georgia, had he lived and died there, the "*attempt*" would have been an "*offense*," for which his estate would have been subjected to a fine of a thousand dollars, and each of his executors, if accepting the trust, a thousand more!

The "Florida slaveholder" before mentioned, with his princely fortune, his educated and accomplished heirs, the children of his parental affection, HIS ONLY ones, but—under the "persecuting" ban of the "Colonization Society," "the pulpit," (Northern and Southern,) and the "legislation" approved by them—outcasts, unable to testify in a Court, against a white man; liable to be colonized to Liberia under force of "flagellations" and untold "enormities;" or even to be kidnapped and enslaved!—the Florida slaveholder, we say, with such a family around his board, presents *another* specimen of the liberty and human right senjoyed by the slaveholder! By no means so rare a case as the Northern reader would, perhaps, imagine.

Nor is it on the plantation alone that such cases occur. We remember a thrifty mechanic in a Southern city, who acquired a comfortable estate, and lived more elegantly than mechanics in Southern cities commonly do. He owned several slaves. But his *family* was of the mixed race. He lived with a quadroon woman, without marriage, of course, for the laws would not permit it. His daughters were elegant, beautiful, and nearly white. They were free, as was also their mother; but they were subject to the vexations that harass "*free* people of color." The father sought for them respectable connections in life, and nothing but the laws forbidding such marriages stood in the way; for they were much admired, members of the Methodist Episcopal Church, and *one* of them was loved and wooed by a *white* member of the *same* church, and a slaveholder; but the *law* stood in the way of their marriage! She might have become his *mistress* without fear of the law, and almost, perhaps, without scandal. Whether she afterwards did so, we cannot tell. We call attention to the legal rights, NOT of *slaves*, but of *slaveholders*, to the holy institution of marriage, and to the sanctities of the family relation.

Having broached the "delicate subject," we will venture one other illustration. A young man, a son of a slaveholder, a graduate of one of our Northern colleges, became enamored, on his return home, of a beautiful girl, *nearly* white, who was the property of his father. She had been piously educated, and had become a member of a church. The young man, too, had made a profession of religion at the North. They had played together in childhood, and were affectionately attached to each other. An illicit or secret connection was not to be contemplated. But she was a slave; and whether bond or free, she could not legally be married to a white man! What could be done? If they eloped without her owner's consent, the slave-catchers and their bloodhounds might be after them. If his consent and her free papers could be obtained, where should they go? Not to the "free North," for the exquisite curl of her hair, so lovely in *his* eyes, would attract the attention and the obloquy of the children of the Puritans.

The sequel we cannot tell, further than that the young man took an exploring voyage to the West Indies, and was said to have returned. Whether they emigrated and were married, or whether, remaining in this "free Christian country," they fell into the current of prevailing usages around them, we cannot tell. The imagination of a Mrs. Harriet Beecher Stowe may fill up the picture—a subject worthy of her pencil.

Are we dealing in romance? Come, then, and we will introduce you to a Vice-President of the United States—a very singular man, to be sure, though *not* singular in being a slaveholder, nor singular in having beautiful colored daughters, to be sought after (in some sort) by white gentlemen; but singular in giving his colored daughters a good education, attending them in public *as* a father, and insisting that whoever admired and sought them should do so only in the way of honorable marriage! The singularity of Colonel Richard M. Johnson attracted the nation's attention. He was *so very* singular as to treat the mother of his colored daughters as though she were his wife, to give her the charge of his household, a seat by his side at his table, addressing her as "Mrs. Johnson"—to do all this, instead of selling her in the market, as some other great statesmen have sold the mothers of their colored children. When "Mrs. Johnson" became religious and wished to unite with the church, the good minister felt it his duty to tell her that there was an obstacle in the way—the scandal of her living as she did with

Colonel Johnson. She immediately communicated the fact to the Colonel. "You know, my dear," said he, "I have always been ready to marry you, whenever it could be done. I am ready now, and will call on your minister about it." He did so, and requested the minister to marry them, after explaining the facts of the case. The good minister was now in a worse dilemma than before! What! marry Colonel Johnson to a *colored* woman! What could he say? He could only say that the law would not permit such a marriage. "Very well," retorted Colonel Johnson, (who was not a Christian,) "if your Christian law of marriage will not permit me to marry the woman of my choice, nor permit her to marry the man of her choice, it must even permit us to live together *without* marriage." So saying, he walked away, and that was the last that was said about the marriage. Whether the lady was received into the church, we cannot tell.

Before the outbreak of the anti-abolition excitement, and the consequent clamor about amalgation, an agent of the New-York State Temperance Society (Rev. Mr. Yale) was sent to New Orleans to promote the cause of temperance. He wrote from thence a letter, published in an Albany religious paper, containing a graphic picture of the state of morals and of society in that city. The cause of temperance could make little progress there without a reformation in other respects: the uprooting of habits of licentiousness, the restoration of the family institution; but *this* can never be, he continued, until the laws are repealed which forbid the intermarriage of the white and colored races. A large portion of the people are of the mixed blood. The women of this class are accounted elegant and beautiful. Many of the first gentlemen of New-Orleans will live with them, whether with or without marriage; the consequence of which is a general depravity of morals.

It is needless to say that the picture is truthful, and that its truthfulness is not confined to New-Orleans. One iron link in the chain of the slave is the denial to him of the rights of the family relation, and of freedom of choice in marriage. But *this* badge of slavery we have found upon the neck of the *slaveholder*. In denying free marriage to his *colored* brother, the white man has denied the same right to himself!

We cannot dismiss this branch of the subject without a further remark. When we contemplate the vast and rapidly increasing extent of intermixture between the races; when we remember that "the noblest blood of Virginia" and of all the slave States "runs in the veins of slaves," and is still more widely diffused among the so-called "free people of color;" and when we remember the *legalized persecutions*, inflictions, and liabilities to which even this latter class are found subject—hunted back into slavery, or driven as exiles from the country of their birth—we are shut up to one of two conclusions: Either the Southern slaveholders must be *almost universally* the most heartless, barbarous, and brutal people on the face of the earth, or else there must be thousands of slaveholders whose hearts are wrung daily with anguish, at the thought of the murderous injustice done by the slave laws to their relations and kindred—to their children, to their sisters, to their brothers, to their nephews, to their nieces, to their cousins—for of *such* are a large portion of the slaves and free colored people composed!

We take the most charitable supposition, and conclude that the same cruel laws that wear out the lives of the proscribed race, are oppressive likewise to a large class of slaveholders, who see their near kindred crushed and murdered continually by them.

If this *is not so*, then the pretense of "humane and Christian slaveholders" is all a delusion! If it is not so, then the slave system has extinguished human nature and religion at the South.

If slaveholders are not *themselves* oppressed by the Slave Code, it can only be because they have become monsters who have no sensibilities to be lacerated, no hearts capable of compassion, no unseared consciences to be outraged. We should be sorry to think thus of the majority of them.

The same may be said of the operation of those laws and usages of slavery that forbid the education, religious instruction, and free social worship of the slaves and so-called *free* people of color. The pious *white* people of the South, the ministers of religion, churches, and church members, are *either* aggrieved and oppressed by these enactments and usages, or else *they are not.* On the latter supposition, we are presented with a Church and ministry disregardful of their high mission, and well-nigh apostate. On the former, we see a Church and ministry under the ban of persecution, and crippled in their operations by the strong arm of despotic power.

Under laws by which *colored* Methodists, Baptists, and Presbyterians are forbidden the free exercise of religion and religious worship, we are warranted in assuming that *white* Methodists, Baptists, and Presbyterians feel themselves insulted and aggrieved; that when they see them dragged from the house of prayer (or on their return home) to the watch-house, or writhing under the lash awarded by law for the offense, *they sympathize with them under their persecutions*, and feel themselves, in the persons of their brethren and sisters, under the same ban. *Or else*, if it be not so, we are compelled to regard them as virtually consenting to the persecution of their brethren. We should be sorry to think thus of ALL the *white* Methodists, Baptists, and Presbyterians of the South. And consequently we are compelled to consider the better portion of them under persecution along with their colored brethren.

If there be any thing that Christianity enjoins on her disciples—if there be any thing in which they are engaged—if there be any thing from which they cannot, without the strong arm of persecution, be driven; it is the free assembling of themselves together for social worship and consultation, for mutual instruction and united prayer; and especially the communication of religious knowledge to others, and promoting the circulation and reading of the

Holy Scriptures among them. If there are professors of the Christian religion who do not feel themselves aggrieved and persecuted under enactments or usages which restrain or forbid these, we need not be at any great doubt where to classify them.

Religious *white* people, at the South, are either in unity with persecutors, or else they are under persecution themselves.

Where were the religious liberties of that Methodist Home Mission Society whose missionaries among the colored people, Messrs. Wightman and Turpin, were driven from the missionary field in South Carolina, in 1838, as related in a previous chapter?

What were the religious liberties of those *white* Christians in Charleston, (S. C.,) in 1818, who established a Sabbath-school for the instruction of colored children, and then were forbidden (under penalty of fines, imprisonment, and the infliction of "twenty-nine lashes") from teaching them?

What is religious liberty in New-Orleans?

From the New-Orleans Picayune, Aug. 16, 1841: "Chauncey B. Blake was brought before Recorder Baldwin, charged with tampering with slaves. It was proved that he was seen conversing with a number of them in the street; that he asked them if they could read and write, *and if they would like to have a Bible.* This was the amount of the testimony against him. In *palliation* of his conduct, it was shown that he was a regular appointed agent of the Bible Society in New-Orleans, to distribute the Bible to such as would accept of it. *The Society, however, disclaimed having the most distant intention of giving the Scriptures to slaves*, and it was said Blake had exceeded his commission in offering it. But as it appeared to be a misunderstanding on his part, and not intentional interference, he was discharged with a caution *not to repeat his offense*." (Furnished by Judge Jay.)

What is civil, religious, or political liberty; or where is the independence of the judiciary under enactments like the following?

Louisiana.—"If any person shall use any language from the BAR, BENCH, STAGE, PULPIT, or in any OTHER place, or hold any CONVERSATION having a TENDENCY to promote discontent among free colored people, or insubordination among slaves, he may be imprisoned at hard labor not less than three nor more than twenty-one years; or he may suffer death, at the discretion of the Court." (Child's Appeal, p. 71. See also Kent's Commentaries, vol. II., part IV., p. 268, Note.)

The lawyer cannot effectively plead the cause of a negro claiming his liberty; the judge, in charging the jury, or in giving his judicial decision, cannot repeat the common law maxims of Blackstone, Littleton, Coke, and Fortescue, appropriate to the case; the actor of a drama cannot repeat the best passages in Shakspeare; the minister of the gospel cannot use the language of Bishop Porteus, of John Wesley, of Jonathan Edwards; nay, of St. James or Isaiah, without incurring the hazards of a condemnation under this statute! When one reads the labored "opinions" of Judge Ruffin and others, in Wheeler's Law of Slavery, where the *man* is seen struggling with the *judge*, and a strong sense of the *wrong* of slavery betrays itself amid forced apologies and decisions in its *favor*, it is difficult to resist the impression that the intelligent judge is *himself* under the yoke of bondage to such statutes as the preceding, or to the proscriptive temper that gave rise to them. The same may be said of such self-contradictory clergymen as Dr. Fuller and others, who, on the slave question, cannot conceal their *knowledge* of anti-slavery truth, nor their *fear* of giving it expression. There is no freedom of speech nor of the press on this subject in the slave States.

"In Mississippi, a white man who prints or circulates *doctrines*, sentiments, advice, or *inuendoes*, LIKELY to produce discontent among the colored class, is fined from one hundred to a thousand dollars, and imprisoned from three to twelve months." (Child's Appeal, p. 71.)

"In North Carolina, 'for publishing or circulating any pamphlet or paper having an evident *tendency* to excite slaves or free persons of color to insurrection or resistance,' the law provides imprisonment not less than one year, *and* standing in the pillory *and* whipping, at the discretion of the Court, for the first offense, and DEATH for the second." (Ib., p. 67.)

"In Georgia, the same without any reservation." (Ib.)

"In Virginia, the first offense is punished with thirty-nine lashes, and the second with death." (Ib.)

Mr. Preston, Senator in Congress, declared, in his place in that body, that any person uttering abolition sentiments at the South would be hanged.

What liberty, then, is there for *white* people at the South? And who knows how much would be said there against slavery if the people dared to speak their thoughts? Let us not rashly and too severely condemn the entire South. The *white* people there do not enjoy freedom. They share deeply in the bondage of the *blacks!*

"Abolition editors, in slave States, will not dare avow their opinions." (*Missouri Argus.*)

Perhaps the editor of the Argus dares not avow his. Perhaps he penned this very sentence to allay suspicions, and save his own life.

A Southern member of Congress was not restrained by manly independence, or by any sense of shame for the lack of it, to avow his fears of punishment under such laws as have been quoted. An editor of a Northern paper, "*The Friend of Man*," at Utica, N. Y., published Mr. Pinckney's Report in the House of Representatives, on a subject involving the slave question, and to the Report he appended a review of its positions. He sent some spare copies to members of Congress at Washington City, among whom was Hon. Adam Huntsman, of Tennessee, who soon after wrote a letter to the editor, requesting him not to send him any such paper (opposed to slavery) *after he should have returned to Tennessee*, lest the bare *reception and use* of it should subject him to "an infamous punishment—a penitentiary offense of five years' confinement!" The request was of course complied with, and the legislator remained unharmed.

Where are the liberties of the citizens of the slave States, when forbidden to "trade, barter, or commerce" with one third, one half, or two thirds of the inhabitants—forbidden to obey God by hiding the outcasts — forbidden to "entertain strangers," to "give food to the hungry"—forbidden to convey their persecuted neighbors to a home of security—forbidden to ease their tortures by striking off their pronged iron collars from their necks? Who will slander the South by saying that none of its white citizens *feel themselves* injured, crushed, persecuted, and wronged by enactments like these? Or can a people be said to enjoy liberty and security who live under such a code as this?

There can be no liberty where there is no security, no protection, no law. And in the presence of such despotic power as that of the slaveholder, there can remain very little of these. A general spirit of lawlessness pervades the slave States.

As to the non-slaveholding whites in the slave States, they are, as a class, and with few exceptions, in an abject and degraded condition. A large portion of them are uneducated and poor. In the presence of slave labor, and with the soil in the hands of slaveholders, there is little of lucrative labor within their reach. And labor is *there* a badge of disgrace, assimilating them with the slaves. It is not strange that large numbers of them become improvident and idle. Mechanics, including some from the North, constitute, to a considerable extent, an exception to these remarks. Even these are looked down upon by the slaveholding planters, who have contrived to monopolize and wield nearly all the political power.

On the whole, it cannot with propriety be said that civil, religious, and political liberty exist in the slaveholding States. Nor can they exist there, so long as "the legal relation of owner and slave" remains. *That* relation blights and destroys all the natural and heaven-established relations of life.

CHAPTER III.

LIBERTIES OF THE WHITE PEOPLE OF THE NON-SLAVEHOLDING STATES.

The Rights of the White People of the Non-slaveholding States are directly and indirectly invaded by the Slave Code of the Slave States. Their Liberties, to a great extent, have already fallen a sacrifice, and can never be secure while Slaveholding continues.

WE open, here, upon a wider field than our limits will permit us to explore as its importance demands. The entire political history of the country, which might occupy volumes, demands attention under this head. But we must pass it by, only asking of the reader that he examine it at his leisure.*

The topics of the last preceding chapter might, for the most part, be introduced here again. The white people of the North and of the South suffer, in common, many of the heavy inflictions of the slave master's lash. If the stroke fall less heavily upon the citizens of the free States, it nevertheless falls, and none the less really because, from stupidity induced by long-standing habit, a callous insensibility

* Some sketches and outlines of this history may be found in the Author's "Slavery and Anti-Slavery, a History," &c.

indicates that it is scarcely felt or perceived. In no other way did ever a people, once free, submit to part with their freedom. "A people," says Montesquieu, "may lose their liberties in a day, and not miss them for a century." Thus it was with the Romans, who, under the reign of the tyrant Nero, had not ceased boasting of their liberties!

So closely connected are the people of the free and of the slave States, that whatever affects the latter can scarcely fail to affect the former.

If the spectacle of human beings bereft of self-ownership and the rights of property is found to undermine the foundations of personal security and the rights of property at the South, they cannot remain perfectly stable at the North.

If brutal inflictions on the slaves beget brutal assaults and encounters between Southern gentlemen, the contamination of the bad example cannot but have its effect at the North.

If slave labor at the South makes manual labor a badge of degradation *there*, such labor will become less respectable in the free States.

If the whites of the South submit to the tyranny that forbids them to hold "commerce, trade, or barter" with one half of their neighbors, the money-making traffickers of the North will scarcely think of the indignity or the immense losses they suffer, in being shut out by the Slave Code from their natural and political right of commerce with millions of their fellow-countrymen.

If the people of the South become debased and

servile, by submitting to the loss of freedom of speech and of the press, those inestimable rights will become less prized at the North, and the natural attempts of slaveholders to extend this feature of their sway over the North will not lack for auxiliaries among editors, politicians, statesmen, lawyers, judges, and ministers of religion, in close affinity with those slaveholders at the North.

If the whites of the South submit to enactments which forbid them to relieve the suffering, to feed the hungry, to shelter the outcasts, to perform the common offices of humanity to those most in need of them, the same ignoble and unmanly servility will be likely to manifest itself at the North, until the despots of the South become emboldened to enact statutes for extending *this* feature of their sway over the entire country.

If churches, church members and ministers of religion at the South (either as persecutors or as persecuted) submit to arrangements by which the rights of free social worship, religious instruction, and missionary labor (including the distribution of Bibles and the teaching of the people to read) are forbidden and suppressed, the churches, church members and ministers of the North connected with them, will be exposed to similar indignities, temptations, and derelictions. And by this process it may come to pass that, while compassing sea and land to convert the heathen abroad, and give to every family on the earth a Bible, and teach them to read it in Sabbath-schools, admonishing their missionaries not to heed the prohibitory decrees of civil governments, they may, nevertheless, be among the first to cry out against the application of their own doctrine to the heathen of America, made such by the slave codes of the South.

And, finally, if the non-slaveholding whites of the South submit to be shorn of their political power, and despoiled of their civil liberties and political rights, the non-slaveholding whites of the North, equally contemned by the same oligarchy of slaveholders, will be likely to imbibe the same spirit of pusillanimous submission, to sink into the same degradation, and share the same fate.

The intelligent reader need not be told that such, indeed, are the facts of the case, as already developed and incorporated into the history of the country. We need not and cannot enter here into the details; nor is it necessary to cite authorities in proof. Whoever has been on the stage of action in this country, and a reader of the public journals for the last twenty years, will be at no loss for the particulars to which we refer.

What has been now witnessed was matter of intelligent anticipation and prediction before it took place. Though the climax of disgrace and ruin has not yet been reached, and may yet be averted by prompt efforts, yet we have come sufficiently near the precipice to recognize the truthfulness of the picture drawn, long since, of the gulf below, by one of our most eminent statesmen. In the House of Delegates of Maryland, in 1789, William Pinck-

NEY (a member of the Convention that had just drafted the Federal Constitution) held the following remarkable language:

"I have no hope that the stream of *general liberty* will flow for ever unpolluted through the mire of partial *bondage*, or that those who have been habituated to lord it over others will not, in time, become base enough to let others lord it over them. If they resist, it will be the struggle of pride and selfishness, not of principle."

If the relation of slave owner and slave is to be continued, all this may be expected to follow, as the natural if not necessary result. By reverting again to the facts presented in the latter part of our chapter on the "origin of the relation and its subjects," it will be seen that the process of *enslaving white people* has already commenced, and is making steady and rapid progress, with the prospect (according to Henry Clay) of becoming prevalent a few generations hence, when the slavery and the existence of the *black* race shall have ceased.

CONCLUDING CHAPTER.

Summary Review of the Slave Code—Its Character and Effects—Inquiries concerning the Duties of Christians, Churches, and Ministers—the Responsibilities of Citizens, of Society, of Civil Government, of Legislators and Magistrates—Scrutiny of the Legality of American Slavery—The Heaven-prescribed Remedy—The Worthlessness of Temporizing Substitutes—Closing Appeal.

If the reader has attentively considered the preceding pages, he will now be able to pass an intelligent judgment upon the character of the *Slave Code*, and of the practice of *slaveholding*, protected and defined *by* it. The so-called "*legal relation of master and slave*" he will have found to be the relation of an *owner* to a *human chattel*, body and soul. The verity and the efficacy of this monstrous claim he will have traced in each successive chapter and topic of the entire treatise. He will have witnessed the legitimate workings of this claim in the connected incidents of slave traffic, seizure of slave property for debt, inheritance and division of slave property, and *uses* of slave property. He will have seen that in the presence of this claim slaves can possess nothing, can make no contract, can neither enter into the *marriage* relation, nor discharge the duties, nor claim the rights, nor share the sanctities of the *family* relation. He will have observed how this claim of absolute proprietorship in the slave involves the claim and virtually secures the exercise of unlimited and irresponsible authority on the part of the "owner;" the enforcement of his labor without wages; the direction of his food, clothing, and shelter; the infliction of discretionary punishment upon him, virtually amounting (in consequence of the incompetency of colored witnesses) to the power of life and death over him. This despotic power of the "owners" he will have seen delegated to overseers or agents, and shared by the members of their families. The same relation of slave ownership he will have seen substituting the legal protection of slave *property* for the *personal* protection of the slaves, leaving them exposed to the most frightful barbarities, without the right of self-protection, or the means of redress by a suit against the "owner;" without power of self-redemption, or even a change of masters. This "relation," hereditary and perpetual, he has found to include the most crushing spiritual despotism over the rights of conscience ever claimed by man on the face of the earth; and he has seen it hunting its fugitive victims as if they were brute beasts. This "relation," as thus developed and systematized, he has found to have been originated by the piratical African slave-trade, as commenced by the infamous John Hawkins, yet extending itself over Indians and white persons, and fostering in the heart of our boasted republic a slave-trade more demoralizing than that on the African coast.

This so-called "legal relation," as thus defined and described, he will have found to be the very same that is daily declared to be a blameless and innocent one, involving no guilt in those who "hold" and "sustain" it.

The attentive reader has *further* seen how this "relation" of slave ownership has shaped and determined the "relation" of the slave to society and to civil government; how it bars his access to the judiciary, denying his capacity to be a party to a civil suit; how it bids the Courts reject the testimony not only of *slaves*, but of *free* colored persons; how it enforces the subjection of slaves not only to their "owners" and overseers, but to *all other white* persons; how it frames and executes unjust and inhuman penal enactments against the slaves; how it forbids their education, their religious instruction and free social worship; and, finally, how it interposes obstacles to manumissions by the master, and to acts of emancipation by the State.

The same "relation" of slave ownership he has found waging successful warfare upon the liberties of the free, degrading the free people of color, and dragging them back into chattelhood; despoiling the free whites of the South, not excepting slaveholders themselves, of some of the essential rights of humanity, freedom of speech and of the press, the right of propagating true religion, and of reducing it to practice by deeds of justice and mercy to the oppressed; extending the same iron sway over the free citizens of the North, and bidding the sons of the Pilgrims dishonor their sires, by joining in the hunt after fugitive slaves.

All this the attentive readers of the preceding pages have witnessed. The writer will not insult them by asking them whether they consider *such* a "relation," with such a paternity, with such a character, and with such fruits, an *innocent* one, reposing upon the foundation of apostles and patriarchs, the Bible its charter, the Founder of Christianity its chief corner-stone! But he wishes to propound to them, for their consideration and decision, a few plain and important practical questions.

Is it not high time that the churches of this country, of all sects, their members and ministry, were purged from the sin of slaveholding, and from the taint of religious fraternity with slaveholders?

If this system and sum of abominations is to be tolerated in the Church, what description of practices, what crimes should be excluded from her pale and debarred from her communion? Is it theft? Is it robbery? Is it cruelty? Is it murder? Is it man-stealing? Is it extortion? Is it adultery? Is it bloody persecution? Is it using a neighbor's service without wages, and giving him naught for his work? Is it violence? Is it fraud? Is it despising the poor? Is it taking away the key of knowledge? Is it proscribing Bibles, and forbidding free religious worship? Is it upholding, abetting, and sustaining all these combined?

If *these* are to be excluded from religious communion and fellowship, must not the so-called "legal relation of master and slave" be excluded likewise, by excluding those who resolutely persist in sustaining it? *Can* the *former* be done without doing the *latter?* And if it be left undone, what must become of the Church? Will not the salt lose its savor? And what will it then be good for, but to be cast out and trodden under foot of men? Is there nothing in the signs of the times that gives significance to these questions? How long shall infidelity be armed with the most powerful of all weapons against the Bible and Christianity, against the Ministry and the Church?

If the reader be a Christian, will not his regard for Christianity suggest to him the proper answer to these inquiries? And if he be *not* a Christian, would he not, nevertheless, desire to see the most potent of all social influences—that of the prevailing religion of the country—arrayed against this stupendous system of inhumanity and wrong?

If the Saviour of men was manifested "that he might destroy the works" of the Devil, and "proclaim deliverance to the captives;" if his disciples are his witnesses, and engaged in the prosecution of his work, are they not bound to "have no fellowship with the works of darkness, but rather reprove them?" Especially, are not his ministers bound to "cry aloud and spare not; to lift up their voice like a trumpet; to show the people their transgression, and the house of Jacob their sin?" If *such* an iniquity as the holding of humanity in chattelhood may escape their rebukes, what form of wickedness may not claim equal exemption? What commandment of the law, what precept of the gospel, what principle of the Christian theology is not set at naught by the enslaver? What meaning can there be in the words *justice* or *mercy*, what significance in the doctrine of human brotherhood, or what force in the precepts, "Love thy neighbor as thyself," "Remember them that are in bonds, as bound with them," and "Go teach all nations," if the practice of enslaving immortal men, for whom Christ died, and of whose nature he is partaker, is not to be condemned; if the cause of the slave is not to be vindicated; if the oppressor is not to be called to repentance; if his victim is not to be taught and disenthralled?

Is it not mockery to pray, "Thy kingdom come," and yet neglect engaging in labors like these? If the work of elevating depressed humanity be Christ's work, should not the "undoing of the heavy burthens," and "letting the oppressed go free," be the work of Christians, the mission of the Church of Christ?

Turning next to the responsibilities of citizens, of society, of civil government, of legislators, and of magistrates, we demand whether the crime of enslaving and embruting a human being ought not to be promptly and vigorously suppressed by the strong arm of penal law? *If not*, what crime or what outrage against humanity ought to be thus suppressed? Shall a man be punished for stealing *an ox*, or for knowingly receiving, appropriating, and using a *stolen ox*, and yet be suffered with impunity to steal or receive, appropriate and use a *stolen man?* Will the law pretend to protect my rights of *property*, and yet refuse to protect my *personal* right to *myself?* By what authority, by what rule, on what principle, with what consistency, and with what ultimate success, will the law, or the administrators and expounders of law, attempt to maintain, by the sanctions of penal infliction, the rights of WHITE men, while they refuse thus to maintain the rights of BLACK, or YELLOW, or SWARTHY, or BROWN men? Upon what maxims of civil law or of the science of jurisprudence will they proceed in doing this? Or will they proclaim to the world that there *is no such thing as* "LEGAL SCIENCE;" that the pretense of it is a cheat; that the belief in it is a delusion; that jurisprudence is a game of chance; that law rests upon caprice, and interposes no obstacle to aggression, no protection from brute force, no guaranties against despotic power? If *this* be the decision of grave jurists, who will care to have jurists? Who will be grateful for the institution of civil government? Who will respect the magistracy? *Who will venerate* LAW? How shall civil government, jurisprudence, and law be vindicated from aspersion and shielded from execration and contempt, but by wielding them for their high and holy ends? How, indeed, shall this be done but by denying to the American Slave Code (instinct, as it is, with all the elements of inherent lawlessness) any just claim to the honors or the authority of valid law? What, after all, becomes of the boasted *legality* of slave ownership, and where is the legal *validity* of the American Slave Code in the presence of such legal decisions and common law maxims as the following?

"*Statutes against fundamental morality are void.*" (Judge McLean. Supreme Court of the United States.)

Is not the Slave Code "against fundamental morality?" If it is *not*, what existing or conceivable statute could come under that description, or of what use is the maxim? But if the Slave Code *is* "against fundamental morality," have not the people a claim upon Judge McLean and the United States Supreme Court for a decision affirming the illegality of slave ownership, whenever a suitable case shall be presented for their consideration and action?

"*If it be found that a former decision is manifestly absurd and unjust, it is declared,* NOT *that such a sentence was* BAD *law, but that it was* NOT *law.*" (Littleton.)

Are not the "decisions" in support of slavery, as cited in this volume, "manifestly absurd and unjust?" If *not*, what recorded or conceivable decisions *could* be thus characterized? But if they *are* of that character, does not the maxim of Littleton call for judicial decisions declaring "NOT *that such sentence was* BAD *law, but that it was* NOT *law?*"

Will it be said that time and precedent have so settled the law on this subject that it must not or cannot be disturbed?

"Where the foundation is weak, the structure falls." "What is *invalid* from the beginning cannot be made *valid* by length of time." (Noyes' Maxims.)

Will it be said that statutes and judicial decisions set aside or modify natural or common law? It is of the very *nature* of natural or common law to contradict this plea! Hear it:

"The law of nature being coeval with mankind, and dictated by God himself, is, of course, superior in obligation to every other. It is binding all over the globe, in all countries, and at all times. *No human laws have* ANY VALIDITY *if contrary to* THIS; and such of them as *are* valid derive all their force, mediately or immediately, from this original." (Fortescue.)

"The inferior must give place to the superior; man's laws to God's laws. If, therefore, any *statute* be enacted *contrary to these*, it ought to be considered of NO AUTHORITY in the laws of England." (Noyes.)

"If any human law shall *allow* or require us to commit crime, we are bound to transgress that human law, or else we must offend against both the natural and the divine." (Blackstone.)

"When an Act of Parliament is against common right or reason, or repugnant, or impossible to be performed, *the common law will control it*, and adjudge such act to be VOID." (Coke.)

Will it be said that common or natural law may possibly allow the practice of slaveholding?

"Those rights which God and nature have established, and which are therefore called natural rights, such as *life and liberty*, need not the aid of human laws to be more effectually vested *in every man* than they are, neither do they receive any additional strength when declared by the municipal law to be inviolable. On the contrary, *no human legislation has power to abridge or destroy them*, unless the owner himself has committed some act that amounts to a forfeiture." (Fortescue.)

"The law, therefore, which supports slavery and opposes liberty, must necessarily be condemned as cruel, for every feeling of human nature advocates liberty. Slavery is introduced by human wickedness, but God advocates liberty by the nature which he has given to man." (Fortescue.)

Much more might be quoted from the great luminaries of common law to the same point. Can there be any *doubt* on the question of the legality of slavery? If so, the common law rule of decision is simple:

"Whenever the question of liberty *seems doubtful*, the decision must be *in favor of liberty*." (Digest.)

THE REMEDY for slavery and its untold abominations and horrors is simple. It is *so* simple, that worldly wisdom (which is foolishness with God, and which bewilders itself in its own never-ending labyrinths) thinks it complex and difficult. It is merely to cease doing evil, and to commence doing right. It is for the Government to "break every yoke and let the oppressed go free"—to "proclaim liberty throughout the land to all the inhabitants thereof"—to "execute judgment between a man and his neighbor," and "deliver the spoiled out of the hands of the oppressor." It is for the citizens to "bring the poor that are cast out to their own house, and not hide themselves from their own flesh;" to welcome them to a residence "among" them "where they shall choose," "where it liketh them best." It is for the "masters" to "render unto their servants that which is just and equal," "for the laborer is worthy of his reward." It is for the voters, who are the sovereign people, to choose "judges and officers" who shall "judge the people with just judgment," remembering that "he that ruleth over men must be just, ruling in the fear of God." If the tenure of slave property be illegal, let the Courts thus decide. If not, or if the judges decline doing their duty, let the legislators abolish slavery by statute. In either case, let them repeal their own unrighteous enactments. Let those who need the labor of the colored people employ them for honest wages, and leave off living by plunder.

This is God's own remedy for slavery. Experiment has fully tested its safety and its benefits, till those who had not learned to confide in God and walk by *faith* have been compelled to recognize historical facts, and may, at least, walk by *sight.*

A moderate measure of historical information and common sense, one would think, might suffice (with the single eye that causes the whole body to be full of light) to detect the folly, the absurdity, and the inefficiency of all those schemes by which, on this particular subject, men have sought to reach the *ends or results* of justice and honesty without the task of their self-denying exercise. The attempt to kill the poisonous tree of slavery by lopping off a few of its more unsightly branches—the subtle but short-sighted diplomacy that seeks to outwit the arch-enemy of humanity and fritter away his power by temporizing expedients and conciliatory compromises—the policy of conceding the innocency of the so-called legal relation while raising an outcry against its component parts, the particulars in which it consists, the incidents by which it is defined—the inveterate day-dream of suppressing the *traffic* in human beings without overturning human *chattelhood*, or of preventing the *extension* of slavery so long as it is suffered to *exist*—the delusion that the circumscribing of its boundaries (if it were practicable) would be equivalent to its abolition or secure its termination—the notion that national neutrality can uproot a national sin, or excuse from its abandonment; or that there *can* be such a thing as a republican Government maintaining neutrality concerning the chattelhood of its citizens—above all, the expedient of exporting the *oppressed*, instead of ceasing from and overturning *oppression*—these are some of the fallacies of our times which, in generations to come, will be cited as exemplifications of the bewilderment introduced by the presence of slavery.

In conclusion, the writer would urge on all classes of his readers the claims of the enslaved. What portion of the community, or what description of human beings should be exempted from the appeal, or excused from earnest efforts in their favor?

Lives there *the man* who could justify himself in the retirement of his own heart, should his own conscience convict him of coldness and indifference concerning the *chattelhood of man?* Could he help despising himself, and sinking, in his own estimate of himself, to the level of the servile slave, or the dulness of the unthinking brute? Lives there the *woman*, with a woman's heart and a woman's love, whose inmost soul does not bleed at the wrongs of the slave? How could the woman be lovely or attract virtuous love who should fail to do this? How could she respect herself, how could a wise and manly husband confide in her, or how could she claim for herself the respect due to a woman, should she be justly charged or suspected of indifference when woman shrieks under the lash, when woman's affections are outraged, when woman is torn from husband and child, when woman is crushed and polluted by lawless and domineering lust, when woman is transformed to a beast? Is there the circumspect and self-respecting woman who would bestow her affections and repose her confiding hopes upon *the man* who should betray an indifference to such wrongs inflicted upon woman?

Is there a patriot, a lover of his country, who can be indifferent to the existence and the sway of the Slave Code; who does not blush at the national disgrace, and tremble, as did Jefferson, in view of impending judgments incurred by the national sin?

Is there a wise statesman who fails to foresee the ruin of his country and the wreck of its free institutions, unless the leprosy can be healed?

Can the political economist be unconcerned, when

he witnesses this incubus upon the pecuniary prosperity of the republic—this paralysis of the nation's strength.

Can the friend of education, the patron of intellectual progress, neglect to protest against the enforcement of ignorance, the proscription of letters, the closing of every avenue to the intellects of increasing millions of his countrymen? Can he do otherwise than deplore and condemn the code that prevents the establishment and prosperity of schools and colleges for whites, while it forbids the elements of literature and science to the people of color?

Is there the wise legislator, civilian, or jurist, who does not see and condemn, in the Slave Code, the opprobrium of legislation, the disgrace of jurisprudence, the subversion of equity, the promotion of lawlessness, the element of social insecurity, and the seeds of every crime which legislation and jurisprudence should suppress or restrain?

Can the moralist look with unconcern upon a system that fosters every vice, and represses every virtue; that opens the flood-gates of immorality, and shuts up every fountain of enlightenment and reformation?

Can the patrons of Christian missions do less than condemn the code that closes the avenues of missionary enterprise against millions of their own countrymen? Can distributors of Bibles and religious tracts fail to remonstrate with the supporters of a system that forbids the distribution and the reading of them? Can Christians, can Christian ministers and churches be silent witnesses of all this enforced heathenism in our midst? Can they regard with apathy or disfavor the effort to relieve from the condition of chattelhood so many millions of precious souls for whom Christ died?

Every dictate of our common humanity, every impulse of unperverted human sympathy, every deduction of unsophisticated reason, every monition of enlightened conscience, every maxim of sound political wisdom, every conclusion of a far-reaching and prophetic prudence, every principle and precept of our holy religion, every aspiration after a likeness to the blessed Redeemer and the Universal Father, every desire and hope of the onward progress and elevation of our country and our species, unitedly impel us to espouse, earnestly and courageously, the cause of the enslaved.

Let each reader be persuaded to do this, by considerations derived from all that is precious in human nature, or sacred in impartial justice; by all that is binding in moral obligation and law, or ennobling and God-like in mercy; by all that is attractive in human virtue, and inestimable in human freedom; by all that is momentous in a state of earthly probation, and solemn in the final judgment, when it will be said to those who withhold needed kindness, "Inasmuch as ye did it not unto one of the least of these, my brethren, ye did it not unto me."

APPENDIX A.

FUGITIVE SLAVE BILL OF 1850.

AN ACT TO AMEND, AND SUPPLEMENTARY TO THE ACT ENTITLED, "AN ACT RESPECTING FUGITIVES FROM JUSTICE, AND PERSONS ESCAPING FROM THE SERVICE OF THEIR MASTERS," APPROVED FEBRUARY 12, 1793.

Be it enacted by the Senate and House of Representatives of the United States of America in Congress assembled, That the persons who have been, or may hereafter be, appointed commissioners, in virtue of any Act of Congress, by the Circuit Courts of the United States, and who, in consequence of such appointment, are authorized to exercise the powers that any justice of the peace or other magistrate of any of the United States may exercise in respect to offenders for any crime or offense against the United States, by arresting, imprisoning, or bailing the same under and by virtue of the thirty-third section of the Act of the twenty-fourth of September, seventeen hundred and eighty-nine, entitled, "An Act to establish the judicial courts of the United States," shall be, and are hereby authorized and required to exercise and discharge all the powers and duties conferred by this Act.

SEC. 2. *And be it further enacted*, That the Superior Court of each organized Territory of the United States shall have the same power to appoint commissioners to take acknowledgments of bail and affidavit, and to take depositions of witnesses in civil causes, which is now possessed by the Circuit Courts of the United States; and all commissioners who shall hereafter be appointed for such purposes by the Superior Court of any organized Territory of the United States shall possess all the powers and exercise all the duties conferred by law upon the commissioners appointed by the Circuit Courts of the United States for similar purposes, and shall moreover exercise and discharge all the powers and duties conferred by this Act.

SEC. 3. *And be it further enacted*, That the Circuit Courts of the United States, and the Superior Courts of each organized Territory of the United States, shall from time to time enlarge the number of commissioners, with a view to afford reasonable facilities to reclaim fugitives from labor, and to the prompt discharge of the duties imposed by this Act.

SEC. 4. *And be it further enacted*, That the commissioners above named shall have concurrent jurisdiction with the judges of the Circuit and District Courts of the United States, in their respective circuits and districts within the several States, and the judges of the Superior Courts of the Territories, severally and collectively, in term time and vacation; and shall grant certificates to such claimants, upon satisfactory proof being made, with authority to take and remove such fugitives from service or labor, under the restrictions herein contained, to the State or Territory from which such persons may have escaped or fled.

SEC. 5. *And be it further enacted*, That it shall be the duty of all marshals and deputy marshals to obey and execute all warrants and precepts issued under the provisions of this Act, when to them directed; and should any marshal or deputy marshal refuse to receive such warrant or other process, when tendered, or to use all proper means diligently to execute the same, he shall, on conviction thereof, be fined in the sum of one thousand dollars to the use of such claimant, on the motion of such claimant, by the Circuit or District Court for the district of such marshal; and after arrest of such fugitive by such marshal or his deputy, or whilst at any time in his custody, under the provisions of this Act, should such fugitive escape, whether with or without the assent of such marshal or his deputy, such marshal shall be liable, on his official bond, to be prosecuted, for the benefit of such claimant, for the full value of the service or labor of said fugitive in the State, Territory, or district whence he escaped; and the better to enable the said commissioners, when thus appointed, to execute their duties faithfully and efficiently, in conformity with the requirements of the Constitution of the United States and of this Act, they are hereby authorized and empowered, within their counties respectively, to appoint in writing under their hands, any one or more suitable persons, from time to time, to execute all such warrants and other process as may be issued by them in the lawful performance of their respective duties; with an authority to such commissioners, or the persons to be appointed by them to execute process as aforesaid, to summon and call to their aid the bystanders or *posse comitatus* of the proper county, when necessary to insure a faithful observance of the clause of the Constitution referred to, in conformity with the provisions of this Act: and all good citizens are hereby commanded to aid and assist in the prompt and efficient execution of this law, whenever their services may be required, as aforesaid, for that purpose; and said warrants shall run and be executed by said officers any where in the State within which they are issued.

SEC. 6. *And be it further enacted*, That when a person held to service or labor in any State or Territory of the United States has heretofore or shall hereafter escape into another State or Territory of the United States, the person or persons to whom such service or labor may be due, or his, her, or their agent or attorney, duly authorized, by power of attorney, in writing, acknowledged and certified under the seal of some legal office or court of the State or Territory in which the same may be executed, may pursue and reclaim such fugitive person, either by procuring a warrant from some one of the courts, judges, or commissioners aforesaid, of the proper circuit, district or county, for the apprehension of such fugitive from service or labor, or by seizing and arresting such fugitive where the same can be done without process, and by taking and causing such person to be taken forthwith before such court, judge or commissioner, whose duty it shall be to hear and determine the case of such claimant in a summary manner; and upon satisfactory proof being made, by deposition or affidavit, in writing, to be taken and certified by such court, judge, or commissioner, or by other satisfactory testimony, duly taken and certified by some court, magistrate, justice of the peace, or other legal officer authorized to administer an oath and take depositions under the laws of the State or Territory from which such person owing service or labor may have escaped, with a certificate of such magistracy or other authority, as aforesaid, with the seal of the proper court or officer thereto attached, which seal shall be sufficient to establish the competency of the proof, and with proof, also by affidavit, of the identity of the person whose service or labor is claimed to be due as aforesaid, that the person so arrested does in fact owe service or labor to the person or persons claiming him or her, in the State or Territory from which such fugitive may have escaped as aforesaid, and that said person escaped, to make out and deliver to such claimant, his or her agent or attorney, a certificate setting forth the substantial facts as to the service or labor due from such fugitive to the claimant, and of his or her escape from the State or Territory in which such service or labor was due to the State or Territory in which he or she was arrested, with authority to such claimant, or his or her agent or attorney, to use such reasonable force and restraint as may be necessary under the circumstances of the case, to take and remove such fugitive person back to the State or Territory from whence he or she may have escaped as aforesaid. In no trial or hearing under this Act shall the testimony of such alleged fugitive be admitted in evidence; and the certificates in this and the first section mentioned shall be conclusive of the right of the person or persons in whose favor granted to remove such fugitive to the State or Territory from which he escaped, and shall prevent all molestation of said person or persons by any process issued by any court, judge, magistrate, or other person whomsoever.

SEC. 7. *And be it further enacted*, That any person who

shall knowingly and willingly obstruct, hinder, or prevent such claimant, his agent or attorney, or any person or persons lawfully assisting him, her, or them, from arresting such fugitive from service or labor, either with or without process as aforesaid; or shall rescue, or attempt to rescue, such fugitive from service or labor, from the custody of such claimant, his or her agent or attorney, or other person or persons lawfully assisting as aforesaid, when so arrested, pursuant to the authority herein given and declared; or shall aid, abet, or assist such person, so owing service or labor as aforesaid, directly or indirectly, to escape from such claimant, his agent or attorney, or other person or persons, legally authorized as aforesaid; or shall harbor or conceal such fugitive, so as to prevent the discovery and arrest of such person, after notice or knowledge of the fact that such person was a fugitive from service or labor as aforesaid, shall, for either of said offenses, be subject to a fine not exceeding one thousand dollars, and imprisonment not exceeding six months, by indictment and conviction before the District Court of the United States for the district in which such offense may have been committed, or before the proper court of criminal jurisdiction, if committed within any one of the organized Territories of the United States; and shall moreover forfeit and pay, by way of civil damages to the party injured by such illegal conduct, the sum of one thousand dollars for each fugitive so lost as aforesaid, to be recovered by action of debt in any of the District or Territorial Courts aforesaid, within whose jurisdiction the said offense may have been committed.

Sec. 8. *And be it further enacted*, That the marshals, their deputies, and the clerks of the said District and Territorial Courts, shall be paid for their services the like fees as may be allowed to them for similar services in other cases; and where such services are rendered exclusively in the arrest, custody, and delivery of the fugitive to the claimant, his or her agent or attorney, or where such supposed fugitive may be discharged out of custody for the want of sufficient proof as aforesaid, then such fees are to be paid in the whole by such claimant, his agent or attorney; and in all cases where the proceedings are before a commissioner, he shall be entitled to a fee of ten dollars in full for his services in each case, upon the delivery of the said certificate to the claimant, his or her agent or attorney; or a fee of five dollars in cases where the proof shall not, in the opinion of such commissioner, warrant such certificate and delivery, inclusive of all services incident to such arrest and examination, to be paid in either case by the claimant, his or her agent or attorney. The person or persons authorized to execute the process to be issued by such commissioners for the arrest and detention of fugitives from service or labor as aforesaid, shall also be entitled to a fee of five dollars each for each person he or they may arrest and take before any such commissioner as aforesaid at the instance and request of such claimant, with such other fees as may be deemed reasonable by such commissioner for such other additional services as may be necessarily performed by him or them: such as attending to the examination, keeping the fugitive in custody, and providing him with food and lodging during his detention, and until the final determination of such commissioner; and in general for performing such other duties as may be required by such claimant, his or her attorney or agent, or commissioner in the premises; such fees to be made up in conformity with the fees usually charged by the officers of the courts of justice within the proper district or county, as near as may be practicable, and paid by such claimants, their agents or attorneys, whether such supposed fugitive from service or labor be ordered to be delivered to such claimants by the final determination of such commissioners or not.

SEC. 9. *And be it further enacted*, That upon affidavit made by the claimant of such fugitive, his agent or attorney, after such certificate has been issued, that he has reason to apprehend that such fugitive will be rescued by force from his or their possession before he can be taken beyond the limits of the State in which the arrest is made, it shall be the duty of the officer making the arrest to retain such fugitive in his custody, and to remove him to the State whence he fled, and there to deliver him to said claimant, his agent or attorney. And to this end the officer aforesaid is hereby authorized and required to employ so many persons as he may deem necessary to overcome such force, and to retain them in his service so long as circumstances may require; the said officer and his assistants, while so employed, to receive the same compensation, and to be allowed the same expenses as are now allowed by law for the transportation of criminals, to be certified by the judge of the district within which the arrest is made, and paid out of the treasury of the United States.

SEC. 10. *And be it further enacted*, That when any person held to service or labor in any State or Territory, or in the District of Columbia, shall escape therefrom, the party to whom such service or labor shall be due, his, her, or their agent or attorney, may apply to any court of record therein, or judge thereof in vacation, and make satisfactory proof to such court, or judge in vacation, of the escape aforesaid, and that the person escaping owed service or labor to such party. Whereupon the court shall cause a record to be made of the matters so proved, and also a general description of the person so escaping, with such convenient certainty as may be; and a transcript of such record, authenticated by the attestation of the clerk, and of the seal of the said court, being produced in any other State, Territory, or district in which the person so escaping may be found, and being exhibited to any judge, commissioner, or other officer authorized by the law of the United States to cause persons escaping from service or labor to be delivered up, shall be held and taken to be full and conclusive evidence of the fact of escape, and that the service or labor of the person escaping is due to the party in such record mentioned. And upon the production by the said party of other and further evidence, if necessary, either oral or by affidavit, in addition to what is contained in the said record, of the identity of the person escaping, he or she shall be delivered up to the claimant. And the said court, commissioner, judge, or other person authorized by this Act to grant certificates to claimants of fugitives, shall, upon the production of the record and other evidences aforesaid, grant to such claimant a certificate of his right to take any such person identified and proved to be owing service or labor as aforesaid, which certificate shall authorize such claimant to seize or arrest and transport such person to the State or Territory from which he escaped: *Provided*, That nothing herein contained shall be construed as requiring the production of a transcript of such record as evidence as aforesaid; but in its absence, the claim shall be heard and determined upon other satisfactory proofs competent in law.

HOWELL COBB,
Speaker of the House of Representatives.

WILLIAM R. KING,
President of the Senate, pro tempore.

Approved September 18th, 1850.
MILLARD FILLMORE.

APPENDIX B.

SLAVERY AMONG THE CHEROKEES AND CHOCTAWS.

SINCE the body of the preceding work was mostly in type, the author has met with a volume containing the Constitutions and Laws of the Cherokees and Choctaws, which embrace many provisions on the subject of Slavery, very similar to those of our American Slave States in their vicinity, and evidently borrowed from them. A few specimens may be interesting, especially as throwing light upon the question whether it is proper to assist in building up churches in those nations that admit and retain as members those who enact, administer, and support such laws, or who uphold them by claiming and sustaining the relation of slave owners.

THE CHEROKEES.

The "Constitution of the Cherokee Nation," formed by a Convention of Delegates from the several districts at New-Echota, July, 1827, contains the following:

"No person shall be eligible to a seat in General Council but a *free* Cherokee male citizen, who shall have attained to the age of twenty-five years. The descendants of Cherokee men by all *free* women, *except* the African race, whose parents may [have] been living together as man and wife, according to the customs and laws of this nation, shall be entitled to all the rights and privileges of this nation, as well as the posterity of

Cherokee women by all *free* men. *No person who is of negro or mulatto parentage, either by the father or mother side, shall be eligible to hold any office of profit, honor, or trust in this Government.*" (Art. III., sect. 4.)

The same provision is retained in the New Constitution of the Cherokee Nation, passed at Tah-le-quah, in Sept. 1839. (Art. III., sect. 5.)

Among the laws of the Cherokees we find one, Sept. 1839, entitled, "An act to prevent amalgamation with *colored* persons," (meaning descendants of Africans,) just as if Cherokees were whites, and *not* "colored." Penalty, corporal punishment, not to exceed fifty stripes, and such intermarriages declared not to be lawful.

Another "Act," under date of Nov. 15, 1843, is "to *legalize* intermarriage with *white* men !"

Another Act, 7th Nov. 1840, declares that "it shall not be lawful for any free negro or mulatto, *not of Cherokee blood*, to hold or own any improvement within the limits of this nation; neither shall it be lawful for *slaves* to own any property of the following description, viz: horses, cattle, hogs, or fire-arms." Provision is made for the seizure and sale of such property, &c.

Another "Act," Oct. 19, 1841, is for "authorizing the appointment of patrol companies," who "shall take up and bring to punishment any negro or negroes that may be strolling about, not on their owner's premises, without a pass from their owner or owners." And any negro not entitled to Cherokee privileges, if found armed, may be whipped, not exceeding thirty-nine lashes.

Another "Act," dated 22d October, 1841, is for "prohibiting the teaching of negroes to read and write." "*Be it enacted by the National Council*, That from and after the passage of this Act, it shall not be lawful for any person or persons whatever to teach any free negro or negroes *not of Cherokee blood*,* or

* "*Not of Cherokee blood!*" It would be quite an improvement, should our Anglo-Saxon slave legislators imitate this by saying, "*not of English blood*," in their statutes of this character.

any slave belonging to any citizen or citizens of the nation, to read or write." The penalty annexed to a violation of this enactment is a fine of $100 to $500, at the discretion of the Court trying the offense.

"An Act in regard to free negroes," Dec. 2, 1842, directs "the sheriffs of the several districts" to notify free negroes to leave the limits of the nation by the 1st of Jan. 1843. If they refused to go, they were to be immediately expelled. "Sect. 4. Be it further enacted, That should any free negro or negroes be found guilty of aiding, abetting, or decoying any slave or slaves to leave his or their owner or employer, such free negro or negroes shall receive for each and every such offense one hundred lashes on the bare back, and be immediately removed from this nation."

Bound up in the same volume with these Constitutions and enactments, we find the "Constitution of the Cherokee Bible Society," in which is the following: "Art. 2. The object of the Society shall be to disseminate the Sacred Scriptures in the English and Cherokee languages among the people of the Cherokee nation; and all funds collected by the Society shall be expended for that object."

From the preceding extracts of the Constitutions and Laws it would seem that "free negroes and mulattoes not of Cherokee blood" were not considered as "entitled to Cherokee privileges," or as constituting a part of "the Cherokee nation." And the teaching of them or the slaves to read or write, as has been shown, is expressly forbidden, under heavy penalties. So that the peculiar phraseology employed by the Bible Society is readily understood. Its object did not include the supply of such persons, and it was intended to guard against any such use of its funds! It is lamentable to see a nation so recently put in possession of the Bible, so forward to withhold it from others, even forbidding its use! But in this the Cherokees only imitate our own nation and our own Bible Societies, from whom they have received the Scriptures! They have only practised the religion they have received from us! We may see in this the fruit of sending to the heathen a gospel that tolerates slave-holding.

CHOCTAWS.

The Constitution of the Choctaw Nation, approved October, 1838, embodies a "Declaration of Rights," the first article of which commences with, "All *freemen*, when they form a social compact, are equal in rights," &c. It is not difficult to trace the parentage of this emendation of the Declaration of '76. It is revealed in the following:

"From and after the adoption of this Constitution, *no free negro, or any part negro, unconnected with Choctaw or Chickasaw blood*, shall be permitted to come and settle in the Choctaw nation." (Art. VIII., sect. 6.)

"No person who is *any part negro* shall ever be allowed to hold any office under this Government." (Art. VIII., sect. 14.)

"The General Council, when in session, shall have the power by law to naturalize and adopt as citizens of this nation, any Indian, or descendant of other Indian tribes, *except a negro or descendant of a negro.*" (Art. VIII., sect. 15.)

The following is an act approved 5th October, 1836:

"*Be it enacted, &c.*, That from and after the passage of this Act, if any citizen of the United States, acting as a missionary or a preacher, or whatever his occupation may be, is found to take an active part in favoring the principles and notions of the most fatal and destructive doctrines of Abolitionism, he shall be compelled to leave the nation, and for ever stay out of it.

"*Be it further enacted, &c.*, That teaching slaves how to read, to write, or to sing in meeting-houses or schools, or in any open place, without the consent of the owner, or allowing them to sit at table with him, shall be sufficient ground to convict persons of favoring the principles and notions of Abolitionism.

It was provided also that no slave should "be in possession of any property or arms;" that if any slave infringed any Choctaw rights, he should "be driven out of company to behave himself;" and in case of his return and further intrusion, "he should receive ten lashes." But "any good honest slave shall be permitted to carry a gun, by having a pass from his master."

In 1838 it was enacted, "That from and after the passage of this law, if any person or persons, citizens of this nation, shall *publicly take up with a negro slave*,* he or she so offending shall be liable to pay a fine of not less than ten dollars, nor exceeding twenty-five dollars, *and shall be separated;* and for a second offense of a similar nature the party shall receive not exceeding thirty-nine lashes nor less than five, on the bare back, *and shall be separated*, as the Court may determine."

"The Constitution and Laws of the Choctaw Nation," from which the preceding extracts are taken, bears the imprint of 1840, and the latest enactments it contains are dated Oct. 1839. But the "American Missionary," New-York, January, 1853, contains an account of some later enactments, taken from a Report made in 1848 by Mr. Treat, one of the Secretaries of the American Board of Commissioners for Foreign Missions. The following is an extract from this statement of the "American Missionary:"

In 1840 "it was enacted that all free negroes in the nation, unconnected with the Choctaw or Chickasaw blood, 'should leave the nation by the first of March, 1841,' and 'for ever keep out of it.' In case of their infringing this law, 'they were to be seized and sold to the highest bidder for life.' It was also enacted that if any citizen of the nation hired, concealed, or in any way protected any free negro, to evade the foregoing provision, he should forfeit from $250 to $500, or if unable to pay this fine, 'receive fifty lashes on his bare back.'

"In 1846 a law was passed, which prohibited all negroes, whether they had 'papers' or not, from entering and remaining in the Choctaw nation. The offenders were to receive 'not less than one hundred lashes on the bare back,' besides a forfeiture of all property found in their possession, one third 'to

---

* "*Publicly take up with.*" The possibility of a *legal marriage* with a slave seems not to have been recognized. The union was only "a *taking up with*," a phrase used among slaves.

go to the light horsemen' who apprehended them, and two thirds 'to be applied to some beneficial purpose.'

"The most objectionable enactment, says Mr. Treat, which he found, having any bearing upon slavery, was approved October 15th, 1846. It is as follows:

"'*Be it enacted*, *&c.*, That no negro slave can be emancipated in this Nation except by application or petition of the owner to the General Council; and *provided also*, that it shall be made to appear to the Council the owner or owners, at the time of application, shall have no debt or debts outstanding against him or her, either in or out of this Nation. Then, and in that case, the General Council shall have the power to pass an act for the owner to emancipate his or her slave, which negro, after being freed, shall leave this nation within thirty days after the passage of the Act. And in case said free negro or negroes shall return into this Nation afterwards, he, she, or they shall be subject to be taken by the light horsemen and exposed to public sale for the term of five years; and the funds arising from such sale shall be used as national funds.'"

LIST OF REPORTED CASES

CITED IN THIS VOLUME.

Allan *vs.* Young, (La.) 188

Banks, Admr., *vs.* Marksbury, 70
Bazzy *vs.* Rose and child, (Lou.) 149
Beatley *vs.* Judy, (Ky.) 70
Beall *vs.* Joseph, (Ky.) 348
Berard *vs.* Berard et al., (Lou.) 241, 295
Bore *vs.* Bush, (Lou.) 318
Brandon et al. *vs.* Merchants' and Planters' Bank, (Ala.) 92, 293
Butler *vs.* Boardman, (Md.) 278
Bynam *vs.* Bostwick, (S. C.) 29, 293

Carroll et al. *vs.* Connet, (Ky.) 71
Commonwealth (Va.) *vs.* Carver, 194, 204
Commonwealth (Mass.) *vs.* Aves, 262
Cooke (colored) *vs.* Cooke, (Ky.) 350
Cornfute *vs.* Dale, (Md.) 202
Crawford *vs.* Cheney, (La.) 205

Davis *vs.* Curry, (Ky.) 238
Davis *vs.* Sandford, (Ky.) 274
Delphine *vs.* Devise, (La.) 650
Dolly Chapple, (Va.) 194
Dorothee *vs.* Coquillon, (La.) 125, 158, 242
Dunbar *vs.* Williams, (N. Y.) 148

Enlaws *vs.* Enlaws, (Ky.) 71
Emmerson *vs.* Howland, 93

Fields *vs.* State of Tenn., 195
Free Lucy *vs.* Frank, 93

George et al. *vs.* Corse, (Md.) 345
Glen *vs.* Hodges, (N. Y.) 235
Givens *vs.* Mann, (Va.) 349
Girod *vs.* Lewis, (Lou.) 107, 293–4
Gomez *vs.* Bonneval, (Lou.) 280

Hall *vs.* Mullen, (Md.) 91, 93, 264, 349
Hamilton *vs.* Cragg (Md.) 349
Harris *vs.* Clarissa et al., (Tenn.) 30
Harvey et al *vs.* Decker and Hopkins, (Miss.) 262, 264
Hilton *vs.* Caston, 168
Hudgens *vs.* Wrights, (Va.) 263, 273–4, 296
Hutchins *vs.* Lee, (Miss.) 235

Icar *vs.* Suars, (La.) 32

Jarrett *vs.* Higbee, (Ky.) 102
Jennings *vs.* Furderburg, (S. C.) 188–9
Johnson et al. *vs.* Barrett, (S. C.) 149
Jourdan *vs.* Patten, (La.) 205

Kittletas *vs.* Fleet, (N. Y.) 347

Labranche *vs.* Watkins, (La.) 235
Lewis *vs.* Fullerton, (Va.) 349
Lunsford *vs.* Coquillon, (La.) 261–2

Markham *vs.* Close, (La.) 187, 195
Marie Louisa *vs.* Marriott et al. (La.) 261–2
Maria *vs.* Surbach, (Va.) 278
Mary *vs.* Morris et al., (Lou.) 349
McCutchen et al. *vs.* Marshall et al., (U. S.) 278
May *vs.* Brown and Boisseau, (Va.) 203–4
Metayer *vs.* Metayer, (Lou.) 266
Moosa *vs.* Allain, (Lou.) 350.

Negro Tom, (N. Y.) 348
Negro Cato *vs.* Howard (Md.) 349
Negro George et al. *vs.* Corse, (Md.) 345

People *vs.* Lervy, 93

Plumpton *vs.* Cook, (Ky.) 70
Prigg *vs.* Pennsylvania, (U. S.) 168

Rankin *vs.* Lydia, (Ky) 467
Richardson *vs.* Dukes, (S. C.) 189

Sawney *vs.* Carter, (Va) 347, 349
Scidmore *vs.* Smith, 205, 236
Seville *vs.* Chretien (La.) 263–4, 266
Sims White *vs.* James Chambers, (S. C.) 168, 202–3
Smith *vs.* Rowzee, 51
Smith *vs* Hancock, (Ky.) 204
Somerset, James, (slave) 259
State of Miss. *vs.* Jones, 192, 204
" N. J. *vs* Waggoner, 28, 265
" N. C. *vs.* Mann, 32, 79, 126, 154, 169, 204
" " *vs.* Reed, 191
" " *vs.* Hale, 192, 204, 207
" " *vs.* Ben, 317
" " *vs.* Jim, 317
" " *vs.* Charity, 317
State of S. C. *vs.* Maner, 453, 193, 204
" " *vs.* Cheatwood, 168, 191, 204
" " *vs.* E. Smith and R. Smith, 190
" " *vs.* Raines, 190
" " *vs.* McGee, 211
" " *vs.* Hannah Elliott, 233, 277
" " *vs.* Davis and Hanna, 277
" Va. *vs.* Carver, 194, 204
Stevenson *vs.* Singleton, (Va.) 347, 349

Tate *vs.* O'Neill, (N. C.) 203

Vaughan *vs.* Phebe, (Tenn.) 266
Victoire *vs.* Dissua, (Lou.) 349

Wells *vs.* Kennerly, (S. C.) 149
Westell *vs.* Earnest and Parker, (S.C.) 189
White *vs.* Chambers, (S. C.) 168, 202–3
Will *vs.* Thompson, 348

GENERAL INDEX.

Advertisements:
Slaves sold for distribution, 75
" wanted by dealers, 54
" for sale by dealers, 54–5
" taken, and for sale for debt, 66–7
" "acclimated," for sale, 81–2
" "breeder" for sale, 84
" "damaged" wanted, 87
" fugitives in search of their families, 119
Reward for evidence to convict a mother of the crime of "harboring" her son, 119
Of a wife in search of her husband, 119
Reward offered for killing a slave for running off with his wife, 120
Describing fugitives scarred, branded, cropped, shot, &c., 219–20
"Negro dogs" and slave hunting, 236–7
"White" slaves, 284–5
Agricultural Societies, Southern, (testimony of,) 81
Alabama: slaves ill clothed, 146; legalized slave discipline, 165; laws *vs.* harboring fugitives. 233; mode of testing claims to freedom, 299; laws *vs.* preaching, 322; laws *vs.* emancipation, 341–3
Alarm at negroes reading, 336
Alexandria, (D. C.) coroner's inquest, 181
Allan, Rev. Wm. T., (Testimony,) 39, 148, 312
Am. Bible Soc. and slave families, 115
Amer. Colonization Soc. (See Colonization Soc.)
Ameliorations impracticable, 293
Ancient slavery, "*peculium*," 96
An aunt in Court, claiming nieces as slaves of *other* nieces, 241–2
Appendix A, Fugitive Slave Bill, 409
" B, Cherokees and Choctaws, 417
Archer, Judge, 345
Avery, George A.,(Testimony,) 148, 214, 216

Badger, Judge, 317
Baltimore Advertiser, (Testimony,)142
Baptism of slaves, 253, 332
Battery on a slave, 32, &c., 168–9, 192
Betting on a negro's life, in a fit, 40
Berry, Mr. (Va.) Testimony, 323
Bibb, Judge, 103
Bible prohibited, 321, 324
Bible Societies do not supply slaves, 323
Birney, James G., (Testimony,) 57
Blackwell, Samuel, (Testimony,) 80
Bliss, Philemon, (Testimony,) 143–4
Bourne, Rev. Geo., (Testimony,) 111, 141
Boudinot, Tobias, (Testimony,) 141
Bouldin, Hon. T. T., (Testimony,) 145
Boyle, Judge, 275
Branding slaves, 219–20
Breckenridge, Dr. R. J., (Testimony,) 368
Breckenbrough, Judge, 194
"Breeders," 30, 55, 84–5
Brougham, Lord. "No property in man," 270
Brodnax, Mr., (Va.) 367
Buchanan, Dr. Geo., (Testimony,) 145, 222
Butler, Gov., (S. C.) 210
Burning and beheading a slave, 118
" a free negro, 316

Calhoun, John C., (Testimony,) 285
Carey, Matthew, (Testimony,) 211
Catechisms "incendiary," 336
Caulkins, Nehemiah, (Testimony,) 142–3
Charles V., 267
Charleston, (S. C). Bap. Asso. 37–8, 40
" " Observer, (Testimony,) 335
Channing, Dr. Wm. E., (Testimony,) 148

Chattel principle, 23, 29
Choules, Rev. J. O., (Testimony,) 133
Cherokee slave laws, 417
Choctaw slave laws, 420
Clay, Henry, on slave property, 34, 349
" slave traffic, 48, 55
" slave breeding, 84
" overtasking, 132
" slaves "fat and sleek," 152
" perpetuity of slavery, 249, 272
" future slavery of whites, 283
Clay, Thomas, (Testimony,) 141-3
Clarke, Judge, 192
Claims to freedom, 295
Clothing of slaves, 145, &c.
Code Noir, its comparative mildness, 44-5, 68, 75
Colcock, Judge, 189, 190
Colonial Slavery, 260, &c.
Color defined, 277
" presumptive of slavery, 276-7, 295
Colored testimony excluded, 300, &c.
Colored seamen imprisoned, 362
Colored people, (See "Free People of Color.")
Colonization Society *vs.* manumission on soil, 351 ; origin and objects of, 364 ; meetings, effects of, 366 ; compulsion, 267 ; Maryland Soc., 369-70 ; N Y. State Auxiliary, 365 ; American, (Testimony of,) 222
Connecticut, slave marriage, 106
Contracts of master and slave void, 346, &c.
Constitutions (State) *vs.* Abolition, 350
Congress, U. S. *vs.* slaves' personality, 106 ; right of petition, 37 ; Fugitive Slave Bill, 168, 234, 409
Cornelius, Rev. Elias, (Testimony,) 148
Cost, per annum, of slaves' support, 153
Cousins in Court, claiming cousins as slaves, 241
Cranch, Judge, (Testimony,) 360; petition, 56
Crandall, Prudence, 366
Craziness or idiocy of slave property sold and warranted, 32
Crenshaw, Judge, 293
Criminal prosecutions to defend slave property, 192, 204
Cropping ears legal, 220
Cruelty, certain kinds, authorized, 159
" philosophy of, 223-4

Daggett, Judge, 366
Damaged slaves, uses of, 86-7
Damages to slave property, 201, &c.
Dayton, Col. (M. C.) 36
"Dead or alive" to be returned, 120
Death from nakedness, 145
" starvation, 141, 145
" "moderate correction," 180
Delegated power of overseers, 197, &c., 204
Delaware, laws to prevent escapes, 229
Deming, Dr , (Testimony,) 79
Derbigny, Judge, 280
Dew, Prof , (Testimony,) 84
District of Columbia, slave-trade, 57 ; slaves may not traffic, 100 ; free negroes sold, 227 ; killing authorized, 230-1
Distribution of slave estates, 74-5
Dorsey, Judge, 345
Dower of widows in slaves, 71-2, 346
Drunkenness of slave property sold and warranted, 31
Dwellings of slaves described, 147

Earl, Judge, 345
Education, slaves no right to, 251
" " prohibited, 319
Edwards, Dr. Jonathan, (Testimony,) 141 143, 221 ; accounted slaveholding man-stealing, 271
Erwin, Mr., (Ala.) slave-trader, 59

Facts, treatment of slaves, 209, &c.
Family relation, slaves', 113, &c.
Fine for killing a negro, 191
Fisher, Mr., (Va.) Testimony, 368
Florida, clothing of slaves, 146
" laws to prevent escapes, 229
"Florida Slaveholder," (Testimony,) 370 ; his liberties, 376
Food, clothing, shelter, 135, &c.
Free people of color sold for jail fees, 227 · enslaved, 274, 352 ; liberties of, 355, &c
Free worship forbidden, 326
French slavery, milder type, 45
Fugitive slaves, 225, &c., 227
Fugitive Slave Bill (of 1850,) 283-4, 409
Furman, Rev. Dr., sale of theological books and negroes, 38

Gadsden, T. N., Esq., slave auctioneer, 60
Georgetown, (D. C.) ordinance, 358
Georgia, Presb. Synod, (Testimony,) 111 ; slaves forbidden to traffic, 98 ; slaves' labor, 130 ; food, 136 ; clothing, 145 ; murder, 182-3 ; "moderate correction," 183 ; slave without "pass," 228 ; harboring, 232 ; slavery perpetual and hereditary, 249 ; origin, 260 ; free negroes enslaved, 276 ; claims to freedom, 297-8 ; punished if fails to prove freedom, 297 ; death to strike white person, 305 ; penal laws *vs.* slaves, 315 ;

education prohibited, 319–22; no free worship, 328; *vs.* emancipation, 341, 342; whites fined for teaching, 359; restriction on right of hiring houses, 361; quarantine of freedom, 363; no freedom of speech or of the press, 385
Gholson, Mr., (Va.) 30–1, 36, 55, 82, 84, 272
Gildersleeve, W. C., (Testimony,) 142, 144
Gillmore, Mary, white, Irish, enslaved, 285
Girls, mulatto, high price, 85–6
Grand Jury of Cheraw, (S. C.) Testimony, 211
Greenville (S. C.) Mountaineer, (Testimony,) 336
Grimke, Sarah M., (Testimony,) 115, 148, 154, 256
Ground of slaves' civil condition, 289

Hall, Judge, 193, 317
Hampton, Gen Wade, feeding slaves, cotton seed, 141–2, 218
Harboring fugitives, 232–3, 236
Hawley, Rev. Francis, (Testimony,) 213
Hawkins, Sir John, 258, 271
Hayne, Gov. R. Y., purchased a man's wife and children, 119
Hebrew servitude, 292
Hereditary and perpetual slavery, 248
Hill, John W., (Testimony,) 214–15
History of S. C., (Testimony,) 132
Hitchcock, Judge H., (Ala.) concerned in slave-trade, 59, 175
Home Mission, Meth., put down, 336–7
Honesty of slave property sold and warranted, 32
House slaves, their condition, 111, 117, 200
Humanity punished more than cruelty, 163
Hunger of slaves, 141
Hunting slaves, 234
Huntsman, Hon. Adam, 386
Hymn books, incendiary, 324

Ill treatment, no legal remedy for, 125, 242–3
Illegal importation of slaves, 260, &c.
Imprisonment of slaves by owner, 166–7
Increase of slaves, 70, 72; belong to ulterior legatee, 72; may be sold by Orphans' Court, 72; subject to mortgage, 64–5
Infants cannot be emancipated, (Md.) 349
Indians enslaved, 28, 267–8, 282, 296
Indiana excludes colored witnesses, 359
Inheritance of slave property, 69
Intermarriage with slaves, 278
Iron collars, according to law, 163

Jackson, Gen. Andrew, a slave-trader, 60
Jamaica, (W. I.) mixed breed free, 249
Jefferson, Thomas, 34, 38, 126–7, 218; his will, 276, 375; his daughter sold, 85
Johnson, Col. Richard M., 378–9
Johnson, Judge, 94, 149, 264
Jones, Rev. C. C., of Geo., (Testimony,) 335
Judson, A. T., 336
Judiciary perverted, 207
Jury trial, why denied, 261

Kentucky: slaves real estate, 24; but sold as chattels, 24; Presb. Synod, (Testimony,) 53, 55, 110, 222, 333; slaves may not traffic, 98 nor hire out, 103; nor carry weapons, 229; free colored degraded, 300: laws *vs.* slaves, 312–15; hopeless ignorance, 323–4; laws *vs.* emancipation, 343
Kidnapping, 279
Knowledge, incendiary, 337

Labor of slaves, 78, 128, &c., 150, &c.
Ladd, William, (Testimony,) 142, 146
Lady advertising a fugitive *wife* in search of her *husband*, 119
Leftwich, Wm., (Testimony,) 144, 146
Legality of slavery, 19, 262, &c.
Legislation, none creating slavery, 261, &c.
Lewis Lillburn, his barbarity, 88
Lexington (Ky.) Luminary, (Testimony,) 111
Liberty of free people of color, 355, &c.
" of whites at the South, 372, &c.
" of whites at the North, 389
License to marry emancipates, 106
Licentiousness produced by slavery, 111
Life of slave in his owner's hands, 125
" taken without jury, 314
Littleton, Lord, 20, 401–2
Louisiana: property tenure of slaves, 23; held as real estate, 24; warranty of slaves, 31; ameliorated code, 46; allows a *peculium*, 90; slave families, 114; law of slaves' labor, 130; food, clothing, &c., 135; of punishments, 161; iron collars authorized, 163; overseer's authority, 198; damages to slave property, 203; slaves on horseback, 229; relief from ill treatment, 246; penal laws *vs.* slaves, 314–15; *vs.* free speech and press, 322; religious privileges of slaves, 322; *vs.* emancipation,

243–4 ; subjection of free blacks to whites, 357
Lowry, Nancy, (Testimony,) 213
Lynch Committee, (Mo.) 316

Madison, James, sister of, (Testimony,) 111
Madison, James, denied the right of property in man, 270
Maltby, S. E., (Testimony,) 146
Mansfield, Lord, 259, 270
Marriage of slaves abrogated, 105, &c.
" of whites restricted, 376, &c.
Martinique, comparative lenity shown to slaves, 45
Martin, Judge, 262, 248
Maryland : chattel tenure, 25 ; issue of female slaves, 30 ; bequests to slaves void, 91 ; slaves may not traffic, 99 ; naked and starved, 145 ; damages to slave property, 202 ; whites and blacks required to have "passes," 227–8 ; slaves rambling or riding, 229 ; killing slaves authorized, 230 ; slavery hereditary and perpetual, 248 ; enslaving white women and their children, 273 ; emancipated negroes reënslaved, 275, 359 ; trial of claims to freedom, 298 ; cropping free blacks, 306 ; penal laws *vs.* slaves, 213—16 ; laws of emancipation, 343 ; relig. privileges of slaves, 322
Mason, Mr., (Va.) 261
Massachusetts, submission to slave law, 363
Matthews, Judge, (La.) 107, 188, 206, 264, 266–7–8, 293
Meade, Bishop, (Testimony,) 334
" Merciful safety-valve," 133–4
Meth. E. Church, exclusion of colored witnesses, 159 ; class imprisoned, 226 ; missions suppressed, 336, 383
Miner, Mr., (M. C.) (Testimony,) 361
Ministry for slaves, 334
Mississippi : slave importation, 48 ; constitutional power of Legislature to relieve ill-treated slaves, not exercised, 168, 246 ; enslaves free negroes, 276 ; penal laws *vs.* slaves, 312–13 ; free worship forbidden, 331 ; laws *vs.* emancipation, 341–3 ; expulsion of free colored people, 356 ; no freedom of speech or of the press, 385.
Missouri : slaves may not traffic, 99 ; laws concerning cruelty, 165, &c. ; masters may imprison slaves, 166–7 ; slaves forbidden weapons, 229 ; testing claims to freedom, 299 ; Lynch law, burning free negro, 316 ; no freedom of speech or of the press, 386
Missionary Society put down, 336
Mixed race, 380, &c.
"Moderate correction," "death under," 180
Mortgage of slaves, 24, 63–4
Mosely, Rev. Mr., (Conn.) sale of wife from husband, 114
Mother (free) cannot sue for relief of a slave daughter from ill treatment, 125
Moulton, Horace, (Testimony,) 142–3
Municipal law, (slavery under,) 262, &c.
Murders of slaves, law of, 177, &c. ; frequency of, 210 ; instances of, 210—12, &c. ; of a slave child, 88 ; impunity of white murderers, 88, 210 ; doubts of Judges whether the murder of a slave be indictable, 192, 194 ; murders punished to protect slave property, 192–3 ; virtually commuted for a verdict for pecuniary damages, 208

" Negro's head " advertised, 39
Negro pew, 370
"Negro dogs" (for slave hunting) advertised, 336–7
New-Jersey, Indians enslaved, 28, 266
New-Orleans Argus, (Testimony,) 81
New-Orleans Bee, (Testimony,) 285
New-Orleans Picayune, (Testimony,) 383
New-Orleans Bible Society disclaims the intention of giving Bibles to slaves, 383
Nieces suing their aunt for their freedom, 241–2
Niles' Register, (Testimony,) 285
No appeal of a slave from his master, 126
No prosecution for battery on a slave, 171
No right of redemption from slavery, 245
No access to judiciary, 295, &c.
No statutes creating slavery, 258, 268, &c.
North Carolina Baptist Convention, (Testimony,) 336
North Carolina : law of slave legacies, 69, 70 ; " slaves cannot take by descent," &c., 91 ; may not traffic, 98–9 ; law of food, clothing, &c., 136 ; of killing slaves, 180, 230–1 ; outlawry of, 180 ; damages to slave property, 203 ; slaves without pass, 229 ; enslaving free colored persons, 276 ; no freedom of speech or of the press, 385 ; freedom quarantined, 363 ; penal laws *vs.* slaves, 312–13–14 ; education prohibited, 321 ; Bibles forbidden, 324 ; laws *vs.* emancipation, 341 ; preaching forbidden, 358 ; free colored people legally plundered,

359 ; expatriation or reënslavement, 361

Obsolete, slave laws not, 20
Obstructions to emancipation, 275, 338, &c.
Ohio, black law, 359
O'Niell, Judge, 168
" Oral instruction," 324-5, 336
Origin of the " legal relation," 258
Ottley, Chief Justice, 302
Ouachita (La.) Register, (Testimony,) 237
Outlawry of slaves, 180
Overseers: their power, 197 ; their character, 200

Parrish, John, (Testimony,) 145
Patrols, regulation of, 329
Paxton, Mr., (Testimony,) 285
Peculium of slaves, 26, 90
Peg, slave, damaged, 52
Penal laws *vs.* slaves, 309, &c.
Persecution for religion, 256, 282
Pickens, Mr., (M. C. 37
Piety of slaves advertised for sale, 42
Pinckney, Hon. H. L., sale of a man's wife and children, 119
Pinckney and Ford, (Testimony,) 211
Pinckney, William, (Testimony,) 221
Pitt, William, 259
Portuguese slavery, milder type of, 45
Powell, Eleazer, (Testimony,) 143
Presby. Church, Gen. Assembly, funds loaned and used in slave-trade, 62 ; definition of man-stealing, 271 ; Synod of Ky. (Testimony,) 53, 55, 110, 222, 333 ; Synod of S. C. and Geo., (Testimony,) 111, 334
" Prescription" no valid foundation for slaveholding, 266-7
Priestley, Dr., maxim of, 17
Protection of slaves in fact, 209, &c.
Property in a slave adjudged paramount to the slave's right to life, 317-18
Punishment of slaves by masters, 155, &c.

Quakers of N. Carolina, emancipation by, 352
Quarantine of freedom, 363

Randolph, Thos. J., (Testimony,) 56
Randolph, John, (Testimony,) 217
" " will of, 146
Rankin, Rev. John, (Testimony,) 141, 145
Rape of female slave, no protection against, 86
Reed, Rev. Dr., (Testimony,) 80
Relation of slave to Society, 287
Religious liberty of slaves, 251, &c., 326, &c.
Religious worship prohibited, 326
Renshaw, Rev. S. C., (Testimony,) 143, 146
Revolutionary service of slave, bounty belongs to his master, 93-4
Roane, Judge, 296
Robinson, Judge, (Ky.) 71
Roman Civil Law, 25-6, 156, 264
Ruffin, Judge, (of N. C.) 32, 79, 126, 154, 156, 165, 170, 317

Sabbath-schools for slaves, 324
Sale of slaves, 23, 25, 54, 66-7
Safford, Judge, 91
Sapington, L., (Testimony,) 118, 127
Savery, William, (Testimony,) 145
Savannah River Bap. Asso. *vs.* marriage, 109, 127, 258
Savannah City Ordinance *vs.* Schools, 321
Schools broken up, 320, &c., 366
Self-defense not allowed, 306-7
Separation of families, 53 ; exceptions to this, 73
Severity not caused by abolitionists, 20
Sharp, Granville, 259
Sheriffs obey orders of slaveholders, 167
Seizure of slaves for debt, 63
Slaves: not considered men, 35-7 ; no right of petition, 37 ; devisable, like other chattels, 72 ; can own nothing, 89, &c. ; can make no contract, 93 ; can be agents for their masters, 94-5 ; no crime to gamble with them, 95 ; laws forbidding them to hold property, 96 ; may not traffic, 95-7 ; nor hire out, 98 ; nor marry, 105 ; nor constitute families, 113 ; nor control their children, 113-17, 198 ; nor appeal from master, 126 ; cost of their support, 153 ; aged sent out to beg, 153-4 ; punished at will, 155 ; cannot testify, 159 ; imprisoned by owners, 166-7 ; battery of them, by owners, no breach of the peace, 168 ; not even by shooting, 170 ; laws concerning murder of, 177 ; outlawry, of, 180 ; controlled by overseers and by children, 198 ; how protected, as property, 201-7 ; branded, cropped, shot, 219-20, 231 ; cannot sue master, 239 ; no right of redemption, 245 ; nor of education, 251 ; nor of religion, 251 ; whipped to death for religion, 256 ; follow condition of slave mother, 273-4 ; civil condition, 289; no access to judiciary, 295 ; whipped by law for failing to sustain suit for freedom, 297 ; subjection to all white persons, 305 ; self-defense not allowed to colored

persons, 306–7; penal laws *vs.* slaves, 309; slave hunts, 231–4.
Slaveholders may not allow slaves to traffic or hold property, 97, &c.; authority of, 162; rights not to be questioned in Courts, 173; self-interest does not protect the slave, 195; not bound to show title to a slave claiming freedom, 241–2; do not enjoy civil and religious liberty, 372, &c.
Smith, Dr. A. G., (Testimony,) 143
Smythe, Gen. Alexander, (Testimony,) 132, 141
Smylie, Rev. James, (Testimony,) 50, 58
Somerset, James, (slave) case, 259
South Carolina: chattel tenure, 23; warranty of slaves, 31–2; slaves can own nothing, 91; may not traffic, 97; law of labor, 128–9; of food and clothing, 137; laws respecting cruelty, 159, 178, 301; damages to slave property, 202–3; slaves without pass, 228–9; enticing slaves, 232; perpetuity of slavery, 248; imprisonment of colored seamen, 362; laws *vs.* emancipation, 341; testing claims to freedom, 297; owner exculpated by oath, 301; death for striking white person, 305–6; penal laws *vs.* slaves, 312–15; education prohibited, 319, &c., 329; Methodist Missions suppressed, 336
Spanish slavery, milder type of, 45, 101, 131, 247, 292, 250, 344
Spiritual despotism, 124–5, 251, &c.
"*Statu liber*," no relief for ill treatment of, 125
Stewart, Mr., (Ill.) Testimony, 58
Stone, A. A., (Testimony,) 133, 141
Story's "Conflict of Laws," 262
Subjects of slavery, 251, &c.
Sugar plantations "use up" slaves, 80
Summers, Mr. (Va.) 35
Swain, Wm. and Moses, (Testimony,) 141

Taylor, Judge, 192
Tennessee: slaves may not traffic, 98; ill clothed, 145; law on killing slaves, 182, and see N. Carolina, 180; slaves without pass, 229; penal laws *vs.* slaves, 312–15; laws *vs.* emancipation, 342–3; expatriation laws, 356
Testimony excluded, 159, 300, &c.
Thome, Rev. James A., (Testimony,) 223
Torrey, Dr., (Testimony,) 285
Traffic in slaves, 44, &c.
Treatment of sick, infirm, and aged, 147–9
Tucker, Judge, (Testimony,) 237–8
Turner, L., (Testimony,) 38, 2 3
Turpin, Mr., (Missionary,) 336, 383

Unlimited power, 27, 122
"Unlawful assemblies," 204–5
"Unusual punishments" prohibited, 161, &c.; defined, 162, &c.
"Used up" in five to eight years, 133–4
Uses of slave property, 77, &c.

Vanderpool, Hon. Mr., 36
"Verbal instruction" for slaves, 324, 336
Violence to female chastity, 220
Virginia: slaves chattels, 24; may not traffic, 98; sold for trading, 101; clothing of slaves, ; 145–6; damages to slave property, 203–4; weapons forbidden, 229; killing lawfully, 231; "literary fund," from sale of emancipated negroes, 275–6; testing claims to freedom, 298; attorneys fined for pleading, if suit fails, 298; free colored persons striking white persons, 306; penal laws *vs.* slaves, 313–15; education prohibited, 320; religious worship forbidden, 330–1; emancipation laws, 341–3; no freedom of speech or of the press, 385

Wages, slaves receive none, 150
Wall, Col., (Ky.) Senator and slave dealer, 59, 60
Warranty of slaves sold, 31–2
Washington City Corporation, 227
Waugh, Bishop, 369
Weld, Angelina Grimke, (Testimony,) 93, 116, 127, 144
Western Medical Reformer, (Testimony,) 143
Western Luminary, (Testimony,) 335
Westgate, G. W., (Testimony,) 146
West Indies, (Brit.) slavery was illegal, 270; free colored people less oppressed, 372
Wesley, John, on "men-stealers," 271
Wheeler's criticism on Stroud examined, 184–5
White men on plantations required, 302
White persons enslaved, 282
White women marrying slaves, 273
White poor supported by colored poor, 99
Whitefield, Rev. George, (Testimony,) 131, 141, 221
Wife no right to manumit, 346
Wills, of personal estates, embrace slaves, 70; may bequeath unborn slaves, and separate the future "increase" from the mother, 70; for emancipation, set aside, 344–5, &c.

Wirt, Wm., Attorney-Gen., his opinion of certain laws, 362 ; his description of overseers, 200
Wilmington, (N. C.) 100, 226
Wise, Hon. Mr., 36, 106
Wives of slaves appropriated by their owners, 118
Woman, with infant, at work on plantation, 118
Woolman, John, (Testimony,) 114, 132, 142, 145, 222, 323

www.ingramcontent.com/pod-product-compliance
Lightning Source LLC
LaVergne TN
LVHW021145110826
845150LV00005B/1127
* 9 7 8 1 4 2 5 5 4 6 9 1 5 *